Advocacy in the
Human Services

Advocacy in the Human Services

MARK EZELL, PH.D.
University of Kansas

BROOKS/COLE
CENGAGE Learning

Australia • Brazil • Japan • Korea • Mexico • Singapore • Spain • United Kingdom • United States

Advocacy in the Human Services

Mark Ezell

Social Work Editor: Lisa Gebo

Assistant Editor: Susan Wilson

Editorial Assistant: Sheila Walsh

Marketing Manager: Caroline Concilla

Project Editor: Trudy Brown

Print Buyer: Robert King

Permissions Editor: Joohee Lee

Production Service: Proof Positive/Farrowlyne Associates

Cover Designer: Yvo Riezebos

Compositor: Black Dot Graphics

For product information and technology assistance, contact us at **Cengage Learning Customer & Sales Support, 1-800-354-9706**

For permission to use material from this text or product, submit all requests online at **www.cengage.com/permissions** Further permissions questions can be emailed to **permissionrequest@cengage.com**

Library of Congress Control Number: 00-037896

ISBN-13: 978-0-534-34861-8

ISBN-10: 0-534-34861-0

Brooks/Cole
20 Davis Drive
Belmont, CA 94002
USA

Cengage Learning is a leading provider of customized learning solutions with office locations around the globe, including Singapore, the United Kingdom, Australia, Mexico, Brazil, and Japan. Locate your local office at **www.cengage.com/global**

Cengage Learning products are represented in Canada by Nelson Education, Ltd.

To learn more about Brooks/Cole, visit **www.cengage.com/brookscole**

Purchase any of our products at your local college store or at our preferred online store **www.ichapters.com**

Printed in the United States of America
6 7 8 9 10   18 17 16 15 14

Contents

Preface *ix*

Introduction *xvii*

Part One:

THE GROUNDWORK FOR ADVOCACY 1

Chapter 1

Motivations for Advocacy 3
Chapter Objectives 3
Advocacy Ideals 5
Why Do Advocacy? 7
Is Enough Time Devoted to Advocacy? 10
Optimism About Advocacy 11
What Keeps Practitioners from Doing Advocacy? 12
Self-Empowerment to Do Advocacy 13
Summary 18
Discussion Questions 19

Chapter 2

Understanding Advocacy 20
Chapter Objectives 20
What Is Advocacy? (and What Isn't It?) 21

Types of Advocacy   25

Analyzing Advocacy Activities   28

Beliefs and Assumptions Underlying Advocacy Practice   31

Summary   *34*

Discussion Questions   *36*

Chapter 3

The Ethics of Advocacy   37

Chapter Objectives   *37*

Ethical Obligations to Do Advocacy   38

Ethical Principles and Challenges Relevant to the
    Practice of Advocacy   40

Advocacy and Cultural Diversity   47

Summary   *49*

Discussion Questions   *50*

Part Two:

ADVOCACY STRATEGIES AND TACTICS   51

Chapter 4

Agency Advocacy   53

Chapter Objectives   *53*

Targets for Agency Advocacy   54

Agency Discretion   58

Tactics   61

Summary   *72*

Discussion Questions   *73*

Chapter 5

Legislative Advocacy   74

Chapter Objectives   *74*

Understanding Legislative Process   75

Advocacy Activities During Legislative Session   79

Non-Session Activities   88

Political Campaigns and Advocacy   95

Summary   97

Discussion Questions   97

Chapter 6

Legal Advocacy   98

Chapter Objectives   98

Case Examples of Opportunities for Legal Advocacy   100

Non-Litigious Tactics   105

Litigation   109

Summary   113

Discussion Questions   114

Chapter 7

Community Advocacy   115

Chapter Objectives   115

Community Education As an Advocacy Strategy   117

Media Tactics   122

Other Community Advocacy Tactics   134

Summary   137

Discussion Questions   137

Chapter 8

Doing Your Advocacy Homework   138

Chapter Objectives   138

Advocacy Needs Assessments   140

Understanding the Problem or Need   142

Establishing Advocacy Targets   146

Mapping the Decision System   148

Selecting Strategies and Tactics   149

Summary   150

Discussion Questions   151

Part Three:

ISSUES, DILEMMAS, AND CHALLENGES   153

Chapter 9

Putting the Advocacy Pieces Together   155

Chapter Objectives   155

Doing Their Advocacy Homework   156

Agency Advocacy   164

Community Advocacy   169

Legislative Advocacy   171

Return to Agency Advocacy   179

Summary   180

Discussion Questions   180

Chapter 10

Advocacy Skills, Challenges, and Practice Guidelines   181

Chapter Objectives   181

Critical Advocacy Skills and Attitudes   182

Advocacy Challenges   188

Practice Guidelines   192

Summary   196

Discussion Questions   196

References   197

Index   201

Preface

As we start the 21st century, the number of individuals, families, and communities that rely on human services continues to rise, but policies and service delivery systems that affect them seem to be less responsive. Likewise, as our society becomes more diverse, the disproportionately high needs and vulnerabilities of ethnic groups are becoming more evident. Even before these recent trends in demographics and in the social welfare, health care, mental health, and education systems, few would have asserted that all was well and that clients' problems and needs were adequately met. It is not a pretty picture, and even the most optimistic among us will have to admit that more and more consumers of human services will be left behind if these trends continue.

There is much that can be done to alter these trends and change the bleak scenarios. That is why I wrote this book. There has always been a need for members of helping professions to advocate for and with their clients and their programs, and there is a greater need today. Unfortunately, as Gibelman and Kraft (1996) point out, "advocacy has thus received less sanction, support, and priority than other interventions with or on behalf of human services clients" (p. 57). Further, Walz and Groze (1991) agree that social work, one of the human service professions, is becoming more conservative and there is "a weakening of the advocacy or political component in social work education and practice" (p. 500). With the new funding schemes such as managed care, there is an ever-increasing focus on reimbursable activities. Sunley (1997) points out that "practitioners within the managed-care system may be able to carry out some case-and-cause advocacy within the limits of company requirements and possible job jeopardy" (p. 84), but more advocacy will need to originate outside the system and address broad issues.

This book is intended to increase both the amount and effectiveness of advocacy done with and on behalf of those served by helping professionals. *The goal of this book is to bring together what is currently a disparate literature of advocacy knowledge and skills and to articulate a comprehensive approach to advocacy*. My hope is that this synthesis will define the bound-aries of advocacy practice, separate it from other commonly used interven-tions, and elevate it as a practice intervention in and of itself. I view advocacy practice as a distinct practice method that can be implemented alone or in combination with other micro-, meso-, or macro-interventions.

As a result of the research I conducted—described more fully in chapter 1—it is clear that more advocacy training is likely to increase the amount of advocacy done by practitioners (Ezell, 1994). This research, which focused on social workers in particular, indicated that one of the reasons social workers hesitate to do advocacy is that they have little or no training in it. This research found that there is a positive, statistically significant relationship between the amount of training and the amount of advocacy conducted. This is true both for on-the-job as well as volunteer advocacy. It is my hope that this book will provide an impetus for more training of human service practitioners, students, and volunteers and, thus, more advocacy.

Several good books have been written covering parts of the ground cov-ered here. Prominent examples include Richan's (1991) *Lobbying for Social Change,* as well as Haynes and Mickelson's (2000) *Affecting Change.* As good as the books are, they don't provide all the advocacy tools needed by human service professionals, which, of course, is a challenge for any single book. They focus on lobbying, which is very important but is not the only way to bring about change on behalf of clients. Other, and possibly more, opportunities for advocacy exist outside the legislative process.

AUDIENCE

There are several audiences for this book. First, there are the students study-ing to become human service professionals, whether their specific field is social work, criminal justice, child care, education, recreation, developmental disabilities, or addictions, just to name a few of the human service fields. Many, probably most, of these students plan to invest most of their time work-ing with families and individuals. On the other hand, there will be some who choose to make jobs and careers of advocacy.

The book will also be useful to helping professionals and volunteers already at work in human services. Helping professionals and volunteers are those who work and volunteer in social and welfare services, education, and health care. Barker (1995) defines **human services** as "programs and activi-ties designed to enhance people's development and well-being" (p. 173). *Human services* is a term used broadly to include education, health care, per-sonal social services, housing, income maintenance, justice, and public safety (Barker, 1995).

THIS BOOK'S CONTRIBUTION

This book describes a comprehensive approach to advocacy, one that includes and goes beyond legislative advocacy. I describe a large number of advocacy tools that can be used in a variety of settings to help clients. This comprehensive approach began to take shape in the 1970s, when I was involved in creating a statewide child advocacy agency that was modeled after the work of the Children's Defense Fund. The approach further matured when the agency received funding from the Office of Juvenile Justice and Delinquency Prevention (OJJDP) to engage in child and youth advocacy. There were approximately 20 projects funded by OJJDP, all being evaluated by the American Institute for Research (1983), and they began to categorize their advocacy strategies as administrative, legal, legislative, and community. David Richart and Stephen Bing (1989), both directors of OJJDP-funded projects, wrote a child advocacy book that has this comprehensive approach at its heart.

Due to the fact that I present a comprehensive advocacy approach that includes four major strategies, I have a lot of ground to cover. A book that concentrates on lobbying, for example, will certainly have more depth than my single chapter on legislative advocacy; but, to the best of my knowledge, no other book describes all these advocacy strategies and tactics in one place and also talks about how to combine them.

I will be very pleased if those who study this book, those who have and have not done advocacy in the past, become more mindful as they implement varying strategies and tactics. I am using the word *mindfulness* in much the same way as Schön (1983) used "reflectiveness." Mindful advocates are those who continually assess, analyze, and strategize as they practice advocacy, changing courses and tactics as need be and as dictated by the many interacting and dynamic variables to be considered. Mindful advocates understand the complexity of change and adapt their tactics to this reality.

Unfortunately, there is not as much empirical research on the effectiveness of different advocacy strategies in different situations as we would like. The science of advocacy practice relies heavily on a growing body of case studies as well as the practical experience of those who do advocacy. I do not mean to be overly critical of the field's failure to produce good research on advocacy, for this is a very difficult undertaking. For example, imagine the challenge of comparing the effectiveness of an advocacy campaign that uses letter writing to get legislation passed to one that involves personal visits to legislators. Hopefully, as the practice of advocacy is better defined, more research will be reported.

Notwithstanding the cautions above, a fair amount of knowledge and experience contribute to this book's approach to advocacy. The framework of advocacy practice described here is based on knowledge of how public policy is created and implemented and how organizations operate. It is based on a review of the relevant literature, including numerous case studies of advocacy efforts, as well as the cumulative advice of many experienced and successful advocates. Reisch (1990) provides empirical support for a multifaceted approach to advocacy such as the one presented in this book. He compared effective advocacy organizations to those considered ineffective, and he found that "effective organizations were more likely to allocate resources to influence legislation or public opinion. . . . Additionally, they were more likely to regard legal action . . . and efforts to influence media coverage . . . as relevant to organizational goals" (p. 74). This book presents a comprehensive and integrated approach to advocacy in the human services that I think will be effective in many situations.

ABOUT THE AUTHOR

My advocacy experience started more than 20 years ago. Very early in my career, I was lucky enough to be associated with a group of experienced human service leaders who recognized that the policymaking process in our state was out of balance because there was no organized voice for children. A concerted effort by the sheriffs in the state had recently succeeded in passing regressive juvenile justice legislation and there had been no counter-balancing advocacy on behalf of youth. These leaders' vision, and my luck at being in the right place at the right time, led to the creation of a statewide advocacy organization for children and youth.

I quickly learned a lot about how to put a nonprofit organization together, what is advocacy, and how to do it. I had completed one graduate degree at that point and I remember thinking, "I could be in big trouble here; I've never had a course in any of this or anything remotely associated with it." We had many successes, as well as some frustrations, as we learned to use our advocacy techniques. The organization we founded continues to advocate effectively for children and youth.

During the time I worked for this advocacy agency, I had not received professional training in any of the human services. The agency, however, dealt with issues of concern to many helping professions, such as education, child welfare, health care, mental health, poverty, hunger, developmental disabilities, and juvenile delinquency. Since then, I have accumulated several graduate degrees, mostly in social work, and I subsequently entered academia. Not only have I studied and taught advocacy, but I have also remained actively involved with various advocacy agencies.

Several facets of my presentation distinctly reflect my personal experiences and preferences. Past and present advocacy has been carried out on behalf of children, youth, and their families, so many of the examples used in the book come from that field. I began to create examples from many different issues and client groups but, by and large, decided to stick with real examples with which I was personally involved. When describing these experiences, I usually don't refer to myself but, rather, use *we*. *We* refers to the staff and volunteers or coalition members associated with a particular advocacy effort. *We* more accurately reflects the fact that advocacy is rarely practiced alone.

Aside from my extensive experience in child advocacy, it also happens that the greatest bulk of writing on advocacy is in this area. Given that I do try to draw together and build on prior work, I refer to a large amount of child advocacy literature. It is important to remember that the systems and decision-making processes that impact children's programs and services are the same as those that impact other client groups.

Another indisputable leaning in the book is toward class advocacy—advocating for a larger number of clients who share a common condition or problem. My experience is with this type of advocacy, which holds great promise to produce change more quickly and to benefit more people.

Finally, readers will be able to see that many examples are about advocacy at the state level, dealings with state legislatures, agencies, and governors. This is where advocates should focus their efforts. Not to the exclusion of federal and local levels, of course, but it is the level of government at which the majority of relevant policy and program decisions are made that affect clients who consume human services.

FEATURES

The book is divided into three parts. Part 1 consists of three chapters that develop several starting points for engaging in advocacy. Getting started means being motivated to do advocacy, having advocacy ideals, and empowering oneself to do advocacy. Those topics are discussed in chapter 1. Chapter 2 presents a starting point involving the understanding of advocacy as a concept, the different types of advocacy, and its underpinning assumptions. The final starting point, developed in chapter 3, is the ethical foundation of advocacy practice. Chapter 3 also uses ethics as a springboard to examine how concerns about cultural awareness and social injustice fit into advocacy practice.

Part 2 presents the essential strategies and tactics of advocacy practice. There are four primary strategies: agency advocacy, legislative advocacy, legal advocacy, and community advocacy. Each chapter of part 2 presents one of these strategies and attendant tactics. The final chapter in part 2 is called "Doing Your Advocacy Homework." Its emphasis is on the often neglected steps of studying client issues, targeting advocacy efforts, mapping relevant decision systems, and the overall planning of an advocacy effort.

Part 3 includes two chapters that integrate and extend earlier ideas and strategies. The entirety of chapter 9 is a case study used to demonstrate step-by-step a multifaceted advocacy effort that lasts for more than a year. The last chapter summarizes advocacy practice by presenting, among other things, a set of advocacy guidelines.

Each chapter starts with objectives and ends with discussion questions. This, in addition to the examples throughout the text, should promote the learning process. Another method I use to engage readers is to ask questions throughout the text. I ask readers to reflect on points I've made and to see if they can add to them. I might ask how my observations compare to their experiences. Sometimes when presenting research findings, I ask whether readers are surprised or if they would have predicted differently.

Because I want this book to be very accessible, I use a somewhat casual tone. This tone might disguise the extensive amount of scholarship that has gone into this work. Dozens and dozens of references are included, which may be examined further if readers wish to pursue certain issues. In this way, I hope the writing style won't intimidate a community college student nor be below that to which graduate students are accustomed.

In this book I use social work as an example of a human service profession and as an entrée to human services in general. I am a member of the social work profession, teach in social work, and conducted my advocacy research with social workers.

ACKNOWLEDGMENTS

This book has been a labor of love and hate. For those who have done much writing, they will understand both sides of the equation. For a humorous explanation of the writing process, Anne Lamott's (1994) *Bird by Bird* is a must read. She very accurately describes what it's like to sit down and try to write. You sit down at your computer, put your fingers on the keyboard, and try to think. But, as Lamott explains,

> Then your mental illnesses arrive at the desk like your sickest, most secretive relatives. And they pull up chairs in a semicircle around the computer, and they try to be quiet but you know they are there with their weird coppery breath, leering at you behind your back. (p. 16)

I love doing and thinking about advocacy. I'll jump on any soapbox in a 10-mile radius to extol its importance. But figuring out how to write a book about it and actually writing it, word by word, is painful.

There are many people I should acknowledge for helping me in some way while I was learning about and doing advocacy and writing this book. I had an outstanding advocacy mentor in my early days in Tallahassee whose importance must be acknowledged. Ms. Budd Bell is a powerful and effective social worker, teacher, and advocate as a result of her knowledge, skill, focus, and personality. I hope she is proud of my work here and sees it as part of her legacy.

I learned many valuable lessons about advocacy from many professionals and volunteers during my days with the Florida Center for Children and Youth. Later, I had a rare opportunity to replicate and increase my observations about advocacy through my association with the Children's Alliance in Washington State.

The book has improved over the course of many reviews and I therefore want to thank those who invested their time and energy to comment on earlier drafts: Denise Davison, Illinois State University; Mark S. Homan, Pima Community College; Rob Lawson, Western Washington University; Sonja Matison, Eastern Washington University; and Merrill Youkeles, Kingsborough Community College. The suggestions, questions, and criticisms were heeded as revisions were made. Lisa Gebo and Susan Wilson at Brooks/Cole/Wadsworth have been patient, wise, and helpful throughout this project. Angela McHaney Brown is a very skillful editor whose suggestions made the book clearer and more readable. Trudy Brown smoothly managed the book through a complex production process.

Ms. Pat Arthur of Seattle was extremely helpful when she reviewed my drafts on legal advocacy. She is a model advocate who taught me a great deal and who I miss.

I mentioned earlier the love and hate mood swings of this project. Thankfully, the vicissitudes of writing were interrupted by a true and very real love. This new love motivated a major relocation, a marriage, and the happy addition of two very special stepchildren, Andy and Lauren. My new bride, Marianne Berry, an outstanding scholar in her own right, has been an ongoing source of support as well as a wise sounding board. I dedicate this book to her.

Introduction

For several decades, human service professionals have been witnessing major shifts in public policy, funding, and programming toward the poor, the needy, oppressed groups, and the vulnerable. Many of these shifts are unfavorable. Neither public nor private funding has ever been adequate to meet the vast array of problems that human service professionals witness on a day-to-day basis. Even in times when human services funding increases, it fails to keep pace with the increasing number and complexity of problems and needs of people who consume and depend on health and human services.

As these trends continue, Congress and the federal government are devolving decision making, service administration, and financing to the states. The states, likewise, are devolving responsibilities to regional structures and local governments. Specifically, in August 1996, Congress passed and the president signed the Personal Responsibility and Work Opportunity Reconciliation Act (PRWORA), legislation intended to overhaul the country's welfare system. Some have called this "welfare reform." A major aspect of PRWORA is that a great deal of welfare decision making and financing is being transferred to the state level.

With decisions on policies, programs, and funding being closer than ever to the front lines of service delivery, this may mean that the decision-making process and decision makers themselves are more accessible to members of human service professions. Whether helping professionals will be able to influence policies and funding remains to be seen. What will make a difference? The individual and collective skills and motivations of human service practitioners are likely to be the primary determinants of successful policy change.

The purpose of this book is to increase the abilities of human service practitioners to make a difference, to influence policy, program, and funding decisions that will positively impact their clients. That is what advocacy is all about. Effective advocacy involves knowing why it is important to do it and when it is the most appropriate intervention. Once the motivation to act is triggered, a set of skills is necessary to determine, for example, whether the target for change is a state law, an agency policy, or a funding decision. The same set of analytic skills are needed to determine how the relevant decision is made, when it is made, and by whom. In this book, this stage of advocacy is referred to as "Doing Your Advocacy Homework." Advocacy homework leads to the selection of targets, strategies, and tactics (defined below), but it should not be assumed that this process is linear. It is very common for advocates who are implementing a strategy to discover the need for more homework, and the new homework may cause them to alter their original plans.

ADVOCACY PRACTICE

The entirety of this book should be viewed as the conceptualization and elucidation of a comprehensive intervention for and with clients,[1] be they individuals, families, classes of individuals, neighborhoods, or communities. That intervention, advocacy, can be practiced by human service professionals, clients, community volunteers, or all three as a unified group. This presentation of advocacy practice collates materials and ideas from disparate fields, but it does not invent advocacy. There have been many books and articles written on different aspects of advocacy in the past and those are invaluable. Oftentimes, a specific approach toward change has gone by different names, such as policy-practice (Jansson, 1999) or community change (Homan, 1999), to just name two.

One of the primary advantages of this book's approach to advocacy is that it can be utilized year-round to promote change in a variety of settings. The type of advocacy probably written about and taught most often, legislative advocacy, is a very important and powerful strategy for change, but unless the relevant legislative body is in session, this type of advocacy cannot be used to address clients' problems. Furthermore, legislative bodies alone cannot solve all the problems advocates confront.

Congress is in session throughout the year except for traditional and sometimes lengthy recesses. School boards and city and county councils generally meet on a regular basis (e.g., weekly or bimonthly) as well. State legislatures, however, where most human service policies and funding originate, do not.

---

1. There is much debate about the correct term to use when referring to the people with whom the helping professions work, the people who use our services. Some have expressed the belief that many of the terms are disempowering. There are many choices, such as *client, patient, student, consumer, service user,* or *service recipient.* I will usually use *client(s),* and the others are used occasionally depending on context. It is not intended to disempower. In fact, I'll give specific attention to empowering the client group for whom you advocate.

The legislatures of only eight states and the District of Columbia meet all year (National Conference of State Legislators, 1999). Seven state legislatures meet every other year.

A simplified depiction of advocacy practice is presented in Figure I.1. It shows, from left to right, the usual progression of an advocacy effort. The process starts with the identification of client problems or needs and proceeds to the homework stage at which the targets for change are identified and the overall strategy or strategies are planned. Advocacy strategies are implemented through the use of a variety of tactics. What is not depicted in the figure is the ongoing reflection and monitoring that advocates do as they seek change. They constantly ask themselves questions, such as "Are we getting the desired short and long term results, or has new information surfaced that requires a change of strategy?"

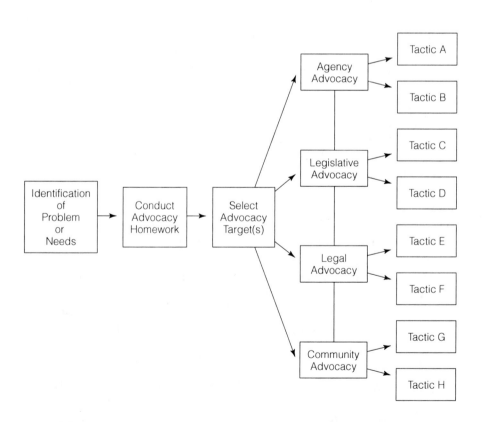

FIGURE I.1

Advocacy practice.

TERMINOLOGY

In order to develop advocacy as an arena of human service practice, a set of terms is used to denote specific ideas. The usage of these terms in this book may or may not be consistent with common usage. It is important, therefore, to clarify their meanings. To some degree, an advocacy jargon is developed to go along with advocacy knowledge and skills.

The conceptual definition of **advocacy** is fully discussed and elaborated on in chapter 2. That articulation gives full meaning to the concept and the intervention. The definition of advocacy used in this book is the following: Advocacy consists of those purposive efforts to change specific existing or proposed policies or practices on behalf of or with a specific client or group of clients.

Four **advocacy strategies** are described in this book: Agency Advocacy, Legislative Advocacy, Legal Advocacy, and Community Advocacy. Strategies are named for the arena in which they take place and, in general, the location of the targets for change. In order to get a law changed to increase access to health services, for example, the advocacy effort takes place in the legislative arena. A strategy is a broad approach toward change, a general plan of action that encompasses numerous tactics. Strategies should be thought of on a larger scale than tactics.

Advocacy tactics are specific change activities such as lobbying legislators, testifying at a committee hearing, persuading an agency executive, holding a news conference, or filing a friend-of-the-court brief in a lawsuit. Thus, several advocacy tactics used simultaneously or sequentially make up an advocacy strategy.

Advocacy targets are the specific entities that need to change. For instance, specific state statutes are frequently the targets for advocates who seek to alter the language of the statutes. Agency policies are frequently the target for change, such as a school board's policies on the process to be used to suspend a student, and advocates often target budgets for change as well. Certain community attitudes and stereotypes frequently need to be changed in order to help clients. These are just a few examples of advocacy targets. If there is anything close to a certainty in advocacy practice it is that the effective advocates are the ones who have clearly and specifically identified their advocacy targets.

A Brief History of Advocacy in Human Services and Social Work

The origin of the human services field dates back to the 1950s (Schram & Mandell, 1994) and 1960s (Burger & Youkeles, 2000) while the origin of the social work profession is traced to the very early 1900s. Neukrug (2000) explains that the human service profession borrows from psychology, counseling, and social work. Of these professions, social work's experience with advocacy is the oldest and has the greatest influence on human service advocacy. That being the case, this section highlights trends in social work's history that influence and support the practice of advocacy. As this very brief historical account reaches the 1960s, attention will be directed to antecedents of human service advocacy.

Kutchins and Kutchins (1978) trace the roots of social work advocacy back to Dorothea Dix and her work on behalf of people who are mentally ill and to Jane Addams as the mother of the settlement house movement. They describe instances in which both case and class advocacy (defined in chapter 2) were performed. For example, social workers helped immigrants negotiate with local governments and also worked on legislation (e.g., child labor, juvenile court, and women's suffrage). During the Progressive Era, social workers and social reformers placed a great deal of emphasis on reforming the social environment of the poor, and advocacy was a prominent method for doing so.

In the 1920s, however, the social work profession became enamored with psychotherapy (Specht & Courtney, 1994) and "Social workers continued to worship at the altar of psychoanalysis into the deepest and darkest moments of the Great Depression and World War II" (pp. 95–96). There were notable exceptions, such as when some social workers were involved in developing the New Deal legislation (Haynes & Mickelson, 2000), but the waning of advocacy lasted several more decades. The political environment of the 1960s, the War on Poverty, the Civil Rights Movement, and the Community Mental Health Movement spurred a reemergence of advocacy in the profession and, to a large degree, created the new profession of human services. As Kutchins and Kutchins describe, in those years advocacy and community organization were frequently coupled, and both were viewed as significant strategies to be used by social workers.

Legislation passed and funded in the 1960s (e.g., the Economic Opportunity Act) created a large number of new jobs for workers who could take over entry-level and basic tasks to let social workers and psychologists focus on tasks that required advanced training. These jobs were the beginning of generalist human service professionals (Burger & Youkeles, 2000).

Again in the 1970s and 1980s, political activism on the part of social workers waned (Haynes & Mickelson, 2000; Reisch, 1986). Several scholars have observed another upswing of political activism by social workers and other human service practitioners in the 1990s (Amidei, 1987; Ezell, 1993; Haynes & Mickelson, 2000). Of necessity, human service professionals used political and advocacy strategies to fight the budget cutting tendencies of the Reagan and Bush administrations.

In addition to the civil rights and antipoverty movements, Richart and Bing (1989) also point to consumer and disabilities movements as sources of ideas and strategies for advocacy. As they rightly point out, "The common thread of these other historic efforts is their attempt to remove barriers from the lives of certain groups of people and to establish a meaningful voice in shaping their own destinies" (p. 27).

As the new millennium begins, human service practitioners are found in a wide range of settings with greatly expanded tasks and responsibilities. They see human suffering daily as well as the shortcomings of the social institutions designed to prevent and respond to it. They are poised to engage in advocacy for and with their respective clients. They can draw from their history and their ethics to do so. With the knowledge and skills this book offers, human service practitioners can and will change the landscape of society.

THE GROUNDWORK FOR ADVOCACY

CHAPTER 1   MOTIVATIONS FOR ADVOCACY
CHAPTER 2   UNDERSTANDING ADVOCACY
CHAPTER 3   THE ETHICS OF ADVOCACY

There are a lot of ideas that advocates need to understand in order to be effective. They must know when advocacy is a useful approach to bring about change and when another intervention will work better. They need to know how to analyze problems, issues, and situations so they can select effective advocacy strategies; and they must be able to plan, coordinate, and implement these strategies. There are so many variables advocates need to take into consideration, variables which change from day to day, that it is impossible to develop a simple recipe that is guaranteed to produce a successful advocacy episode. That's the reason the first three chapters are devoted to the ideas behind advocacy—definitions, concepts, and assumptions—so you can learn how to do advocacy while also becoming an effective "thinking advocate" who can select or change strategies when confronted with different situations, and who can alter his or her tactics in midstream if necessary. To engage in successful advocacy, you will need to be a reflective practitioner of advocacy (Schön, 1983).

Instead of starting the book with definitions, however, chapter 1 starts with an examination of the reasons for doing advocacy and what motivates advocates. In general, practitioners do advocacy because they want to achieve certain goals with and for clients and they wish to see positive changes take place. It is important to never lose sight of those goals. It's important to stay well grounded in your personal and professional reasons for doing advocacy. This will be your touchstone, especially on those frustrating days when it seems as if little progress is being made.

The reasons why many human service professionals do little or no advocacy are also explored. These reasons represent real barriers advocates face whenever they do advocacy or try to recruit others. These constraints may be real or illusory; either way, they keep us from doing more and better advocacy.

Chapter 2 introduces important conceptual material that makes up advocates' operating theories and the underpinnings of the mindful practice of advocacy. Not only does this chapter present and discuss a useful definition of advocacy, it organizes types of advocacy and guiding assumptions into workable, sensible tools.

Chapter 3 discusses the ethics of advocacy, a topic of great importance and complexity. The ever-present dilemmas of when advocacy practice is ethically obligatory and those relevant to the immediate practice of advocacy are analyzed and discussed. The *Code of Ethics* of the National Association of Social Workers (1996) and the *Ethical Standards* of the National Organization for Human Service Education (2000) are used as a backdrop for these discussions. The final section of chapter 3 explores the challenge of culturally sensitive advocacy practice.

After studying these three chapters and responding to the discussion questions included, the reader will be ready for the presentation of the four primary advocacy strategies, each of which constitutes a chapter in part 2.

MOTIVATIONS FOR ADVOCACY

CHAPTER OBJECTIVES

By the time you finish studying this chapter, you should

1. Be able to describe common goals of advocacy.
2. Understand several reasons why we do advocacy.
3. Think about whether human service professionals do enough advocacy.
4. Be familiar with common barriers to advocacy, both at the individual and organizational level, and possible ways to overcome them.
5. Be aware of several self-empowering tips.

The book starts with the reasons for doing advocacy and by articulating a set of **advocacy ideals,** or what advocates hope to accomplish as a result of their hard work. This chapter examines the question "What motivates advocates and what are their goals?" In addition, the amount of time social workers devote to advocacy both on the job and as volunteers is analyzed. Besides examining prevalent attitudes about advocacy, the reasons why practitioners might not advocate is presented. The chapter ends with suggestions for empowering yourself to do advocacy.

It is very important to be aware of the feelings and values that motivate you to engage in advocacy. Successful advocacy takes time. Advocates rarely get legislation passed on their first attempt and, even if they do, this is only the beginning of the change effort. When advocates succeed and get legislation passed, whether it's their first, second, or third try, they need to monitor the implementation of the new law to see that it works as intended and reaches the people for whom it was designed.

The whole advocacy process may seem never-ending, frustrating, and tiring at times, and involving too many compromises along the way. But it is a process of critical importance if human service professionals and volunteers are to serve fully their clients. Values, ideals, commitment, and hope fuel the tenacity needed by advocates. Personal awareness of one's values, ideals, and commitment is critical; and periodically revisiting them, especially in times of low energy, disappointment, and frustration, helps keep advocates going. This awareness helps you keep your eye on the prize.

Besides knowing your reasons for doing advocacy, it is equally important to be aware of your hesitancies, or why you might drag your feet. Obstacles to advocacy are both real and imagined, but both have the same effect: you don't advocate. One of the only ways to keep obstacles, fears, and doubts from overwhelming you is to identify them, appreciate them for what they are, reframe them, and strategize how to get around or through them. For example, some advocates are not comfortable with one-on-one lobbying of legislators and, therefore, avoid it. In most lobbying situations, advocates have about 30 seconds to make their point. With so little time, it can feel as if the descriptions of the clients' problems and proposed solutions are grossly over-simplified. One alternative is to avoid this advocacy tactic, but most advocates would agree that one-on-one lobbying of legislators is essential. Among the many ways that advocates resolve this dilemma is to tell legislators that they are only being given a thumbnail sketch of the issues, and that a position paper with more details is available for their review.

Believe it or not, there are good reasons to be optimistic about advocacy. I'm not sure I was optimistic when I started doing advocacy. I had idealistic hopes about creating a better, more just society and world, and I was somewhat cynical about the possibility of being successful in such an enormous venture. After my first legislative session working for a child advocacy agency, however, I saw that advocacy could be effective and could contribute to significant change.

To this day I'm not quite sure how we did it, or what forces came together to assist us. Child advocates throughout the state of Florida were concerned about youth dropping out or skipping school, about large numbers of expulsions and suspensions, especially since a disproportionate number were youth of color. A coalition of advocates was able to get legislation passed (and $10 million of funding) for school districts to set up alternative school programs that would be responsive to youth who had trouble in mainstream programs. Passage and funding of the legislation was only the beginning, but I had seen the process work. This is what can happen when organized advocates seek targeted change.

Research on Advocacy   Very little research has been done on advocacy. There are numerous case studies describing and analyzing advocacy efforts but almost no comparative studies that examine which advocacy strategies work best under differing circumstances. Throughout the book, I include findings from a study I did on social work advocacy (Ezell, 1991, 1993, 1994). I use the findings as a springboard toward more in-depth discussions of the practice of advocacy.

I surveyed a random sample of social workers in one state to collect data on advocacy. The research is limited by the fact that it focused on social workers and did not include other human service professionals; it was done in one state only; it used survey techniques; and it was done almost 10 years ago. Notwithstanding the limitations, the findings are useful as grist for one's mill.

ADVOCACY IDEALS

One of the things that members of the helping professions have in common is the desire to make a difference. They hope to shape communities, societies, and the world in certain desirable ways. They want to rid the world of undesirables such as injustice, oppression, suffering, ignorance, and poverty. This is why advocacy should be done. When people focus their mind's eye, they can see both the ugliness they wish to eliminate and the dream they want to reach. In other words, they hold to a set of ideals; and when an agency, city, state, or country falls short of those ideals, they want to act.

What is your personal version of this? What will the world look like if your advocacy efforts succeed? What end results or ideals are your high priorities? Some advocacy ideals are listed below. As you read them, think about whether you agree with them or if you would need to edit them to match your vision. These ideals articulate the desired long-term results of advocacy and what you hope the world looks like when you are finished.[2] They are interdependent and not mutually exclusive. Some need explanation and others do not. They are listed in Figure 1.1.

We advocate to create a society that is just, in which all persons have equal opportunities to pursue their potential. Advocates get involved in many issues because clients haven't been treated fairly, or because their opportunities are blocked or are unequal. For example, those who advocate for school desegregation or for equal pay for those of comparable worth are doing so in order to make society more just and to equalize opportunity.

We advocate to ensure that programs and services are accessible, effective, appropriate, flexible, comprehensive, adequate, and efficient. Programs are accessible if the neediest of clients can be served conveniently at the service sight, their home, or both, and there are no barriers that prevent the receipt of services. They are effective if they satisfy client needs and eliminate

---

2. The following ideas were influenced by the work of Richart and Bing (1989). In their work, they conceptualized these as goals.

We advocate to

1. create a society that is just, in which all persons have equal opportunities to pursue their potential.

2. ensure that programs and services are accessible, effective, appropriate, flexible, comprehensive, adequate, and efficient.

3. protect existing individual rights and entitlements and to establish new rights and entitlements as needed.

4. eliminate the negative and unethical impact that social institutions, organizations, programs, and individuals may have on people.

5. assure that the least intrusive intervention is utilized to meet the client's needs and achieve the service goal.

FIGURE **1.1**

Advocacy ideals.

or reduce the clients confronting problems. Services are appropriate if they are addressing the real, high-priority problems and needs of clients, and if there is a logical match between the service and the need. They are flexible if they can adapt to different kinds of clients who have different circumstances, challenges, and locations but the same essential issues. Services are comprehensive if they effectively address all aspects of a problem and issues frequently bundled together. Programs are adequate when they are able to serve all who require their services. Finally, they are efficient if resources are expended wisely.

We advocate in order to protect existing individual rights and entitlements and to establish new rights and entitlements as needed. Although federal and state constitutions and laws have created many rights and entitlements, they are not always observed. Many advocates feel that more rights and entitlements should be created if, for example, a right to treatment has been established in some service arenas but not in others. Agencies can and do create rights for their clients. For example, some agencies have established clear procedures on how to terminate program eligibility, as schools do when they expel students. Their policies might dictate that a neutral arbiter is to make the decision after holding a hearing that allows both sides to present their cases. The policies might further articulate when and how to appeal.

We advocate to eliminate the negative and unethical impact that social institutions, organizations, programs, and individuals may have on people. Some agency practices inappropriately or negatively label people while others exclude, under-serve, or deny eligibility to them. There are agencies that, through acts of either omission or commission, cause physical and psychological damage. There are organizations that have neglected to maintain their facilities or have failed to assure the appropriate qualifications of staff members. Sometimes clients are not treated with respect and are not empowered to have input into decisions that impact them. Advocates labor to reduce and eliminate these negative impacts and interactions between their clients and agencies.

We advocate to assure that the least intrusive intervention[3] is utilized to meet the client's needs and achieve the service goal. This is similar to physicians' Hippocratic oath to do no harm. We hope to have services that are not disruptive, that minimize invasions of privacy and maximize client self-determination and autonomy. We don't want the cure to be worse than the cause.

Are there other advocacy ideals you can add to this list? Which ones of these are particularly meaningful for you? Why? Answering this question will help you identify the specific values that fuel your desire to bring about change.

Advocates also use these ideals as assessment criteria when monitoring the operations of various programs and policies. Each implies a set of questions to ask. For example, is this policy or program just, does it promote equal opportunity? Is this service accessible to parents who work from 8:00 a.m. until 5:00 p.m.? If you go through the advocacy ideals and turn them into questions, you will have a valuable advocacy tool. When we identify a gap between an advocacy ideal and the actual operation of a program, we are motivated to advocate.

WHY DO ADVOCACY?

Before you read any further, take a moment and jot down several reasons for which you might do advocacy. If you haven't had a chance to engage in advocacy, make a short list of your potential motivations for doing it.

How do your reasons compare to the research? The author's survey included a list of possible reasons for doing advocacy and respondents were asked to rank their top three reasons. In an exploratory study on advocacy, Epstein (1981) found that "many advocates seem to have entered the field through personal experiences of stigmatization and through involvements in self-help movements" (p. 6). Other reasons were chosen more frequently in the author's study, however. More respondents wanted to see things change and considered advocacy the best approach for certain problems. Many respondents advocate because they feel it's their professional responsibility to do so. The code of ethics of the National Association of Social Workers (NASW, 1996) outlines an expectation that social workers will advocate for their clients, as do the codes of ethics of other professions (e.g., National

---

3. Others refer to the "least detrimental alternative."

Organization for Human Service Education, 2000). The ethics of advocacy will be discussed at length in chapter 3.

Very few social workers do advocacy because of peer pressure or because they wish to avoid feelings of guilt, and previous work or volunteer experience are also infrequently chosen as reasons (see Table 1.1). Less than 3% say their primary reason for doing advocacy is "because it's my job to do it" and even fewer do it because they enjoy it.

The reason that far outranks all others is "because of my personal values." Strong personal beliefs, values, and standards motivate those who engage in advocacy. Upon reflection, the response, "because of my personal values," may not go far enough to identify the particular beliefs that motivate advocates. This response could be inclusive of some of the other reasons listed in the question; one's personal values might derive from experiences of oppression, prior work or volunteer experience, or professional ethics. Nevertheless, respondents are saying that they do advocacy because of personal principles or standards in order to achieve something worthwhile.

For Whom to Advocate

By examining the types of client groups for which practitioners advocate, we can get a hint about specific motivating values. Children and youth is the client group most frequently advocated for, and no other group even approaches this

TABLE 1.1   REASONS FOR DOING ADVOCACY

"I want to do advocacy because . . ."	Primary Choice (%)	First, Second, or Third Choice (%)
of my personal values.	43.3	70.0
I think it's the best approach for certain problems.	13.9	51.8
it's my professional responsibility.	13.0	49.8
I'd like to see things change.	8.8	41.6
I've personally experienced oppression.	2.5	8.8
it's my job to do it.	2.3	6.5
I enjoy advocacy activities.	.6	7.1
of my previous work experience.	.6	4.5
of previous volunteer experience.	.3	3.4
I'd feel guilty if I didn't.	0.0	3.4
of peer pressure.	0.0	.3

frequency (see Table 1.2). To varying degrees, the groups listed in Table 1.2 have two things in common: (1) many helping professionals may perceive them to be vulnerable because they have little power; and (2) they may not be able to advocate effectively for themselves.[4] This being the case, it is reasonable to deduce that one of the reasons to advocate is to try to balance differences of power, to increase the influence of and protect vulnerable groups. It also seems to be the case that every client group deserves to have one or more spokespersons, advocates who look out for their best interests when they are unable to do so. Put together, these ideas form a very basic advocacy belief: everyone should have a voice in policymaking processes so that their interests are represented, whether the voice is that of the clients themselves or advocates representing them.

There are other reasons for doing advocacy that haven't been mentioned. Many people explain that they feel so frustrated or angry over the ways certain client groups are short-changed they simply have to do something to change things. Others have explained that their desire to advocate wells up from deep inside because their sense of justice has been offended by some action or

---

TABLE 1.2 FOR WHOM DO YOU ADVOCATE?

Client Group	Primary Choice (%)	First, Second, or Third Choice (%)
Children and youth	33.1	49.3
Other[a]	10.0	n/a
Older people	8.5	18.4
People with chronic mental illness	8.5	15.6
People with emotional disturbances	4.8	21.8
People with low incomes	4.2	24.6
Women	4.0	21.8
People with developmental disabilities	3.4	9.6
Minorities	3.1	9.1
People with chronic illnesses	1.4	2.5
Victims of abuse	.8	1.7

[a]Includes unspecified groups, homeless people, gays and lesbians, crime victims, people with AIDS, and people charged with crimes.

---

4. It is important to note that perceptions of powerlessness or vulnerability might not reflect reality for all members of these groups. These perceptions are sometimes based on historically outdated information, but even though they are inaccurate, they are powerful shapers of behavior.

omission; they feel outraged and must do something. I remember feeling moved to act when a colleague pointed out the disturbing notion that everyone is an advocate, but the problem is that most people advocate for the status quo. Attempting to change things requires great energy and focus.

IS ENOUGH TIME DEVOTED TO ADVOCACY?

When asked, "How much time do you devote to advocacy?" approximately 90% of the social work respondents advocated for clients on the job and slightly more than 65% did so as volunteers. Approximately one third of the respondents said they did no volunteer advocacy and another third did less than an hour per week.

What are your reactions to these findings? Are they consistent with your experience and observations as you've worked in the field, done internships, or volunteered? Your reactions may depend on whether you're a person who sees the glass as half *full* or half *empty*. The part of me that I'll label the "advocacy lunatic" was very disappointed with these findings. I just don't understand why practitioners don't work around the clock doing advocacy and then do more in the evenings and on weekends. Who needs sleep when you're working on such noble causes?

On the other hand, an hour a week adds up over the course of a year or two, and if practitioners are working together in teams and coalitions as they do advocacy, this can have a positive impact. Similarly, advocating for half a day per week, either through work or as a volunteer, is 26 days of advocacy per year. If every one of those advocates would increase this by an hour a week, this would add more than a workweek to the yearly total.

It is not possible to say whether this amount of volunteer and job advocacy is a lot or a little, or whether this is an increase or decrease from 10 or 20 years earlier. There is, however, some indication that the political activity of social workers has been increasing in the last decade (Ezell, 1993). A lot could be learned if another survey could be administered to the same respondents five years later.

What are your impressions of advocacy trends? Are practitioners doing more, less, or the same amount of advocacy? For you, what is the right amount of time to devote to advocacy on the job and as a volunteer?

Being an Advocate Versus Doing Advocacy

This is a good time to point out an important distinction implicitly being made. Note that the survey didn't ask respondents to indicate if they consider themselves to be advocates or not, but sought to determine how much time they devoted to *doing* advocacy. Phrases such as *doing advocacy,* or *engaging in advocacy* are being used here as opposed to *being an advocate*. It is likely that almost all of the respondents, as well as everyone in the helping professions, think of themselves as advocates because they all have the client's best interests in mind and do all they can to make sure their needs are being met. It is important to think of advocacy as something one does, an intervention for one or more clients, or a type of practice, as opposed to a set of thoughts, feelings, or attitudes (e.g., a proclient viewpoint). This idea is more fully discussed in chapter 2.

OPTIMISM ABOUT ADVOCACY

Besides some of the questions already discussed, the advocacy survey mailed to social workers included a list of statements on which respondents were asked to indicate their level of agreement. Table 1.3 includes the results. As you review the findings on each of the items, think about how you would respond.

Respondents strongly believe that advocacy should be one of their official duties (see Table 1.3). Almost all of those who are in jobs involving some advocacy are happy with that.

Item 2 indicates that the vast majority of respondents believe that advocacy is a social worker's professional responsibility. They weren't asked whether this professional responsibility has to be acted on at work, as a volunteer, or both. That would have been an interesting follow-up question. What do you think? Should everyone be expected to do advocacy, and should they be expected to be happy about it?

Are social workers optimistic about advocacy? In general, yes. More than 60% agreed that advocacy will produce major change, and 80.4% said that they are successful helping clients through advocacy.[5] Furthermore, almost 90% said that we have a better chance of success if we work together in coalitions or organizations. In Item 6, respondents were given a chance to express any reservations they might have about doing advocacy compared to other types of interventions. Surprisingly, almost 75% say that advocacy does not detract from other helpful activities. Are your impressions different from these data? Many respondents seem to think that advocacy holds great promise for helping clients.

Respondents expressed a high level of optimism that advocacy can meet the challenge of improving our social service system and also expressed that their peers are supportive of their advocacy work. Without this support, one

---

5. You may be wondering about the wording of these statements and why some are worded positively and others negatively. This is a technique used in survey research to assure that the respondent reads the item closely. If all of the items are worded positively, for example, the respondent starts to expect this and may not pay close attention after several items.

TABLE 1.3	PREVALENT ATTITUDES REGARDING ADVOCACY			
Attitude Regarding Advocacy		**Agree (%)**	**Neutral (%)**	**Disagree (%)**
1. Advocacy should be part of my official duties.		82.5	7.4	10.1
2. Advocacy is part of being a professional social worker.		92.7	5.3	2.0
3. Advocacy will produce change, but it will be minor.		25.3	12.5	62.2
4. I am rarely successful at helping clients through advocacy.		5.4	14.2	80.4
5. Advocates have the best chance of succeeding if they work together in a coalition or organization.		88.1	8.7	3.3
6. Devoting time to advocacy takes away from other job activities that would help clients more.		7.2	20.3	72.5
7. The social service system is so big and complex that advocates won't be able to change it.		6.3	6.9	86.8
8. The attitudes of other social workers support my advocacy efforts.		68.2	24.7	7.1

might feel isolated doing advocacy and would tend to do less. Figure 1.2 summarizes these findings.

What Keeps Practitioners from Doing Advocacy?

When asked their reasons for *not* doing advocacy, by far the most frequent reason social workers gave was a lack of time. Other frequently cited reasons included the following: lack of energy to do advocacy, lack of resources, advocacy is not the best approach to use, and a lack of training in how to do advocacy. (Obviously, this book is intended to deal with this last one.) Are these just a bunch of excuses being made by guilt-laden respondents? In a few cases this might be true, but taking these statements at face value is a better approach. The lack of time, energy, resources, and training are real barriers that can and must be dealt with if we are to increase advocacy.

Predictors of Advocacy Involvement

Two questions previously discussed turned out to be very important predictors of the amount of time devoted to advocacy and they provide a clue as to how to increase the number of practitioners doing advocacy. Those who said that

IN GENERAL, SOCIAL WORKERS FEEL THAT

1. advocacy should be expected of them in their jobs and as professional social workers.

2. advocacy can have a major impact for clients, and advocates can be successful, especially if they work together.

3. advocacy can help clients more than other job activities.

4. they receive their colleagues' support for advocacy.

5. our social service system is changeable.

FIGURE **1.2**

General attitudes about advocacy.

advocacy was part of their official duties spent more time doing advocacy than those who said it was not (Ezell, 1994). A person's job description and assignments are critical factors. Furthermore, those who indicated that advocating for clients was one of their agency's primary functions did more advocacy than those who worked for nonadvocacy agencies. Agency function and a person's job description are important factors that can determine whether and how much advocacy a practitioner will do.

This is a huge dilemma experienced by thousands of practitioners who see the need for advocacy and wish they could do more. A substantial majority thinks that advocacy should both be part of their duties and be expected of professional social workers. Even then, they say, "How in the world can I try to change anything with the workload I have, with limited access to information, and the constraints my agency puts on what I can do?" That is a good question. What would you recommend?

SELF-EMPOWERMENT TO DO ADVOCACY

There are real constraints and obstacles to advocacy in almost every agency, including situations where advocacy is neither included in job descriptions nor considered an agency function. These decrease the chances of doing advocacy. Nevertheless, there are many practitioners who do advocacy anyway. They seem to have four things in common: (1) they see the need for advocacy; (2) they believe that advocacy will work to improve client situations; (3) they know how and when to do advocacy; and (4) they do not feel overwhelmed by it. These four characteristics interact with each other in the sense that if, for example, a person feels unsure of his or her advocacy skills, he or she is likely to be pessimistic about its prospects.

This book can help deal with knowing how and when to do advocacy, and it should convince readers that advocacy can be effective. Hopefully after studying this book readers will feel motivated to do it, but let's first deal with those who already know they want to do it but are faced with agency constraints.

Reducing Barriers to Advocacy

There are many things you can do to reduce the barriers to advocacy in your agency. Taylor (1987) wisely points out that you should expect some resistance in your agency and that this is usually based on your colleagues' fear and lack of knowledge and experience. Several ideas are described below.

Talk to your supervisor or director about adding advocacy to your job description or increasing the amount of time you can devote to advocacy. This is a conversation you could initiate at any time, but it would be logical for it to arise during your evaluation, when you agree on your professional development plan. There are many ways to convince a supervisor that this is a good idea. First, if there are several of your colleagues who share your views and will join you when discussing it with your supervisor, your chances of success are improved. Second, document the client needs that will go unmet if advocacy is not undertaken. Third, underscore the fact that your professional ethics require you to advocate. Fourth, demonstrate the positive impacts you already achieved from your advocacy efforts. Finally, explain how doing advocacy will make your program more successful and make your supervisor and agency look good (see Homan, 1999, pp. 67–70 for other suggestions).

Talk to your director about making advocacy an explicit goal of the agency, and about making arrangements for training in advocacy. Many of the tactics used above are useful here, too.

Write a grant to fund advocacy positions in your agency or to allow you to use more of your time for advocacy. A local foundation or corporation could be persuaded that advocacy would complement what you currently do, is greatly needed by your clients, and has the potential of helping a lot of clients.

Locate an advocacy organization with which you can cooperate. If nothing else, they will value your perspective on the problems clients face, the strengths and weaknesses of current policies and programs, and suggestions for solutions. Bringing issues to the attention of other advocates who are in a better position to act is an important contribution. Work with them or do advocacy after hours. Volunteer with your local advocacy agency or professional association or coalesce with other workers to advocate for change.

You might consider looking for a new job. This is not said lightly and it is complicated because few people feel they have the economic freedom to leave a stable job. When it is time for you to look for a promotion or a new job, however, you can ask about the opportunities for advocacy. If you've been offered a new position, you might negotiate for more time to do advocacy. You have the most leverage at this point.

Personal Hesitations

If you are truthful with yourself, you might discover that the reason you do very little advocacy has more to do with your own hesitations than job or agency constraints. It's natural to occasionally blame others and avoid taking responsibility. Just like the resistance you may encounter from others, your own hesitation may come from doubts and inexperience. The question, then, is how to get past those feelings and thoughts that are holding you back.

Homan (1999) says you have to give yourself permission to act and you have to believe that you will be successful. Although it may sound paradoxical, you also should give yourself permission *not* to act. First, give yourself a break and don't put so much pressure on yourself about all the things you *should* be doing. This sounds like heresy—especially because motivating more advocacy is a goal of the book—but maybe your strengths lie in other areas, you don't like advocacy, or you don't think it's effective. Believe it or not, that's fine. You can't do everything and shouldn't be expected to do so.

There are ways for everyone to contribute to advocacy efforts without necessarily doing advocacy oneself. We are better off if we let people choose to do advocacy instead of using strong-arm tactics, guilt-tripping, and insisting that they absolutely *must* do it (or else they'll be an evil person). More will choose to do it and will do it effectively if it remains a personal choice than if we coerce these behaviors. (Remember this when you get involved recruiting and organizing advocates. Giving permission to choose and respecting a person's choice mobilizes more advocates than not.)

Keep Clients' Needs in the Forefront

A necessary condition for doing advocacy is that you have to know that action is necessary, that the unmet needs of current and future clients are not and will not be addressed without an advocacy intervention. This knowledge is derived from your observations of clients, the quality of the services they get, and those that are not available. Systematic documentation of these observations adds credibility to your case.

As was pointed out earlier, it is important to stay in touch with your advocacy ideals. It is equally important to keep client needs in the forefront. Let me give you an example of this from my advocacy experience. We wanted to do something about the fact that many youth charged with delinquent acts are held in adult jails and commingled with adult prisoners. (This is an issue I come back to frequently in the book and use as an example of many different things). This is a problem for many reasons, not the least of which are the psychological and physical risks youth experience in these settings.

During the time when we were studying the extent and nature of this problem, two juveniles committed suicide while in adult jails, which was unfortunately a predictable occurrence. We documented the problem and its causes, proposed solutions, and many of our recommendations were included in a large legislative bill to reform juvenile justice. As the bill to resolve the problem was moving through the legislature, some groups opposed it and others wanted to compromise or limit it. We found ourselves in the heady situation of negotiating with powerful legislators, lobbyists, and representatives of the governor's office.

It was overwhelming to be in this situation and it was difficult to know how to evaluate various proposals, when to compromise, or when to draw the line. We found it helpful to keep these juveniles in our thoughts, frequently reminding ourselves of their situations and the all too frequent consequences of being commingled with adult prisoners in jail. It was also of strategic benefit to remind others that there would be very important consequences for real people for our actions; we weren't just altering amendments and statutory language.

Feeling the need for action is necessary, but it is not always sufficient to move practitioners into an action mode. You need to know what to do and to have some confidence in your skills. This doesn't just happen because you see a need to advocate and want to do something. One of the primary ways to empower yourself to do advocacy is to learn about advocacy. There are many ways to do this, including courses, workshops, books, and volunteering. It is also very beneficial to work with your colleagues as a team of advocates. Some members of the team will have more experience using certain tactics. You can make your unique contribution to the effort and learn as you go. Another benefit of team advocacy is that there is safety in numbers; unless you feel safe, you are unlikely to engage in advocacy.

Unsafe to Do Advocacy?

What makes people feel unsafe? Maybe the thought that they alone must know the answers, that the stakes are high, and that they better not make mistakes. First, one of the primary advantages of working with a team of advocates is that you don't have to know everything. You can rely on others. Advocacy is a process that unfolds as you move forward; you will not have all the information you need from the beginning and you won't even know all the questions. The stakes are high and, realistically, you can make mistakes. However, the biggest possible mistake occurs when you do nothing—the status quo is reinforced. Doing nothing, sitting on the sidelines, insures that nothing will change for your clients.

Without becoming reckless, keep a healthy perspective about what many would label "mistakes." No one can predict how others will react to a particular advocacy tactic. In hindsight, advocates might decide that someone's reaction was undesirable and different than that for which they had hoped. While some might say that using the tactic was a mistake, it is more functional to view it as new information one can use to make decisions about a continuing strategy.

For example, I used to dislike being second-guessed about what I said during legislative committee testimony. Every now and then, you might have to deal with an aggressive question or comment. Later your colleagues may be full of advice about what you should have said, which can be very frustrating. You might agree that your response didn't turn out as you had hoped, but all is not lost. You can visit or write to legislators to clarify your position. This visit might result in legislators having a better understanding of the issue and some might be persuaded to your position. So, how big of a mistake did you make?

Who Gave You the Right?

Knowing that advocacy is needed and knowing what to do are critical pieces of the motivation puzzle. In addition, advocates need to feel confident that their effort is legitimate. There are many sources of legitimacy, but as Patti (1974) and Bateman (1995) point out:

> The most obvious source, for the professional worker at least, is his [sic] ethical commitment to the primacy of client welfare. (Patti, p. 538)

> The driving force behind the use of advocacy skills is the advocate's ethical stance. (Bateman, p. 59)

We therefore rely heavily on our professional and personal codes of ethics as sources of legitimacy. I have been known to argue (in jest) that we have a constitutional right to complain, and then I came across a wonderful quote from W. E. B. Du Bois that seems to legitimize complaining:

> We must complain, yes plain, blunt complaint, ceaseless agitation, unfailing exposure of dishonesty and wrong—this is the unerring way to liberty, and we must follow it. (Du Bois, 1905)

Another important source of legitimacy is thorough and systematic documentation of clients' problems and needs. This documentation is usually accompanied by a description of the costs and consequences for the client and the community if these issues remain unaddressed. This analysis lends credibility and urgency to your efforts.

Several reminders that might empower practitioners to do advocacy are summarized in Figure 1.3. A final and important source of legitimacy has been

SELF-EMPOWERING REMINDERS

1. Focus on your clients, what they are experiencing, and what they're not getting. Their unmet needs give legitimacy to your efforts.

2. You don't have to do it all yourself.

3. The fear that you'll make a mistake is a good reminder of how important the issue is.

4. The only way to avoid mistakes is to do nothing. The same approach is used to maintain the status quo.

5. Advocacy is an unfolding process. You do not need to have all the answers before you start.

6. Anxiety is created by trying to make decisions too soon and before you have the information you need for those decisions. Move forward and many solutions will be obvious.

7. Excitement and anxiety feel very similar. Label those feelings in your stomach as excitement.

8. You absolutely have the right to question the system for your clients.

9. Don't assume the target system will resist.

10. Think of the outcome of advocacy as a victory for your clients *and* for the target agency (not a win-lose scenario).

FIGURE 1.3

Self-empowering reminders.

implied earlier. If it is part of your job to do advocacy or one of your agency's goals, you are on solid ground to engage in these efforts. Others, both inside and outside your organization, will not question your motives and will tend to give you the benefit of the doubt regarding the legitimacy of the issues for which you advocate.

SUMMARY

This chapter identified and discussed several ideals that advocacy hopes to achieve. These ideals describe optimum conditions for people, communities, and society as a whole. Advocacy practice involves the elimination of problems and the achievement of these ideals. As was discussed, advocates are motivated by many different feelings and goals and intend to assist many different client groups, children and youth being the most common.

One section of the chapter asked whether enough time is devoted to advocacy and analyzed different ways to answer. Another analyzed prevalent attitudes about advocacy and found that there is a great deal of optimism about advocacy. Even though there is optimism about advocacy, there are some common barriers to advocacy practice, the most common being a lack of time. Finally, the chapter presented several self-empowering suggestions to move practitioners into an advocacy posture.

DISCUSSION QUESTIONS

1. What is the difference between doing advocacy and being an advocate? Why is (or isn't) this distinction important?
2. What are some of your reasons for wanting to do advocacy? Do they correspond with those discussed in the chapter?
3. Can you add to the list of reasons why some people don't do advocacy? Imagine being in a situation with the same barriers to advocacy. What could you do to eliminate or reduce these barriers?
4. Are there wrong reasons for doing advocacy? Are there reasons for doing advocacy that might compromise effectiveness? Explain your answers.
5. Do you think the results of the survey would have been different if the respondents had been members of human service professions besides social work?

UNDERSTANDING ADVOCACY 2

CHAPTER OBJECTIVES

By the time you finish studying this chapter, you should

1. Be able to define advocacy and distinguish it from other macro interventions.
2. Be able to distinguish between different types of advocacy.
3. Be able to give examples of what advocates do (i.e., advocacy activities).
4. Be able to discuss and debate several ideas and assumptions that underpin the practice of advocacy.

Specific ideas and assumptions shape the practice of advocacy. It is also influenced by lessons learned from previous advocacy efforts. This chapter starts with a presentation of a conceptual foundation for advocacy practice. The framework defines advocacy and discusses its underlying assumptions. In addition, different types of advocacy will be explained in this chapter.

Devoting time to this foundation work is important for several reasons. First, to be certain that communications are clear, it is important to ensure that we use the same terms in the same way. It is not unusual for two people having a conversation to use the same words but find out later that they really meant very different things. Second, as advocacy matures as a definable practice intervention and as knowledge about it and its effectiveness accumulates, it is important to be able to distinguish it from other interventions. To conduct research on the effectiveness of advocacy and to teach it as a distinct approach, boundaries need to be placed around a set of activities and behaviors with the understanding that they meet the definition of advocacy and those outside the boundary do not. This is equally true of other interventions.

Those who want to roll up their sleeves and do advocacy are usually impatient and want to skip the kind of material presented in this chapter. They say they want very practical skills with no theory. On the one hand, the energy and enthusiasm to get out there and bring about changes that benefit clients is admirable. On the other hand, advocates such as these might not be as effective as they would be if they paid more attention to the conceptual foundations of advocacy practice. This is because advocacy can't be learned or practiced effectively by following a recipe. A recipe only provides the steps and how much of each ingredient to include. They presume constancy of conditions, problems, and participants. The targets and contexts of advocacy are complex and dynamic, however. The critical, first skill an effective advocate needs is the ability to analyze issues, targets, and surrounding circumstances.

The comprehensive advocacy approach in this book is based on a set of assumptions that are usually true, but not always. If advocates don't fully understand these assumptions, they won't know when they don't apply and when the situation calls for a shift of strategies. The following quote from Melton (1983), which can be generalized beyond child advocacy, summarizes the reason for this chapter:

> If child advocacy is to be effective, it needs to be conceptualized better, with particular attention to selection of strategies for making bureaucracies, courts, corporations, etc. responsive to children's needs. (Davidson & Rapp, 1976, p. 91)

Kurt Lewin, a well-known psychologist, once said, "There is nothing so practical as a good theory." Polansky (1986) used this as a title for a very instructive article in which he quotes Lewin and explains that theory tells us what factors to attend to in practice situations and can also organize our efforts. Theories summarize and condense into generalizations the knowledge of those who came before us. As you will see, the set of interconnected definitions, assumptions, concepts, and ideas explained below become a theory of advocacy practice that provides practical guidance as advocacy challenges are confronted.

WHAT IS ADVOCACY? (AND WHAT ISN'T IT?)

While teaching this material in the past, I have found that everyone usually agrees that it's a good idea to have a clear definition of advocacy. Then an interesting phenomenon usually occurs: many students and practitioners try to find a way to fit just about everything they do into the definition of advocacy. The typical statement is: "I do a lot of X in my job. That's advocacy, isn't it?" They seem to feel slighted, or as if what they do is unimportant, if all of their practice activities don't fit within the definition of advocacy. Their thought seems to be that if their activity is intended to help clients, it must be advocacy. The definition of advocacy developed in this book, however, moves away from one that relies on practitioners' intentions and uses a more behaviorally specific definition.

Clearly, helping professionals serve many roles and do many important things to help clients. Sometimes this includes advocacy (as defined later), and sometimes it doesn't. All of these services (or interventions) are important and do not lose their value if they fail to meet the definition of advocacy presented below. Depending on the nature of the client problem or need, there are many situations in which advocacy is not the appropriate intervention. Advocacy is intended to help clients, and not everything a helping professional does is advocacy.

The desire to sweep many disparate helping actions under the rubric of advocacy may stem from professional norms that say that everyone should be doing advocacy (and lots of it). The high value placed on advocacy—although there have been scholars who questioned whether this was just lip service—is a good thing, up to a point. The powerful, albeit unspoken, downside of this norm is the message that if you're not doing advocacy then you are being unethical or falling short in some other way. That's ridiculous! Practitioners should be proud of all the different interventions and activities they use to help people. Choosing one intervention over another shouldn't give a practitioner more or less status; the choice should be based on the needs of the client and what is known about the relative effectiveness of different interventions in different situations. If there were a status system in the helping professions, it should be based on effectiveness. If the chosen intervention effectively meets clients' needs, it doesn't matter whether it fits the definition of advocacy.

Definition

Many definitions of **advocacy** have been suggested over the years. "To defend or promote a cause" is a simple and frequently used definition (McCormick, 1970; Panitch, 1974; Weissman, Epstein, & Savage, 1983). This definition emphasizes action in the phrase "to defend or promote." Hepworth and Larsen (1986) developed a very useful definition of advocacy:

> the process of working with and/or on behalf of clients (1) to obtain services or resources for clients that would not otherwise be provided, (2) to modify extant policies, procedures, or practice that adversely impact clients, or (3) to promote new legislation or policies that will result in the provision of needed resources or services. (p. 569)

This definition underscores the fact that advocacy is goal seeking, that it is a process, and that the process of advocacy involves "obtaining," "modifying," and "promoting."

Kutchins and Kutchins (1978) as well as Sosin and Caulum (1983) pointed out that the definition of advocacy should focus on advocacy activities, not on the advocate's role. Likewise, we should have a definition that allows us to examine what helping professionals are doing to determine whether it is advocacy or some other practice intervention. All too often, it is concluded that practitioners are advocates because they philosophically support the client, are on client's side, or have intentions that are in the best interests of the client. The National Association of Social Workers (NASW) Ad Hoc Committee on Advocacy (1969) asserted that "good intentions are not enough for the fulfillment of the advocacy role" (p. 20).

Besides having a definition that is behaviorally specific and can be used to determine whether an activity is advocacy, it should be clear and simple, and should encompass many different types of advocacy. The following is the definition used in this book:

> **Advocacy consists of those purposive efforts to change specific existing or proposed policies or practices on behalf of or with a specific client or group of clients.**

To Change   Embedded in this seemingly straightforward definition are a number of important elements, each of which deserves a few clarifying comments. The first element of the definition to notice is the primary verb, "to change." Advocacy is about change and this is central to the practice of advocacy. Social policies and agency practices need to be changed in order to attain the advocacy ideals articulated in chapter 1.

It is important to remember that everyone is an advocate. While this sounds good, the problem is that most of them advocate for the status quo. Advocacy can be used no matter which side of an issue you are on, and strategies will differ depending on your assessment of the status quo. The status quo has very powerful inertia, partially derived from all the justifications built around it, and because of this it can be an uphill battle to change it.

Generally, but not always, the energy goes toward advocating for change in the status quo. Sometimes advocacy is used to prevent seemingly negative changes to existing policies and practices. There are times when advocacy strategies are used to defeat proposals not thought to be in the best interests of clients, when the status quo—although still less than perfect—is better than the new proposal. Imagine, for example, a scenario in which advocates successfully procured funding from their legislature for a new service for their client group but, during the subsequent legislative session, they must engage in advocacy to maintain their progress and to fight an effort by unsympathetic legislators to cut the funds. In this case, advocates work to maintain the status quo and prevent change.

Purposive   The second important element in the definition is that advocacy is purposive. The term and idea are borrowed from Sunley (1983) when he refers to advocacy as "a planned and purposive change effort composed of study, planning, action, and evaluation" (p. 1). Bateman (1995) also says that advocacy is structured. It is systematic like other interventions in that it involves a thorough assessment of client problems and strengths, planning the intervention, implementing the advocacy plan, evaluating the results, and deciding how to proceed.

There is another very important aspect to advocacy's purposiveness. It is purposive in that it uses the four strategies described in this book—agency advocacy, legislative advocacy, legal advocacy, and community advocacy—as well as the specific tactics associated with these strategies. Those are the tools available to those who practice advocacy. Without this distinction, one might argue that the work human service managers do to change the policies and practices of their agencies is advocacy. The means by which they create change, however, is planning, organizing, staffing and supervising, raising and managing funds, and designing programs rather than using agency, legislative, legal, and community advocacy strategies. They are involved in advocacy (Ezell, 1991), but management practice is not advocacy practice.

Related to the purposiveness of the change effort, is that the definition separates means from ends. Advocates engage in purposive efforts, and the goal is improved policies and practices. The implication of this is that when evaluating an intervention to determine whether it is advocacy, not only the efforts, or activity, must be considered, but so should the goal of the activity.

Targets for Change   The definition of advocacy also identifies two targets for change, policies and practices. They can be either proposed or existing policies and practices (but for ease of presentation, the repetitive reminder will be dropped). First, it is important to note that the target of intervention is not the *client* but an agency policy or practice or a policy of the service system within which agencies operate, such as the child welfare system. Epstein (1981) explained that advocates generally work on problems that "are in the relationship between the client and an unresponsive 'system'" (p. 8).

Second, there is a distinction between a policy and a practice. Policies are usually formally stated, such as federal or state laws and local ordinances. Practices of agencies or individual practitioners are rarely formalized in writing, and these practices may or may not be consistent with agency or system policies. More extensive discussions of targets for change are included in chapters 4 through 7, which explain the four major advocacy strategies.

With and on Behalf of   Another element of the definition that deserves comment is the phrase "with and on behalf of." First, the definition does not indicate, and therefore does not limit, who engages in an advocacy change effort. It could be alcohol counselors, family support workers, social workers, doctors, nurses, teachers, or citizen volunteers. It most certainly could be a client or group of clients advocating on their own behalf, or it could be a coalition that includes professionals, citizen volunteers, and clients.

Second, it is not always possible for clients to engage in advocacy or to be fully involved as partners in a change effort (e.g., infants). Some may infer a disempowering meaning in the phrase "on behalf of" that is not intended. The dilemma of client involvement and permission will be discussed in chapter 3. For now, be assured that this book does not assume that professionals always know what's best for clients or that advocacy is something we have to do for clients because they can't do it for themselves. Clients should always be involved in advocacy in an empowering manner.[6]

TYPES OF ADVOCACY

The number of clients for whom one advocates is the first major factor used to draw distinctions between types of advocacy. If you are advocating for one client, a family, or a small, identifiable group of clients, this is known as **case advocacy.** McGowan (1987) defines it as "partisan intervention on behalf of an individual client or identified client group with one or more secondary institutions to secure or enhance a needed service, resource, or entitlement" (p. 92). Case advocacy has also been explained in the following way:

> The typical case advocacy situation involves a caseworker. . . . In trying to help a family, child, or youth . . . the direct service worker encounters a blockage. An agency is unresponsive, no service is provided, or a promised service does not materialize. Then, as the client's champion, the worker attempts to correct the situation. (Kahn, Kamerman, & McGowan, 1972, pp. 65–66)

Class advocacy, on the other hand, is an intervention to change a policy or practice on behalf of a group of clients who share the same problem or status (Epstein, 1981). The term *class* is borrowed from law as in "class action litigation." One might engage in class advocacy by seeking policy change that would benefit all abused children or all people with chronic mental illness, for example.

The distinction between case and class advocacy is not cut-and-dried. A helping professional might have a client who is not receiving appropriate services because of a particular agency's policy. The practitioner seeks to alter this

---

6. The phrase "with or on behalf of" may be shortened to avoid awkward wording.

policy to enable the receipt of services. If this advocate is successful, all similarly situated clients—a class—are likely to benefit. In this instance, a successful case advocacy effort has resulted in benefits for an entire class of clients. Generally, however, case advocacy doesn't seek change on the same scale as class advocacy. Case advocates may seek clarification or reinterpretation of an agency's rules denying their client's eligibility. They might argue that the rule has been misapplied, that relevant data has been ignored or misinterpreted, or that extenuating or special circumstances exist, but they aren't trying to change the rule. The distinction between case and class advocacy is based on who is identified as the client(s). It may be, for example, Ms. Jones and her children who have been inappropriately denied benefits (case advocacy) or all female-headed welfare families in the county whose benefit payments are insufficient (class advocacy).

Internal advocacy is another important type of advocacy. According to Patti (1974), internal advocacy is conducted by employees of an agency to change policies or practices of their agency. Examples he gives include the following: efforts to remove deleterious conditions or practices of their organization, and working to change their agency's policies to increase client access or to improve service effectiveness.

External advocacy occurs when change is sought in agencies other than one's agency of employment. Volunteers aren't employed in the same sense as staff, nor are clients. Both, however, are affiliated with some agencies and not others. If change is sought in their agency of affiliation, this is internal advocacy. If it is pursued in other organizations, with which there is no affiliation, this is external advocacy. This leads us to conclude that the nature of the advocate-agency affiliation, in a broader sense, is more useful in distinguishing between internal and external advocacy than merely looking at employment status.

Internal and external advocacy present advocates with different opportunities and challenges. Even though they are biting the hand that feeds them, internal advocates often have credibility because of their program expertise and access to information. Whether this gives internal advocates more leverage is debatable, but it is likely to impact the choice of strategies. Internal advocates, largely because of their employment status, are far more likely to use conservative tactics. Analogous with this, Melton (1983) identified stylistic differences between governmental versus private advocacy projects. Private (and external) advocacy projects tend to focus on class issues and use more adversarial strategies such as legal action. Government-sponsored advocacy projects are more conciliatory, case-oriented, and likely to use administrative negotiations.

There are many other types of advocacy, but few are clearly defined or mutually exclusive. They are listed and briefly defined in Table 2.1. The list represents apples and oranges in that strategies are mixed together with types.

The discussion to follow should help to clarify and simplify these divergent definitions.

Citizen, clinical, self, and **direct service advocacy** are similar in their focus on individual cases and are distinguished by who does the advocacy, a

TABLE 2.1	TYPES OF ADVOCACY

Type	Definition
Case Advocacy	"Partisan intervention on behalf of an individual client or identified client group with one or more secondary institutions to secure or enhance a needed service, resource, or entitlement" (McGowan, 1987, p. 92)
Class Advocacy	An intervention on behalf of a group of clients who share the same problem or status (Epstein, 1981)
Internal Advocacy	Is conducted by employees of an agency to change policies or practices of their agency (Patti, 1974)
Systems Advocacy	Is promoted to change policies and practices affecting all persons in a certain group or class (Schloss & Jayne, 1994, p. 230)
Policy Advocacy	Efforts to influence those who "work with laws, public programs, or court decisions" (Amidei, 1991)
Political Advocacy	Seems to be the same as class, policy, and systems advocacy
Self Advocacy	1) Clients/consumers learn their rights and how to protect them;
	2) "[A] process in which an individual, or a group of people, speak or act on their own behalf in pursuit of their own needs and interests" (Bateman, 1995, p. 4)
Clinical Advocacy	The delivery of services accompanied by efforts to alter "ecological mismatches" at the root of problem behaviors (Melton, 1983, p. 98)
Direct Service Advocacy	Making agencies accessible and accountable to those they serve
Citizen Advocacy	1) When a citizen "befriends" a service user and acts to understand, respond to and represent the other person's interests as if they were the advocate's own (Bateman, 1995)
	2) "[I]ndividual and broader-based efforts by members of the public to effect changes in both the formulation of policies and their implementation" (Hudson, 1982, p. 109)
Legal Advocacy	Representing clients before the courts or other legal tribunals
Legislative Advocacy	Promoting and influencing legislation that will benefit the deprived populations that social work represents
Community Advocacy	1) Educate the community, define and document problems, and organize the community (Schloss & Jayne, 1994);
	2) Advocacy on behalf of a composite of individuals in a community who have similar problems or needs but may not be known to each other (Coates, 1989)

citizen, a practitioner, or a client. In this book, all of these will be considered case advocacy. When clients take collective action on their own behalf, they are engaged in class advocacy. Who is doing case advocacy, and whether they are inside or outside the targeted agency, has implications for the choice of strategies, but the focus remains on individual cases.

Systems advocacy (Schloss & Jayne, 1994) and **policy advocacy** are the same as class advocacy. **Legal, administrative**, and **legislative advocacy** are viewed as *strategies* in this book (rather than *types*), and they can be used for either cases or classes. They are usually associated with class advocacy because the goal is broad change for many clients. Administrative advocacy is the most likely of this group to be used to resolve issues for individual cases. These three strategies identify the target system and incorporate the use of particular tactics. An entire chapter is devoted to each and more specifics will be discussed then.

Haynes and Mickelson (2000) wrote about **political advocacy** but have not defined it in a way that can be differentiated from class, policy, or systems advocacy. They say that political strategies are social action strategies used to intervene with government. They focus on "methods of influencing social policy" (p. xii) and suggest that legislative, judicial, and administrative interventions are appropriate. One can understand why legislative interventions might be labeled "political," but Haynes and Mickelson do not explain why judicial and administrative strategies would be. They frequently refer to two interventions: lobbying, which is equivalent to legislative advocacy in this book, and campaigning for candidates. Others have written about involvement in political campaigns (e.g., Salcido, 1984) but haven't necessarily called it political advocacy.

ANALYZING ADVOCACY ACTIVITIES

A list of specific advocacy activities was included in the survey the author sent to social workers (reviewed in chapter 1) and respondents were asked to indicate how often they engaged in each activity while advocating for their clients (activities listed in Figure 2.1). In order to move from the conceptual world to the world of advocacy practice, it is useful to see how well these advocacy activities fit into the definition of advocacy. Each of these activities will be discussed in greater detail in subsequent chapters, but, for now, a brief examination of them will help to crystallize the definition of advocacy.

Take a minute and review the definition of advocacy: Advocacy consists of those purposive efforts to change specific existing or proposed policies or practices on behalf of or with a specific client or group of clients. Now evaluate each of the activities in Figure 2.1 by asking yourself this question, "If I was engaged in this activity, would I be doing advocacy as defined here?" Does it

ACTIVITIES

1. Arguing for better services
2. Pushing for increased clients' rights in the agency
3. Negotiating with agencies
4. Giving testimony to decision makers
5. Lobbying individual policymakers
6. Litigating or seeking legal remedies
7. Representing a client in an administrative hearing
8. Influencing administrative rule making in other agencies
9. Teaching advocacy skills to clients to solve a problem
10. Educating clients on their rights
11. Educating the public on an issue
12. Monitoring other agencies' performance
13. Conducting issue research
14. Organizing coalitions
15. Influencing media coverage of an issue
16. Mobilizing constituent support
17. Political campaigning

yes

maybe

FIGURE **2.1**

Advocacy activities.

appear that the specific activity is seeking to change a policy or practice on behalf of or with clients?

For items 1 through 8, the answer is "yes, almost always." In each case, the practitioner is seeking change by "arguing, pushing, negotiating, giving, lobbying, litigating, representing, or influencing." It's true that because short phrases are being analyzed, one has to assume a lot. For example, one could reasonably argue that negotiating with agencies is not necessarily intended to change policies or practices for clients, but in most instances that is why the practitioner is doing it.

The answer for items 9 through 17 is "maybe." If a helping professional is teaching advocacy skills to clients because one or more of the clients need to negotiate with the Housing Authority, for example, the practitioner is doing advocacy training and the clients will be engaged in advocacy. The practition-er is not seeking to change a policy or practice directly, even though the results of his or her efforts might eventually lead to change. What this person is doing is important, but it is one step removed from direct advocacy.

Educating clients on their rights is similar to teaching advocacy skills in that the practitioner is seeking to improve the clients' knowledge. The clients may change as a result, but no policy or practice has been directly altered. This activity may be part of an advocacy strategy or part of service delivery, but the two distinct roles shouldn't be commingled (Herbert & Mould, 1992). If prac-titioners were providing services to these same clients, then educating them about their rights would seem to be an important facet of service delivery. If, however, the clients are getting services from another program (or are being denied services), teaching them about their rights will allow the clients to advocate for themselves and is part of an advocacy strategy.

Educating the public on an issue could also be considered one step removed from direct advocacy if it intends to change public attitudes that are supportive of ineffective policies or practices. It may be part of a strategy that seeks to change welfare policies and programs, for example, but until public misconcep-tions are neutralized or reversed, the context for change is unsupportive.

None of the next five items—monitoring agencies, conducting research, organizing coalitions, influencing media, or mobilizing constituents—directly seek to change policies or practices but, as above, are one step removed from direct advocacy. Advocates usually engage in these activities as part of an advocacy strategy. Advocates monitor agencies to gather information on the implementation of policies and practices, but monitoring, itself, doesn't pro-duce change.[7] Neither issue research nor the development of coalitions directly produces change in policy, but both are frequently necessary for effective advocacy. Advocates frequently seek to mobilize policymakers' con-stituents so they will communicate their support or opposition of an issue to their representative.

Participating in political campaigns is very important but is several steps removed from direct advocacy. Campaign activities are intended to garner enough votes to get a candidate elected or reelected. They are intended to change voter behavior not policies or practices that impact clients. Frequent-ly the reason for supporting certain candidates is that they have expressed their interest in changing policies and practices. By campaigning for these can-didates, practitioners hope that certain policies will eventually change, but many intervening steps must occur for this to happen.

---

7. Some would argue that agencies will behave differently because they know they are being scrutinized by advocates, and, therefore, monitoring has produced change. Be that as it may, monitoring is generally a technique used to collect information on service delivery and on how clients are being treated.

After reviewing all these activities, some of which are examples of advocacy while others are important steps in advocacy strategies, it should be obvious that advocates need many different types of skills to produce change.

BELIEFS AND ASSUMPTIONS UNDERLYING ADVOCACY PRACTICE

Assumptions are those things thought to be true about how people, society, social institutions, and the world work. Generally, people have been operating under these assumptions for so long they reside at a subconscious level; packaged together, they become our worldview. Every conceptual framework, theoretical model, or practice intervention operates on a set of assumptions; sometimes they are identified explicitly, but not usually. It is important for practitioners to be aware of the assumptions upon which they operate because very few are valid in all circumstances. In situations when previously reliable assumptions don't apply, advocates will need to alter their practice of advocacy. As the assumptions and beliefs are described below, ask yourself whether practitioners could do advocacy without making each assumption or whether advocacy approaches would differ markedly.

Other scholars have discussed advocacy assumptions and the following discussion relies on their work. Knitzer (1976) listed several "principles," and Melton (1983) referred to them as underlying assumptions. Designs for Change (1983) presented "basic beliefs," and Richart and Bing (1989) spelled out thirteen assumptions. This section discusses many of the inherent advocacy assumptions and their implications for practice. Seen in print, the wording of the assumptions may seem too strong—they are stated in absolute terms. When an advocate acts, he or she proceeds as if these assumptions are unquestionably true, without a second thought. These assumptions are summarized in Figure 2.2.

Every person has fundamental rights to a reasonable quality of life, to be free from harm, and to have opportunities to develop. These rights are more basic than constitutional or legal rights, or statutory entitlements—which are largely enforceable—and touch on values about how every human should be treated. How could a practitioner engage in advocacy without this assumption about how the world should be?

Social justice is yet to be achieved in society, and, therefore, society's status quo is unacceptable to advocates. Were the opposite the case, there would be little need for change. By extension, it is assumed that social inequities will continue unless advocates speak out and do something. Problems and needs will not correct themselves over time. Problems persist, if for no other reason than inertia has momentum, because individuals and groups have invested

1. Every person has fundamental rights to a reasonable quality of life, to be free from harm, and to have opportunities to develop.

2. Social justice is yet to be achieved in our society, and, therefore, society's status quo is unacceptable to advocates.

3. Human problems are rooted in social institutions.

4. Government should and will respond to the needs of clients.

5. Policymaking, and therefore policy change, operates in a known, consistent fashion.

6. Changes in policies will stimulate improvements in services, rights, and entitlements.

7. Organizations, and therefore organizational change, operate in a known, consistent fashion.

FIGURE **2.2**

Advocacy assumptions.

heavily in the status quo, and because powerful rationalizations and belief systems develop around the status quo. Consequently, as advocates seek change, some conflict is inevitable.

Advocates operate from the belief that human problems are rooted in social institutions. That is why advocates target policies and organizations for change, and that is why advocacy is not direct service to clients.

Advocates assume that the various levels and branches of government (i.e., local, state, and federal; judicial, legislative, and executive) should and will respond to the needs of clients. This is why advocates take advantage of the many built-in mechanisms available in the branches and levels of government to influence the development and implementation of policy. If advocates assumed the opposite, that government would be unresponsive, practitioners seeking to achieve advocacy ideals would probably use more radical techniques and might seek to alter current forms of government.

Not only do advocates assume that government will be responsive, they make assumptions about how the policymaking process works. The specific strategies and tactics used by an advocate are based on these assumptions. Haynes and Mickelson (2000) discuss several policy models intended to explain what factors determine and predict policy outcomes. According to the "elite model," public policy reflects the preferences of society's elite because the remainder of the population cares little and does less. Those who believe that the preferences of the elite influence policy won't waste their time mobilizing a large number of citizens to persuade legislators to vote a certain way on a piece of legislation. Instead, they will locate some of the community elites and persuade them to contact their legislators.

The "group model" asserts that political groups influence policy, that individuals have little power but can gain influence by banding together with other similar persons. The process of policymaking involves the skirmishes of these groups with one another. Policy outcomes occur as the power and number of political groups shift. Advocates who assume that this model represents the true operation of policymaking will not emphasize working with individual citizens or community elites, but will build a political group by forming a coalition. They will work to increase the power of groups to which they already belong, or will negotiate with other powerful groups to take a policy position consistent with that of the advocate.

The last example, which could be called the "democratic model," holds that all voters have equal influence and that the preferences of the majority determine public policy. Imagine a scenario in which the legislature is nearing a vote on an important bill. Many constituents contact individual legislators to indicate which way to vote. According to the democratic model, the legislator should take the same position as the majority of his or her constituents. Advocates who base their strategies on this model will spend time and energy educating and mobilizing large numbers of individuals. As previously mentioned, advocates ascribing to the elite model would not use this strategy.

The point is not that any of these models is wrong, but that advocates need to be aware of their assumptions about the policymaking process. Evidence is available to support all of the models. For example, there have been many instances in which the majority of constituents urged their legislator to support a piece of legislation and a few, powerful elites expressed their preference to oppose it. Sometimes the legislator votes with the majority of constituents and other times with the elite. The models oversimplify a very complicated process. The problem with many advocates is that they take it for granted that the policymaking process fits their preferred model all the time.

A belief related to the responsive government assumption is that changes in policies will stimulate improvements in services, rights, and entitlements. This could be called the "trickle down" belief. Advocates work to alter policy, believing that those changes will trickle down to clients in the form of new and better services. Since improved services are a major goal of advocacy, this belief directs advocates to focus on the policy level. If advocates didn't believe that policy changes would trickle down to clients, or felt the opposite, very different advocacy approaches would be used.

Advocates use assumptions about the process of how organizations work and how to change them. Similar to policy models, there are many models of how organizations operate. Advocates' assumptions about agencies are generally consistent with a bureaucratic model of organizations. It is assumed that the top person in the agency has the most authority and the bottom persons the least, and those at the bottom follow the policy preferences of the top person. This model would lead advocates to negotiate with the top person to bring about changes in agency policies and practices.

On the other hand, Lipsky (1980) presented the "street-level bureaucratic model" which asserts that it is the direct services workers, who are on the street every day, who make policy. This being the case, advocates would negotiate policy changes with the street-level bureaucrats, not the agency executives. Another organizational model called the "collectivist model" asserts that everyone shares power equally, there are no levels of hierarchy, and everyone participates and has an equal say in policymaking. Adhering to this model has obvious implications for advocacy practice.

Just like policy models, organizational models are often subconsciously adopted by advocates as part of their worldview. This is the way they think the world, society, policymaking, and organizations work, without question. A point made earlier in this section bears repeating. To the degree that advocates' assumptions are valid, so shall their strategies be effective. None of these beliefs are absolutely valid in all circumstances. Being reflective about assumptions and beliefs will help advocates alter strategies when necessary.

Framework for Advocacy Practice

The framework for advocacy practice used in this book is depicted in Figure 2.3. It shows the connections between assumptions, the definition of advocacy, and advocacy strategies and tactics. All of these are combined in a set of practice guidelines that are fully articulated in chapter 10 as a way to summarize the practice of advocacy.

SUMMARY

This chapter has covered a lot of ground by first presenting a conceptual definition of advocacy and discussing important elements of the definition. The definition of advocacy used in this book is the following: Advocacy consists of those purposive efforts to change specific existing or proposed policies or practices on behalf of or with a specific client or group of clients. A list of advocacy activities was analyzed in order to clarify further what is and is not advocacy.

In addition, numerous types of advocacy were defined and discussed. Clearly, there is overlap among many of the types, and the need for greater agreement on terminology is obvious. For this book, the distinctions between case and class advocacy are key, as are the distinctions between internal and external advocacy.

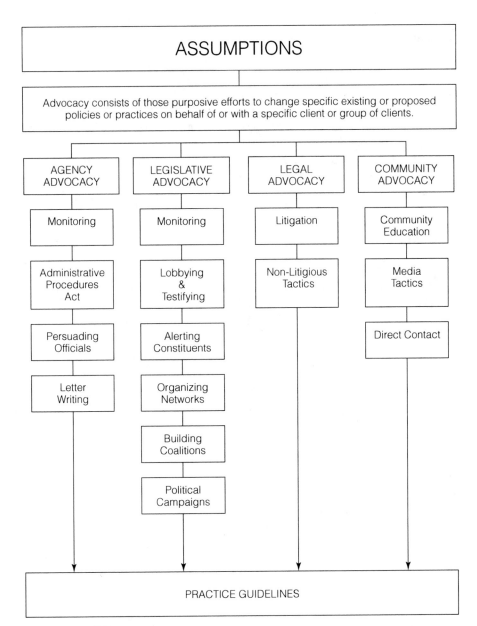

FIGURE 2.3

Framework for advocacy practice.

Finally, a number of beliefs and assumptions that underpin the practice of advocacy were discussed. The assumptions cover fundamental human rights, incomplete progress toward the achievement of social justice, and the nature of human problems. Advocates also make important assumptions about the role and function of government, about the policymaking process and how a change in policy trickles down to the service level, and about how organizations operate.

Ideally, upon completing this chapter, readers will have new or improved conceptual tools to use during the practice of advocacy—tools that are highly effective in the hands of mindful advocates. This presentation is based on the belief that for advocates to be effective as they work with and for their clients, they first have to understand their clients' situations, the context for the advocacy effort, and the nature and underpinnings of advocacy practice.

DISCUSSION QUESTIONS

1. In your opinion, what are the two key elements in the conceptual definition of advocacy? Explain your answer.
2. Are there other types of advocacy you've heard of or practiced? What are they, and which types discussed here are most similar to them?
3. Describe two situations in which clients will need someone else to advocate for them. Is there ever a time when clients must advocate on their own behalf?
4. List several other fundamental rights that advocates should act to protect.

THE ETHICS OF ADVOCACY

CHAPTER OBJECTIVES

By the time you finish studying this chapter, you should

1. Understand ethical issues relating to the decision whether to engage in advocacy.
2. Be familiar with ethical dilemmas that arise during the practice of advocacy.
3. Appreciate the complexity of ethical concerns and be able to apply a code of ethics in order to resolve quandaries.
4. Understand the importance of cultural awareness in the practice of advocacy.

Many helping professionals would agree that a major factor in the choice to do advocacy is ethics. Almost all would agree that when doing advocacy, many ethical issues arise. About the only certainty that we can count on when discussing ethics and advocacy is that there are many reasonable and different points of view, and there will be disagreements. The purpose of this chapter is to examine the ethical mandates on when and whether to do advocacy. In addition, once advocates decide that advocacy is the best approach for their clients, their strategies and tactics need to remain within the bounds of ethical standards. These, too, will be discussed. The final section of the chapter discusses the ethical obligation of human service professionals to be culturally aware as they engage in advocacy practice.

The practice of advocacy presents practitioners with **ethical dilemmas** in the sense that they often face "a choice in which any alternative results in an undesirable action" (Rhodes, 1991, xii). Years of practical experience has taught many practitioners to analyze ethical dilemmas with a mindset that

37

advocacy activities are best classified on a continuum of "ethicalness" rather than viewed as a dichotomy: clearly ethical or clearly unethical. There are simply too many variables, too many stakeholders in ever-changing contexts, and too many competing short- and long-term consequences to allow one to classify an action as absolutely ethical or absolutely unethical. To engage in the type of analysis necessary for this kind of classification is to create a situation that is anathema to advocates: to spend too much time analyzing and not acting. (Some practitioners refer to this condition as "paralysis through analysis.")

Engaging in advocacy from an ethical base is wise because ethics raise the question of moral "rightness" and how things ought to be (Loewenberg & Dolgoff, 1996, p. 6). Many human service professions have codes of ethics that summarize members' obligations, such as the American Counseling Association, American Medical Association, American Psychological Association, National Association of School Psychologists, the National Organization for Human Service Education, and the Society for Applied Sociology.

There may be no better way to sort through ethical issues than to go directly to a code of ethics to see what is outlined. In this case, the *Code of Ethics* of the National Association of Social Workers (NASW, 1996) and the *Ethical Standards of Human Service Professionals* (National Organization for Human Service Education, 2000) will be used to see what, if anything, is said about whether advocacy is an ethical obligation and how to do advocacy ethically.

The National Association of Social Workers (NASW) rightly points out that their code is a guide and doesn't include prescriptive rules that cover all situations; simple solutions are frequently unavailable. Furthermore, while the NASW *Code of Ethics* outlines a set of values, ethical principles, and standards, it does not dictate which of these takes precedence when there is more than one relevant, competing standard for a situation. (Unfortunately, nobody said this would be easy!)

ETHICAL OBLIGATIONS TO DO ADVOCACY

Do these two codes of ethics address this question? The answer is yes, they address this issue both explicitly and implicitly. In fact, the NASW Ad Hoc Committee on Advocacy (1969) asserted that the "obligation of social workers to become advocates flows directly from the social worker's Code of Ethics" (p. 18). For example, the preamble mentions several goals for social workers to promote: social justice, social change, and "the responsiveness of organizations, communities, and other social institutions to individuals' needs and social problems" (p. 1). Advocacy is specifically mentioned as one form of social work practice through which these goals are promoted. There are numerous other ethical beliefs articulated in the NASW *Code of Ethics* that make a strong case for the idea that social workers are ethically obliged to advocate for their clients.[8] For example:

- Social workers' primary goal is to help people in need and to address social problems. (Ethical Principles)
- Social workers challenge social injustice. (Ethical Principles)
- Social workers' primary responsibility is to promote the well-being of clients. (Ethical Standard 1.01)
- Social work administrators should advocate within and outside their agencies for adequate resources to meet clients' needs. (Ethical Standard 3.07[a])
- The social worker should work to improve the employing agencies' policies and procedures, and the efficiency and effectiveness of their services. (Ethical Standard 3.09[b])
- Social workers should advocate for living conditions conducive to the fulfillment of basic human needs and should promote social, economic, political, and cultural values and institutions that are compatible with the realization of social justice. (Ethical Standard 6.01)
- Social workers should engage in social and political action that seeks to ensure that all people have equal access to the resources, employment, services, and opportunities they require to meet their basic human needs and to develop fully. Social workers should be aware of the impact of the political arena on practice and should advocate for changes in policy and legislation to improve social conditions in order to meet basic human needs and promote social justice. (Ethical Standard 6.04[a])
- Social workers should act to prevent and eliminate domination of, exploitation of, and discrimination against any person, group, or class on the basis of race, ethnicity, national origin, color, sex, sexual orientation, age, marital status, political belief, religion, or mental or physical disability. (Ethical Standard 6.04[d]).

The first three beliefs cited above are quite broad in nature and don't necessarily say that advocacy is the means to achieve these lofty goals. There are many ways to act on this responsibility, advocacy being just one, and advocacy certainly aims toward these ends. Ethical Standard 3.07(a) explicitly identifies an ethical duty for administrators, whereas Ethical Standard 3.09(b) essentially endorses internal advocacy in the workplace. The last three come from the section of the code titled, "Social Workers' Ethical Responsibilities to the Broader Society," and two of them specifically use the verb *advocate*.

---

8. There are many statements in the NASW *Code of Ethics* that are explicitly and implicitly related to the practice of advocacy, and many of them overlap with one another. Due to space constraints, not all statements have been cited and discussed. Reprinted with permission from the National Association of Social Workers, *Code of Ethics*, 1996.

The National Organization for Human Service Education's (NOHSE) *Ethical Standards of Human Service Professionals* (2000) also makes it clear that human service professionals are expected to advocate for their clients. The standards make it clear that human service professionals should advocate when regulations and statutes are inconsistent with client rights (Statement 10), and when there are unmet client and community needs (Statement 13). Human service professionals are given a broad mandate to engage in advocacy in Statement 16: "Human service professionals advocate for the rights of all members of society, particularly those who are members of minorities and groups at which discriminatory practices have historically been directed."

Is It Unethical Not to Advocate?

While a strong case can be made for the assertion that both codes create an expectation to engage in advocacy, a vexing question remains: Are practitioners who do not advocate for and on behalf of their clients—when circumstances indicate a need to do so—unethical? As discussed earlier, it's rarely that simple; each case would require an individual assessment. Recall from chapter 1 that the vast majority of social workers think there are a lot of situations in which advocacy is the best approach, and that it can be effective. Remember, too, that many of them either don't do advocacy or do very little, primarily because they don't have time to do it. Do you think this is a valid justification for not taking what is considered to be the ethical course of action?

Another reason that many helping professionals don't do advocacy is that they lack the knowledge and skills. It can be argued that the NASW *Code of Ethics* supports this position (i.e., "Social workers should provide services and represent themselves as competent only within the boundaries of their education, training, license, certification, consultation received, supervised experience, or other relevant professional experience," Ethical Standard 1.04[a]). These issues could be argued forever.

ETHICAL PRINCIPLES AND CHALLENGES RELEVANT TO THE PRACTICE OF ADVOCACY

There are many statements in the NASW *Code of Ethics* and the NOHSE *Ethical Standards* that practitioners should heed as they engage in advocacy practice, or any other type of practice. Those will be described and discussed in this section, as will several common ethical dilemmas advocates face.

Some of the most pertinent ethical precepts relevant to advocacy include the following:

- Respecting and promoting clients' right to self-determination (NASW, 1996, Ethical Standard 1.02; NOHSE, 2000, Statement 8).
- Providing services only when valid informed consent has been obtained (NASW, 1996, Ethical Standard 1.03[a])
- Informing clients of risks, alternatives, and their right to refuse or withdraw consent (NASW, 1996, Ethical Standard 1.03[a]; NOHSE, 2000, Statement 8)
- Performing advocacy only if competent to do so (NASW, 1996, Ethical Standard 1.04[a]; NOHSE, 2000, Statement 26).

In broad terms, the *Code of Ethics* and the *Ethical Standards* require practitioners to operate simultaneously in the best interest of clients, the employing agency, colleagues, the profession, and society as a whole. This is a tall order, and tensions and conflicts are predictable when trying to satisfy the interests of all parties. Although many of the concepts and advocacy strategies discussed in this book are relevant when engaging in case advocacy, the major focus is on class advocacy. This being the case, several ethical dilemmas inherent in the practice of class advocacy need to be discussed.

Informed Consent

Advocates who seek change on behalf of a class of clients may be representing the interests of 100, 1,000, or even 10,000 clients, including those presently experiencing a social problem as well those who might be clients in the future. In addition, the class of clients for whom one advocates might be comprised of infants or other individuals unable to express their needs or directly exercise their rights. Obviously, getting informed consent, fully informing clients about risks, and respecting each client's right to self determination are difficult challenges to surmount.

A specific example will illustrate the point. Many of the national and state offices of the helping professions have lobbyists who push for legislation and funding that is thought to be beneficial to clients and work actively to oppose proposals thought to be detrimental. In circumstances such as these, it rarely happens that the clients these lobbyists are serving have given informed consent, been apprised of the risks associated with attempted legislative change, or been able to self-determine what is in their best interests. It raises a very difficult question, but one that deserves much thought: Are these lobbyists acting in an unethical manner? Be assured that raising the question is not meant to imply the affirmative.

Practitioners engaged in many different types of service delivery frequently believe they are acting in the best interests of their client(s). Notwithstanding their good intentions, we know all too well that good intentions don't automatically result in services that are in the client's best interest (for example, see Gaylin, Glasser, Marcus, & Rothman, 1978, *Doing Good: The Limits of Benevolence*). Caution should be exercised whenever a service provider's (including an advocate's) judgment replaces client decisions. To say that these are complex issues is to understate the situation. For example, how does one resolve the dilemma when an action or a service may be in the client's best interest in the short run but is thought to be detrimental in the long run?

A very common dilemma faced by those doing case advocacy is that the resolution of the problem, such as increased funding for a program or improved eligibility rules, will take a long time to take effect. The immediate client may not benefit, even though people with the same issue in the future will. Put succinctly, "To what extent does one risk injury to his [sic] client's interests in the short run on behalf of institutional changes in the long run?" (Ad Hoc Committee on Advocacy, 1969, p. 19).

Client Self-Determination

How do practitioners know what is in their client's best interest, both in the long and the short run and balanced against society's best interest? The best way to know is to be sure that alternative actions have been clearly explained, risks discussed, and permission granted by the client to pursue a particular direction. When this explicit consent cannot be achieved, the NASW *Code of Ethics* suggests that consent should come from an appropriate third party (e.g., parent or legal guardian). The code explicitly states, "When social workers act on behalf of clients who lack the capacity to make informed decisions, social workers should take reasonable steps to safeguard the interests and rights of those clients" (Ethical Standard 1.14). Practitioners may wish to extend this approach beyond "clients who lack the capacity" to situations in which the class of clients is large, is geographically dispersed, members are not individually known, or there is no practical way to get informed consent. Even then, "reasonable steps to safeguard the interests and rights of those clients" must be taken. Several ideas on how to do this are suggested below.

Many of the "reasonable steps" are related to how advocates select the specific issue in the first place. Was the advocacy problem identified by communicating with a substantial number and cross-section of clients, their spokespersons, or those who provide services to them?[9] Maybe needs assessments, key informant surveys, analyses of service data, or focus groups were conducted. On the other hand, in those situations in which a handful of advocates decide among themselves which client issues are most important without verifying their perceptions in a systematic manner, there are grounds for worrying whether their direction and strategies are in the best interests of this particular class of clients.

---

9. More specifics on how to identify advocacy problems are discussed in chapter 8.

Even if a systematic, open process has been used to identify problems needing resolution, how does an advocate know which of many different solutions is in clients' best interest? For example, a problem has been identified in that some investigations of alleged child abuse and neglect fail to confirm the occurrence and children remain in or are returned to dangerous living situations. Advocacy efforts throughout the country have succeeded in creating multidisciplinary teams of investigators to minimize the problem. The theory behind this approach is that one person investigating a report of child abuse cannot have enough knowledge and skill to identify all aspects of abuse or neglect. A team composed of physicians, psychologists, social workers, nurses, and others will be better able to assess the allegations comprehensively.

How do advocates know this is the best solution, that it is in clients' best interests, or that funds expended in this way would not produce better outcomes if spent on another approach? Infants who have been or might be abused can't advise advocates. Some parents of these children might think this solution makes sense, but many others will be opposed to this approach, feeling that the state already does too much snooping into their families. Other advocates take the position that law enforcement officials should conduct investigations. Is it reasonable to increase the number of identified abused children when in-home services are underfunded and foster care is less than perfect? These are all difficult questions to answer.

Advocates don't have to be wizards with crystal balls, but they do have to be or have access to experts.[10] They need to know a lot about their client group, the nature and frequency of various challenges, the strengths and weaknesses of various service approaches, and be familiar with the research on all of these. They absolutely must be humble about what they know and don't know, and distinguish between opinions and facts. The track record of benevolence, good intentions, and altruism is too spotty for a person to be confident that because an advocate means well, all will turn out well (Gaylin et al., 1978). Be wary of advocates who act as if these issues are simple—they're not.

Since the dilemma of determining what's in the client's best interest is so complex, due to incomplete knowledge and an uncertain future, advocates' attitudes play a large part in the resolution. Fernandez (1980) captures the idea when she explains, "Too often the 'child savers' are certain that they are acting in the child's best interests rather than struggling to ascertain the child's best interests by weighing the complexities and by listening intently to the child's feelings and opinions" (p. 25). The advocacy process, and its early stages in particular, should include questioning and struggling, listening carefully and struggling, weighing options and struggling, and struggling some more over choices of issues, solution, strategy, and, always, clients' best interests.

---

10. This issue comes up again and will be addressed in greater depth when discussing coalitions.

It is important to note that these choices are not advocates' final decisions; they should never close their eyes, ears, hearts, and minds. Closely monitor every step of the process and use information that comes to you along the way to reassess prior decisions. Monitoring client outcomes is especially crucial when changes are being implemented. Things do not work out perfectly, for unpredictable reasons. If the changes do not seem to be in clients' best interests, it is an opportunity to do more advocacy, not a reason to beat yourself up.

Overstating the Case

Another ethical dilemma frequently faced by advocates arises when they try to draw attention to their clients' problems and their proposed solutions. Sometimes they feel as if the problem is being viewed as an unimportant issue that the public and policymakers won't be motivated to address. This can lead to a situation in which an advocate overstates size, frequency, gravity, and consequences of the problem. There is a strong temptation to present extreme case examples as opposed to more usual cases.

Similarly, solutions may be overstated. For example, advocates may be tempted to request funding for 750 new, specialized group-home beds when their best estimates indicate that 600 would suffice. They do this because experience has taught them that the legislature almost never fully funds such a request, and they hope that the downward compromise will come close to meeting the need.

In both cases, advocates may feel as if the end justifies the means—as long as they have good intentions, whatever it takes to accomplish their goals is fair. They wouldn't describe these actions as unethical but, rather, as strategic and realistic. The NASW *Code of Ethics* includes several statements related to this dilemma. It indicates that one of the profession's core values is integrity, and the accompanying ethical principle insists that, "Social workers behave in a trustworthy manner." Further, Ethical Standard 4.06(c), Misrepresentation, indicates that "Social workers should ensure that their representations to clients, agencies, and the public of professional qualifications, credentials, education, competence, affiliations, services provided, or results to be achieved are accurate." This doesn't exactly fit the situations being discussed here but clearly articulates a spirit that applies.

There are other practical reasons, besides ethics, for not overstating the case, one of which is the risk of losing credibility. Credibility may be one of the most important resources that advocates must garner and protect. Imagine a situation in which you are seeking to change a policy that adversely affects your clients, and you have captured the attention of a few policymakers who wish to look into it further. You have gladly provided them with your documentation of the problem, its consequences, and the specific solutions needed. They (or members of their staff) are going to examine this information closely and, if they discover that the logic you used to make estimates is faulty or your numbers are inflated, you will likely lose their cooperation. You may not have totally lost their support on future issues, but it will be given more cautiously, and it will take a long time for you to reestablish the lost credibility.

On Behalf of Clients Versus Empowering Clients

Is there an ethical dilemma when choosing whether to empower clients to advocate for themselves or to represent them? There doesn't seem to be any relevant language in the ethics codes to provide specific guidance in these matters. In case advocacy, practitioners have an identifiable client with whom they are working, and to the greatest degree possible this should be discussed with the client. Practically speaking, a good choice is to do both—empower clients *and* advocate for them. There are real constraints on clients and their advocates in terms of time, energy, finances, skills, and knowledge. It is not impossible, but it is difficult for clients and advocates to attend all the meetings and speak with all the people necessary to bring about the intended change. Working as a team makes a lot of sense ethically and practically.

In class advocacy, it is more difficult to decide whether to advocate on behalf of clients or empower them, because the advocate does not always know every member of the class of clients. However, significant numbers can be identified and empowered to speak on their own behalf (assuming they have the capacity to do so). Many advocates don't do this because they believe that the change goal can be reached more quickly and at less cost if they represent the class of clients themselves. They may be right in many cases and it is reasonable to wonder if "doing for" clients is disempowering and creates dependency, while more empowering approaches are better in the long run (even if the specific change goal is accomplished slowly or not at all). It is probably more useful to view this dilemma as a strategic rather than ethical one.

Another complexity of this dilemma is that in the name of client empowerment, clients may be put in a situation to advocate for themselves against formidable, entrenched, and well-financed opposition. The clients don't have a chance to accomplish their goals and may suffer losses.

One Class of Clients Versus Another

That which is in the best interest of one group of clients may not be in the best interest of another. Advocating for increased rights and options for one class of clients will likely impinge on those of another class. The classic example of this is the ongoing battles regarding parents' rights, children's rights, and family autonomy. Child welfare workers know all too well that the goal of preserving families and the goal of protecting children are frequently compatible, and that one of these two important goals sometimes has to be compromised in pursuit of the other.

The NASW Ad Hoc Committee on Advocacy (1969) provides advice for practitioners faced with the dilemma of competing claims. Their illustrations are based on case advocacy situations, however, and are difficult to apply to class advocacy. The first scenario involves advocates seeking services or benefits for clients (e.g., immediate placement in a group home, housing subsidies) and other people needing the same services. The all too common dilemma is that the supply is inadequate to meet the demand. The Ad Hoc Committee recommends that the advocate "should be seeking to increase the total availability of the scarce resource" in these situations (p. 19). Second, they advise that advocates weigh the competing claims, and the client(s) with the most urgent needs should prevail. The latter advice, while seemingly logical, might leave advocates tied in knots as they try to follow it. Who does the weighing, the advocate or the client or both? It would be surprising for a client to agree to abandon their claim because the claims of others are deemed more urgent, and if the client still wishes to pursue it but the advocate decides otherwise, is the client's right to self-determination being respected? Next, what criteria should one use to assess urgency, and will all parties agree to those criteria and their application? "Urgency" seems to point us toward a short-term view when longer term consequences may be equally or more important. In this case, it seems clear that the Ad Hoc Committee has offered inadequate advice.

Other Difficult Ethical Matters

Selecting advocacy strategies and tactics raises debates about the relative efficacy of alternative approaches. In addition, there are ethical considerations that must be weighed as part of the decision-making process. For example, Homan (1999) bluntly asks, "If you allow a serious problem situation to persist because you will only engage in polite tactics, how does your mannerly approach honor those whose suffering is prolonged?" (p. 345). That is a very humbling question for human service professionals, one that cannot be given full treatment here. Two solutions immediately come to mind. One underscores the value of working in concert with a team of advocates who have expertise in a variety of tactics. Advocates can trade assignments when necessary. Second, when practitioners do not have the skills necessary to meet clients needs, the most common practice is to refer clients to other practitioners. Advocates who are only comfortable using conservative change tactics would be well served by having alliances with those willing to use more radical tactics.

ADVOCACY AND CULTURAL DIVERSITY

The final section of this chapter includes a discusson of a very important topic, engaging in advocacy with cultural awareness. While it is too much to expect that one section of a chapter can review all pertinent cultural awareness skills and knowledge, it is fair to expect that readers' consciousness will be raised. There are many definitions of the term *culture*. Culture is a collection of behaviors and beliefs (Rivera & Erlich, 1995), and in this book the concept will be treated broadly to go beyond ethnic groups. The groups whose cultures are of great concern to advocates are generally those who have suffered the consequences of oppression and discrimination, predominantly people with disabilities, women, older people, people who are poor, gays and lesbians, and ethnic and racial minorities.

Treating People with Respect

It is very common for principles in the codes of ethics of several human service professions to mention that professionals should be "knowledgeable about the cultures and communities within which they practice" (NOHSE, 2000, Statement 18) and that they should acquire the skills needed to practice effectively with culturally diverse client populations (Statement 21). Similarly, the NASW *Code of Ethics* (1996) insists that "social workers treat each person in a caring and respectful fashion, mindful of individual differences and cultural and ethnic diversity" (p. 5). There is similar language in the *Code of Ethics* of the American Counseling Association (2000) and that of the Society of Applied Sociology (2000), just to mention a few.

What does this mean for advocacy practice? When one closely analyzes advocacy tactics and reduces them to their most basic elements, one will find that communication and relationship are essential. While practicing advocacy in an ethical manner is important, if advocates want their communications and relationships to be effective, they must take into consideration the cultural differences of the parties with whom they interact. Figure 3.1 was developed to help you think about the various relationships necessary to engage in advocacy.

Imagine yourself as an advocate who is providing leadership for a particular change effort. The Advocacy Leaders circle and the Clients circle overlap because clients can be advocates. As an advocate, you need to have effective communications with other leaders of your effort. To do so, you need to be aware of cultural similarities and differences in leadership style, how to hold meetings and reach decisions, disagreement and conflict, negotiating, and other communication patterns.

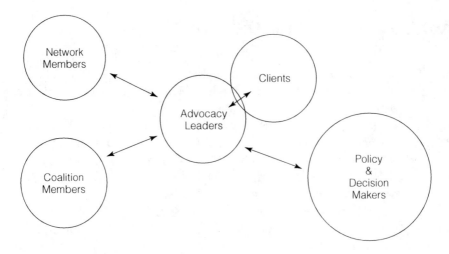

FIGURE **3.1**

Relationships between various actors in an advocacy effort.

A key relationship is the one between advocates and clients. The client group may or may not be culturally homogenous, and the advocate may interact with clients in groups or one-on-one. The challenge of communicating clearly is heightened when advocates meet with culturally heterogeneous groups of clients. Many practitioners have raised the challenging question whether advocates can effectively represent clients from different cultures. Austin and Lowe (1994) include a debate on a similar issue in their book.

Chapter 5 discusses developing advocacy networks and organizing coalitions at length. As advocates use these two approaches to increase their numbers and their influence, it is necessary to engage a wide variety of individuals, groups, and organizations. Just as above, effective communication is necessary for these advocacy partnerships to work, and that includes being culturally aware.

Advocates' interactions with policymakers are central to any change effort. Advocates have to convince legislators to vote in specific ways, to persuade agency leaders to change policies or operate programs differently. It is likely that policymakers will be members of the dominant culture. In this country, power rests disproportionately in the hands of men and Whites. Culturally diverse advocates should treat policymakers with respect and consider their cultural differences when interacting with these individuals.

Without fail, scholars and practitioners who have written about human service practice with diverse populations warn practitioners that "it is a mistake to regard all individuals solely in terms of the general traits of their culture" (Homan, 1999, p. 17). There are as many differences between individuals within cultural groups as across groups. Advocates therefore need to be aware of the differences among individuals within any given cultural group as well as the differences between various cultures.

Challenging Social Injustice, Racism, Discrimination, and Oppression

Not only do the codes of ethics discussed in this chapter call for respect and cultural awareness, many of them state that human service professionals have an ethical duty to advocate on behalf of cultural minorities and for the elimination of social injustice. The NASW *Code of Ethics* (1996) is particularly strong in both regards. It states, "Social workers challenge social injustice. Social workers pursue social change, particularly with and on behalf of vulnerable and oppressed individuals and groups of people" (p. 5).

The *Ethical Standards* of the National Organization for Human Service Education (2000) includes a very similar statement. Advocates are ethically required to give preference to clients who come from groups toward which discriminatory practices historically have been directed. They should direct their work towards the eradication of the powerful and destructive forces of racism, sexism, and other forms of injustice. As was discussed in chapter 1, historically oppressed groups are relatively powerless. A lot of what advocacy is about is increasing certain groups' access to power.

SUMMARY

The dilemmas raised in this chapter are frustrating and difficult to solve. Specific, answers to the questions raised are in short supply. General solutions can't be provided because every ethical dilemma one faces in practice is accompanied by a unique set of circumstances, but suggestions can be made about how to sort through the issues and come up with a reasonable, ethically justifiable course of action. This complexity leaves advocates with a choice over two options: (1) do nothing because an ethical dilemma can't be solved satisfactorily; or (2) proceed with the advocacy effort after making an ethically defensible, less than perfect decision and continue to manage the tension that occurs when one tries to balance the rights and interests of several stakeholders.

Homan (1999) offers the following good advice to advocates:

> Don't get caught up in meaningless arguments over whether the ends are justifying the means. Your time is much more wisely spent firmly rooting yourself in a fundamental code of ethics. Review your commitment to ethics and keep it alive.

Your behavior may very well change from one situation to another, not, one hopes, because you lack ethics but because they inform and drive every important decision you make. (p. 345)

DISCUSSION QUESTIONS

1. Identify several changes you'd make to either the NASW *Code of Ethics* or NOHSE's *Ethical Standards* to give advocates clearer direction. What are the disadvantages of making these changes?
2. Are other human service codes of ethics more or less helpful when being applied to advocacy practice?
3. Describe several specific techniques advocates could use to accomplish client self-determination and informed consent.
4. If one of your colleagues was working with clients and it was clear that advocacy was the appropriate course of action, but your colleague did not engage in advocacy, would you report your colleague for a breach of ethics? Why or why not?

two

ADVOCACY STRATEGIES AND TACTICS

CHAPTER 4   AGENCY ADVOCACY
CHAPTER 5   LEGISLATIVE ADVOCACY
CHAPTER 6   LEGAL ADVOCACY
CHAPTER 7   COMMUNITY ADVOCACY
CHAPTER 8   DOING YOUR ADVOCACY HOMEWORK

Many new ideas were introduced in part 1, including a definition of advocacy, descriptions of different types of advocacy, and common ethical dilemmas advocates face. A framework that can be used to guide advocacy practice was also introduced. Part 2 builds on the previous chapters by describing in a step-by-step fashion how to do advocacy. Advocacy strategies and tactics, what they are and when to use them, are discussed. The strategies are placed in four broad categories: Agency Advocacy; Legislative Advocacy; Legal Advocacy; and Community Advocacy. A chapter is devoted to each strategy, and each identifies and discusses the change targets for which the strategy is best suited and describes the specific tactics necessary to implement the strategy.

The topic of chapter 8, "Doing Your Advocacy Homework," may be the most important step for conducting effective advocacy. The chapter discusses the necessary steps toward planing and targeting an advocacy effort. This includes several types of research (or homework) that must be done to increase the probability that advocacy will be successful. This chapter is out of order when compared to the actual practice of advocacy; in practice, research and targeting precede the implementation of a strategy. Advocacy homework—the research, targeting, and planning—leads to the selection of strategies. However, it is best to learn how to do advocacy homework in this out-of-order fashion because it will have much more meaning if an understanding of the major advocacy strategies has already been developed.

AGENCY ADVOCACY

CHAPTER OBJECTIVES

By the time you finish studying this chapter, you should

1. Have an increased understanding of problems that agency advocacy can address.
2. Be familiar with useful tactics to change agency policies, programs, and practices.
3. Be aware of common agency excuses for inaction and be able to present countering responses.
4. Understand how to team with internal advocates.

Agency advocacy[11] refers to a set of tactics and activities used to bring about change in programs and agencies that will benefit clients. It is one of the four major advocacy strategies covered in this book. It involves identifying needed changes in program policies and practices and influencing agencies to make the needed modifications. In general, it should be the first strategy advocates consider as they advocate with and for the benefit of clients. Agency advocacy can be implemented alone or in combination with other advocacy strategies, such as legal or legislative advocacy.

This chapter is divided into three sections. The first section presents information on the potential agency targets that advocates can challenge by discussing common program shortcomings. The next section seeks to increase advocates' knowledge of agency discretion, or how far agency decision makers' authority extends. The largest section of the chapter is devoted to a presentation of advocacy tactics associated with agency advocacy.

---

11. Previous writers have used the terminology of "administrative advocacy" as the approximate equivalent of agency advocacy.

Public policies materialize and take on tangible properties through agencies. Programs are implemented and services delivered at the agency level, not the policy level. While policymakers are frequently accused of micro-managing agencies, in reality they are not the ones who plan and implement programs on a day-to-day basis. Many organizational factors associated with the design and administration of programs influence the quality of services. For example, the number and qualifications of staff, as well as their ongoing training, determine the effectiveness of services, and funding and eligibility policies dictate which and how many clients will receive services. Agency practices establish how many services clients will receive and for how long.

Even though legislative bodies (Congress, state legislatures, school boards, and city or county council), boards of directors, or owners approve funding plans, it is the agency staff who play a major role preparing proposed budgets. Once the budget has been approved, staff usually have some decision-making flexibility on how funds will be utilized on a day-to-day basis. Advocates may eventually need to influence the policymakers, but they should first try to work with the agency to increase, decrease, or alter spending plans.

TARGETS FOR AGENCY ADVOCACY

What are some of the problems for which agency advocacy is relevant and potentially effective? First and foremost, when trying to answer this question, attention should be directed toward what is and is not happening for clients. To what degree have the issues for which clients sought services been resolved? For example, did they get the quality medical care they needed for what was bothering them? Are clients satisfied with service outcomes and their interactions with staff while receiving services? Are appropriate services available and accessible to clients in need? Is the program having a negative impact on clients? These are the kinds of questions to raise in order to focus on client outcomes.

Second, advocates should figure out what's going on in the agency that is causing or contributing the unsatisfactory client outcomes. How to do that is discussed in depth in chapter 8, "Doing Your Advocacy Homework." Figure 4.1 presents a list of these issues, which will be explained in more detail below. Each of these represents one of the many reasons for which clients may not be achieving desired outcomes, and these issues, therefore, become targets for advocacy.

Ineffective Agencies   Clients may not achieve their desired service goals for many, interdependent reasons, one of which is because the staff with whom clients interact may be unable to deliver the intended intervention effectively. This might be the result of the weak hiring practices of agency

---

PROBLEMS

1. Ineffective agencies

2. Inappropriate behavior by worker(s)

3. Ineffective intervention/service approach

4. Failure to coordinate program with other services

5. Inaccessibility of program/services

6. Outreach inadequate or misdirected

7. Program implementation inconsistent with legislative intent

8. Plans to scale back or eliminate a program

9. New program/service(s)

10. Lack of accountability on service use and outcomes

FIGURE **4.1**

Agency problems amenable to agency advocacy.

---

administrators or insufficient funds to attract qualified staff. Whether initially qualified or not, insufficient or faulty pre- and in-service training may be the reason for which staff members lack adequate knowledge and skills. Ongoing supervision may be weak or quality-control mechanisms deficient. In addition, caseloads may be too large to allow even appropriately trained staff to be effective, or staff members may have other duties that distract them from service delivery. In these cases, the targets for change may be hiring policies, budget allocations, training policies and practices, and supervisory practices. Another option is to seek the termination or transfer of agency administrators.

Inappropriate/Ineffective Workers   This might include unethical, disempowering, or otherwise unprofessional conduct. If workers are chronically late, unprepared for meetings with clients, unmotivated, fail to follow protocols, or neglect to follow through on commitments, they are behaving in an unprofessional manner. Other examples of inappropriate behavior include failing to respect clients, to be culturally sensitive with clients, and to maximize client self-determination and participation in decision making. Termination of these workers should be considered a target for advocates.

Ineffective Intervention   For a variety of reasons, such as failing to remain up-to-date on professional research, agencies use service approaches that are either inappropriate for their clientele and their issues or have been shown to be less effective than others. For example, a juvenile justice agency might use a "scared straight" approach, by which they take youth to visit a prison and interact with convicts serving life sentences. This approach became very popular in the 1970s because of a television documentary espousing its benefits. However, systematic evaluation research has shown that the approach tends to be counterproductive. Yet this program is still being used. Another example, albeit a controversial one, is Drug Abuse Resistance Education or DARE. This is a very popular in-school program to educate children about drug abuse. There have been quite a few research studies that have questioned its effectiveness.

Failure to Coordinate   It is rare for any given agency to have all the services necessary to meet the needs of its clientele. This being the case, it is imperative for agencies and programs to work together. The worst case scenario occurs when two programs are independently working toward noncomplementary objectives with the same client. More commonly, agencies don't have mechanisms in place to identify clients' needs other than those they address and, even if they do, little is done to refer clients to other programs. Similarly, agencies working with the same client (e.g., a family) don't work as a team and fail to communicate with each other in a manner that would optimize resources.

Inaccessibility   If there are barriers to accessibility, it doesn't matter how effective an agency's interventions are or how well coordinated they may be. There are numerous types of barriers: (1) barriers that prevent people with disabilities from accessing or taking full advantage of services, (2) language barriers, (3) geographic barriers, in which the agency location is too far from high-priority clients and transportation issues are not addressed, (4) hours of operation may be different from when needy clients are free, (5) the lack of child or dependent care makes it impossible for certain clients to leave the dependent and go to an agency, and (6) prohibitive service costs.

Inadequate Outreach   Some agencies with excellent programs fail to find or attract the clients most in need of their program. Due to the fact that needs almost always outstrip service availability, caseloads remain full even though the most needy aren't being served. Frequently the clients who are the most difficult to find also have intractable issues and complex circumstances, making them a service challenge. Also, public information campaigns and outreach workers are often viewed as luxuries programs can't afford.

Implementation Inconsistent with Purposes   Every now and then, programs are implemented and operated in a different fashion than instructed or implied by the enacting legislation. Advocates are frequently involved and have significant input at the legislative level when programs and services are being designed and funded. Later, when comparing the implementation of the program to the idea legislators (and advocates) had in mind, advocates may observe that the program is headed in a different direction than was intended.

For example, when legislation and funding was passed in one state for school districts to operate alternative schools, it was explicitly stated that these programs should be positive alternatives. In some instances, alternative schools became in-school suspension programs where youth served time in study halls. (This is not to say that in-school suspension programs are automatically a bad thing, just that this approach is inconsistent with the enabling legislation and funding).

Other examples of this type of inconsistency are when client eligibility rules make the program more or less restrictive than anticipated; the type or extent of services is different than intended; or staffing patterns and qualifications are unlike those discussed during the legislative process. This is not automatically a bad thing; various adjustments almost always need to be made.

Program Elimination   Agencies may be forced to close programs or to implement dramatic cutbacks. As a result, many current clients will lose services, and the needs of future clients will go unmet. Advocates must determine why these decisions have been made, the degree to which the agency could influence the decision, and who in the agency is the ultimate decision maker on the issue. Sometimes these decisions are in the hands of the agency, and at other times a combination of actors are involved. Certainly, if the agency's governing body has ordered the cutback or termination, advocacy strategies should be targeted in its direction. What is frequently the case, however, is that the funding body has reduced the agency's budget without specifically identifying where and how the cutbacks should be made. The agency itself must make the decisions on how to absorb the funding cuts.

New Programs   Occasionally the client group being served by an agency has related needs and issues that are unmet. Advocates (and probably some of the agency staff) recognize that the agency needs to create a new, complementary program or set of services. Most likely, advocates will need to impact the process used to develop funding proposals to ensure that requests are made to create the needed services. At other times, when client needs are urgent, advocates will seek to alter the current allocation of funding within the agency to address these needs. Advocates may need to perform both functions, meeting urgent needs in the short run with a reallocation of funds and developing longer term solutions by impacting the agency's funding proposals.

Lack of Accountability   A problem that advocates frequently encounter is the difficulty of discerning to whom the agency is delivering services, what services are being used by how many clients, and what are the results of service delivery (e.g., Are the concerns for which the client sought services better, worse, or the same?). Even when advocates are in contact with clients who can provide feedback, it is almost impossible for them to compile this information on their own. While it may be the case that an agency that fails to keep and report this type of information is providing quality services to the appropriate number of clients with good results, one wonders. Every agency is accountable in some way (usually regarding its use of funds) to a governing or funding organization, but it is not usually accountable to the clients it serves, advocates for its clients, or the public at large. A lot of what advocacy is about is putting clients in the picture and increasing their influence on the delivery of services.

In situations in which agencies are not being accountable, advocates may seek to have their existing reports put in a digestible format and made public. Agencies generally collect far more information on clients and services than they bother to aggregate, summarize, and report. If agencies are not collecting this type of information, advocates may encourage them to do so, to conduct program evaluations and client satisfaction surveys, and to make this information available. All agencies should continually ask themselves how they are doing and how they can do better, and advocates may have to remind agencies to do so. Having this type of information is a significant advocacy tool.

AGENCY DISCRETION

Tactics associated with agency advocacy are useful only when advocates have identified and focused on specific targets for change. Advocates need to develop an extensive tool kit to use when circumstances dictate. Chapter 8, "Doing Your Advocacy Homework," discusses how to investigate advocacy issues to determine the change targets, what advocacy strategy to use, and which tactics are implied. Agency advocacy should be utilized when the advocate determines that agency rules and regulations as well as formal and informal policies, procedures, and practices need to change.

Agency Regulations

Public agencies and programs usually establish formal rules and regulations in a manner consistent with the state's Administrative Procedures Act (APA).[12]

---

12. It is not always clear—especially to advocates with no legal training—when an agency has to follow the Administrative Procedures Act when developing rules and regulations, and when agencies can use their own decision-making processes to develop operational policies. Advocates might consult with an attorney familiar with the APA or involve attorneys in the advocacy coalition.

These rules, when adopted properly, are the equivalents of law. They might cover areas such as criteria for client eligibility, fee schedules, the confidentiality of records, and clients' due process rights. Advocates must be familiar with their state's Administrative Procedures Act, because it will describe how advocates can comment on and influence proposed rules and seek changes in existing rules. How to use a state's APA to change agency rules will be discussed in more depth in the next section.

An example of when advocates have sought rule changes might be helpful at this point. Advocates in one state engaged in a major advocacy effort to prevent juveniles from being held in adult jails. Their advocacy effort included a combination of strategies and tactics and had great success. The effort was not a *total* success, however, because in certain, rare circumstances juveniles could still be held in adult jails. Therefore, one goal of their advocacy effort was to guarantee the safety of the few juveniles held in jail. They sought changes in the rules of the Department of Corrections (DOC) because the DOC had statutory responsibility to inspect and maintain standards in all jails throughout the state. State law dictated that when juveniles were held in adult jails, they should never be commingled with adult inmates.

Unfortunately, DOC rules, which served as de facto operating standards for jails, said very little on this subject and neglected to define how juveniles and adults in jail should be separated (e.g., physically, by sight, by sound). Therefore, when jail inspectors visited jails to perform audits, they did not routinely check to see if juveniles and adults were commingled. Advocates who were concerned about this problem decided to seek changes in DOC rules so that inspections would cover these issues and the DOC would enforce the state law that prohibited commingling.

This example illustrates a common problem faced by advocates. Even though a good state law was passed and is "on the books," the day-to-day treatment of clients has not improved. There has been a major slip because the agency responsible for implementing and monitoring compliance with the law has not developed the necessary rules and policies to require staff to do their jobs differently.

Agency Policies

Besides official rules and regulations, there are other agency policies that dictate how services will be delivered and how programs will operate. They are developed by the agency using whatever planning and decision-making process it chooses, be that a unilateral, top-down decision-making style or a highly participatory, consensus-based approach. To paraphrase *Webster's Dictionary* (Soukhanov et al., 1984), a policy is a guiding principle meant to shape decisions and actions, and a procedure is an assemblage of agreed-upon methods for carrying out the program. These cover personnel issues (e.g., hiring steps, vacation leave, performance appraisals), financial matters (e.g., what paperwork and whose approval is necessary to get a check written), accountability and forms (e.g., information required at intake, client consent), and matters relating to clients. Agency policies relating to clients might describe intake steps, what to do in case of an emergency, how often clients should be monitored while in their rooms, visiting hours, how cases are assigned, or the treatment regimen.

Agency policies and procedures are usually formalized in writing and kept in an operations or policy and procedures manual, but this is not always the case. To distinguish this type of policy from broader social or public policies, such as those created by legislative bodies and courts, this level of policy will be referred to as **agency policy** or **operational policy**. When an agency policy is identified as the change target, there are a number of advocacy tactics that can be used to change it. They'll be discussed in detail in the next section.

Advocates are frequently interested in proposed and current agency budgets. An agency's budget includes, both explicitly and implicitly, many of its policy statements. They indicate what programs are funded, at what level, and whether there has been growth or decline from previous years. Of great importance to advocates, funding levels determine the number of people who will receive services and the number of staff to deliver them, becoming, in a sense, the agency's policy on caseloads. If advocates closely study the relative funding levels of an agency's various programs, they can frequently ascertain that agency's priorities.

Agency Practices

Finally, advocates need to focus on changing the practices of agencies as well as those of individual practitioners. Agency practices are rarely recorded and they may or may not be consistent with agency or system policies. For example, notwithstanding laws and school district policies, in day-to-day practice, some youth are expelled from school without a fair hearing. As a result of the work of advocates, laws and policies were established requiring fair hearings, and advocacy work continues in order to ensure that agency practices are consistent with policy.

At other times, agency practices, although unwritten, are statements of de facto policy. Agencies frequently standardize the delivery of services, whereby all the practitioners offering a service approach their clients in similar, specific ways. For example, a particular residential program for children has been using individual counseling with a psychodynamic perspective for many years. Advocates may wish to see this treatment approach—a set of practices that comprise an unstated policy—changed because they believe it is not effective and that behavioral and group approaches are more effective.

Advocates shouldn't worry too much about determining whether the target for change fits the specific definitions of **agency policy, procedure,** or

practice used here. Very few people use these terms in a specialized manner, and most interchange them frequently. What one practitioner may call a policy, another in the same agency may call a procedure. It is more important to determine whether the unsatisfactory agency behavior or the absence of services is based on a policy created through an explicit decision process (e.g., rule making through an Administrative Procedures Act) or through less formal processes and tacit agreements, such as the way that cases are customarily handled.

TACTICS

This section discusses several advocacy tactics that fall under the category of agency advocacy. As indicated above, advocates should select their tactics based on the specific change they wish to effect as well as relevant circumstances both internal and external to the agency, including the history of advocacy with the agency. Usually, several of the tactics are used in sequence. A piece of advice that approaches being a law of advocacy is that a strategy and its inherent tactics should be commenced only when advocates know exactly what they want for clients.

Monitoring the Agency

The ultimate success of (or even the opportunity to do) agency advocacy largely rests on advocates' monitoring of agency activities, including their planning and decision making, budget preparation, service delivery, and client outcomes. Performing a watchdog function, advocates should remain aware of the decisions being made and how they'll affect clients. Sometimes it is not possible to keep a constant eye on all relevant agencies and programs, or to read all their reports, especially if practitioners can only devote a small amount of time to advocacy; but full-time advocates should definitely invest time to monitor agencies. As advocates become familiar with an agency's customary patterns of decision making and planning, such as the budget preparation stage, their monitoring can be more selective.

Monitoring can have beneficial effects for clients in and of itself, because agencies and staff know that someone is looking over their shoulder. There have been numerous monitoring projects over the years, from "court watch" programs to frequent visits to institutions and other residential programs. Clients in institutions, in particular, have benefited from these monitoring efforts, because large institutions tend to be located away from population centers, and operations that intend to secure clients also act to keep the public out.

We organized a monitoring program in several regions of the state of Florida that was similar to visitation programs by other civic groups (e.g.,

National Council of Jewish Women, League of Women Voters). Groups of volunteers visited secure juvenile detention facilities daily to collect information and talk to youth. The results of these efforts were impressive. First, a large number of volunteers became very knowledgeable about delinquent youth and detention centers, gaining a rare perspective on these youth and the system that deals with them. These individuals became very effective advocates. Second, the data collected was used to demonstrate to the agency and the legislature that some of the youth held in detention were not dangerous and needed other services, rather than secure confinement. Third, they witnessed the underfunding of the detention centers and, during the legislative session, gave support and testimony to their budget requests. The latter is an important consideration because many agency directors are hesitant, if not resistant, to have volunteers spend time in their programs. The wise program director, however, is aware that 9 times out of 10 their agency, the staff, and the clients will benefit from this.

Table 4.1 lists several agency activities advocates should consider monitoring and suggests specific ways to do this. In every instance, one of the best monitoring techniques is to have good professional relationships with agency staff and to talk with them periodically to be updated on agency activities. Many agencies produce statistical reports, some of which are distributed

TABLE 4.1 AGENCY ACTIVITIES TO MONITOR

What to Monitor	How to Monitor
1. Proposed Rule Changes	✓ Review official publications (e.g., the Federal Register) for announcements
	✓ Talk to agency staff
2. Budget Preparation	✓ Meet with agency staff
	✓ Request copies
3. Client Outcomes	✓ Review annual reports
	✓ Listen to clients
4. Changes in Policy or Programs	✓ Communicate with staff
	✓ Visit agency
	✓ Listen to clients
5. Policy and Program Implementation	✓ Communicate with staff
	✓ Visit agency
	✓ Obtain copies of reports
	✓ Listen to clients

externally and others maintained internally, which are very useful monitoring tools. For example, advocates in one state were interested in investigations of child abuse by a state child welfare agency. Among many other things, their statistical reports included the percent of reported cases that were investigated within 24 hours, as well as the percent of investigated reports that were determined to be valid ("substantiated"). After reviewing and charting several years worth of data, we noticed a steady decline in the percentage of cases that were investigated within 24 hours and that were substantiated. We subsequently met with agency officials to inquire about the decline. The agency agreed to make some changes in policy and practice, and, eventually, we partnered with the agency to lobby for increased funding for more staff and improved training.

Using the Administrative Procedures Act (APA)

As described above, public agencies must follow their state's APA to create and change their rules and regulations. Since most states' APA laws are very similar, Washington's may be used for illustrative purposes. The basic steps in the rule-making process are listed in Figure 4.2. In-depth knowledge of the process empowers advocates and creates advocacy opportunities. Advocates may comment on the subject of possible rule making, provide oral and written comments, encourage the agency to adopt or withdraw proposed rules, or appeal that the final rule is substantially different from the proposed rule. In

---

BASIC STEPS[a]

1. The agency solicits public comment on subject of possible rule making before publishing notice of proposed rules.

2. The public must be notified at least 20 days before a hearing on proposed rules.

3. The hearing must provide an opportunity for oral comments.

4. Before the agency adopts rules, it must summarize all comments received and provide substantive comments.

5. The agency may withdraw a proposed rule, and they may not adopt a rule that is substantially different from the proposed rule.

---

[a] This list is based on an analysis of Washington's APA. Advocates should compile a similar list for their state.

FIGURE 4.2

Steps in Administrative Procedures Act's rule-making process.

---

order to take advantage of these opportunities, advocates must know which publications are used by the state, city, county, or school board to advertise rule making and continuously monitor them.

Frequently, advocates have had their greatest impact while the agency is developing their proposed rules and before they are published. Agencies are not soliciting official input at this point, but if advocates are in touch with agency staff, have good relations with them, and have demonstrated expertise on the issues, staff members are generally quite open to suggestions from advocates, especially if it makes their jobs easier. If the interested advocates have a history of competence and effective advocacy practice, and they are known to be tenacious and willing to go to the next level and beyond to effect change, agency staff will be aware of this and usually will try to find common ground to prevent having confrontations with the advocates later. This is not always the case, however; every advocacy opportunity must be assessed and tactics chosen accordingly.

Any person may petition the agency to change its rules. If advocates choose to do this, the agency has 60 days to respond by either denying the request with reasons, or initiating the rule-making process. The APA has an important caveat in it encouraging stakeholders to settle matters informally if possible and avoid elaborate, expensive procedures. Also, the law says that if it's not feasible for the agency to adopt rules, it should advise the public of its current opinions, approaches, and likely courses of action by means of interpretive or policy statements. Advocates should always get copies of these statements.

There are still other ways to change and improve agency rules. If administrative remedies have been exhausted, and if a person has "standing" (a legal term that means the person is aggrieved or adversely affected by the agency's action), he or she may seek judicial review of the rule. Clearly, having an attorney as part of the advocacy team is beneficial if this avenue is pursued. Also, the designated legislative committee could initiate a legislative review if a majority of its members vote that an agency's rules fall outside legislative intent. Advocates could contact relevant legislators and lobby them to undertake a review. (Figure 4.3 summarizes the points of intervention advocates may use in the rule-making process.)

Meeting with Appropriate Officials

Advocates can request meetings with agency officials for several purposes. As discussed earlier, advocates might meet with agency staff in order to get information on agency operations, to be updated on program plans and progress, or to review client outcomes. They might seek a meeting to present agency officials with problems they've observed, or they might meet to propose a specific change that will solve observed problems. Of course, a single meeting

WHEN INPUT/INTERVENTION IS POSSIBLE

1. Informally during the drafting of propose⌐
2. During hearings to receive comments on ⌐
3. Petitioning for amendment or appeal of exi⌐
4. Seeking judicial review of rules
5. Seeking legislative review of rules

FIGURE **4.3**

Points of intervention in the rule-making process.

FACTORS

1. With whom should you meet?
2. Who should request the meeting?
3. When should you meet?
4. Who should go?
5. How should you present your case?
6. For what should you ask?
7. What should you send in advance?
8. What type of follow-up is required?

FIGURE **4.4**

Factors to consider when visiting an agency director.

---

might serve all three purposes. There are two primary ways to have meetings: in person or over the phone. In both cases, they can be one-on-one or with multiple participants. Figure 4.4 lists the factors advocates should consider when planning such meetings.

With Whom to Meet?   While there are no hard and fast rules about with whom to meet, there are some guidelines. Advocates should try to meet son(s) who has direct responsibility for the problem, the decision has been made or needs to be made. Generally, advocates should low in the bureaucratic hierarchy and, if necessary, request additional meetings with those higher up in the chain of command. This advice brings up the need for advocates to understand an agency's organizational chart. Organizational charts depict chains of command and areas of responsibility.

For example, if advocates wish to see a new service started by the local office of the state human service agency, they should meet with the local or regional director to explore the possibility of including funding in their budget request. It will probably be necessary at a later date to communicate with the staff in the state office who review the regional budget requests. This example underscores an idea that is specifically discussed in chapter 8, the necessity of doing advocacy homework on the chain of command and decision-making process in an agency. This research informs advocates about with whom to meet and when to meet with them.

Frequently, all that is required for a meeting is a phone call or letter requesting one, although sometimes it is more difficult, depending on how busy the person is and how high he or she is in the chain of command. At times, it may be best if a person with some influence requests the meeting, especially if advocates have no prior relationship with the agency official. Practitioners can rely on their agency director, members of their boards of directors, or influential members of their advocacy coalition. The agency official will want to know the subject of the meeting so they can prepare properly and have other relevant staff attend. Advocates should be prepared to inform officials in a general manner about their concerns, but it is probably best to avoid excessive details at this point.

Who Should Go? Deciding which advocates and clients should go to the meeting involves judgments from experience. This is one of many areas of advocacy that is an art form. There are several issues to think about when making the decision regarding who should attend. Advocates should try to impress the agency official that the problem is important, and they are serious about solving it; this can happen through what is said, how it is presented, and who is there. Persons who can clearly and persuasively present advocates' concerns should attend. Their credibility is a primary consideration. Sometimes this is an advocate, a client, or both. The influential person who requested the meeting should attend, if possible, but may ask someone else to review the details.

When deciding who should meet with agency officials, some consideration should be given to the level of the official in the organization and the structure of the organization. For example, if a new runaway shelter is being developed in the community, advocates will need the cooperation of law enforcement, including some policy changes, to accomplish their goals.

They need to convince the local law enforcement agencies that when runaways are picked up, they should be transported to the shelter instead of detention centers and jails.

Law enforcement agencies are organized with quasi-military chains of command with highly formalized rules, job descriptions, and authority structures. The sheriff, for example, being at the top of the chain, expects to meet with top officials from other agencies. Therefore, when meeting with sheriffs, it will work well if the director of the shelter or a prominent board member attends the meeting with the sheriff as opposed to a caseworker. This is not to say that the caseworker would necessarily fail to be effective in this situation; it is a reminder to be aware of factors that increase the probability that advocates' concerns will be heard and acted on.

When to Meet and When Not to Meet   Meeting with an agency director to lobby for the inclusion of new funds in the budget request is ineffective if the budget proposal has already been submitted to the legislative body or to the next level of the bureaucracy. This is why advocates need to understand budget and decision-making processes, time lines, and deadlines. There are other more subtle factors to consider when trying to decide when to meet. Certainly, advocates should complete their background research before meeting with agency officials, because they risk looking foolish if they don't have as many facts as possible. Other factors both inside the agency and in the agency's environment should be considered when scheduling meetings. For example, advocates should consider how much time is left in an official's tenure in office, or whether a new governor is soon to take office and is likely to replace appointed officials. Sometimes officials who are about to leave office are unwilling to make policy changes, while others like the idea of making one last improvement before they leave.

Presenting Your Case   Like the other suggestions given here, there are no absolute rules about how to present your case, what kind of tone to set, or how aggressive to be. Most experienced advocates suggest that it is best to assume that the agency and advocates share the same goals for clients and that a collaborative relationship will be effective in achieving the objectives of the advocacy effort. There are times that the agency and advocates have the same goals but the agency is on a time line for implementing changes that is too slow in the opinion of advocates, or they agree that the changes are needed but they don't have the resources to implement them.

The tone of a meeting is important and advocates do not have total control of this. For their part, one helpful way to think about the meeting atmosphere is that there are two important, potential outcomes: (1) to convince the official to make the change you seek; and (2) to develop an ally for future advocacy efforts. Try not to make an enemy or burn any bridges.

It is likely that in the not-too-distant future, there will be a need to revisit the official for another advocacy effort. Also, it's a small world, and individuals in the helping professions move from agency to agency, position to position. However, this is a difficult balancing act, and if advocates are to fault in one direction or another, it is better to fault in the direction of helping clients. James Thurber's advice is apropos here: "You might as well fall flat on your face as lean over too far backward" (Bartlett, 1992).

Follow-up   It's a good idea to follow up on the meeting with a letter that serves several purposes. First, you should thank the people who met with you. Second, you should use the letter to restate the purpose of the meeting as well as the outcomes. Any agreements that were made should be listed in the letter, including a designation of who is responsible for each task discussed at the meeting. Whatever next steps or additional meetings were agreed upon should be summarized.

If advocates are not satisfied with the outcome of the meeting, they may choose to meet again with the same person or a higher level official. Other advocacy tactics can be brought into play here too. If the agency official wasn't persuaded by your argument (or seemed to be but the situation hasn't changed), he or she may be persuaded by different people using different tactics. Advocates may be able to get one or more influential people to express concern about the same issue. Working with the media to highlight the situation that concerns you also may be considered.

Going Up the Chain of Command   Advocates may have to go to the top to plead their cause. For state government, the governor is the chief administrative officer of state agencies, for counties it may be a county executive, and for cities it may be a mayor or city manager. In general, the higher one goes in the chain of command, the more politically minded the person is, and tactics used by advocates must be attuned to this. Even though it is easy to become cynical about the motives of elected or politically appointed officials, it is best to operate on the assumption that they share your goals and want the best for clients.

Differences of opinion usually occur based not on goals but on the means to achieve them. Experienced advocates have learned many general guidelines for being persuasive and having leverage in situations like this, and they quickly caution that there is no absolute "always" or "never." For example, some might say that top-level agency officials will do anything to avoid a public controversy that might make them or their bosses look bad. If this were true, the veiled threat of going public could wield great influence. However, many politicians believe that there is no such thing as bad publicity, and citizens' memories are short. The point here is that multiple, dynamic factors must be weighed when choosing tactics and that experience is priceless. Failing to learn from experience is deadly.

Predictable Responses from Agencies

There are many ways that agency officials could respond to your proposals. Ideally they'll say, "You're absolutely right, and we'll get on it right away." The opposite response would be, "You're wrong, everything is fine, and we see no reason to change." Unfortunately, advocates rarely get either of these responses; they usually get something in between. If an agency disagrees with you or does not want to do what you suggest, they rarely tell you this directly. You might even leave your meeting thinking that they're going to address the problem, but nothing happens. They've got inertia on their side; you have to shift the direction of the inertia.

It is wise to be prepared for the variety of responses you might get so that you can counter or neutralize unsatisfactory responses. The following material is adapted from the work of Fernandez (1980) and includes some of the more frequent "excuses" you're likely to hear, as well as some arguments to make in response (see Table 4.2). Anticipating these excuses and practicing responses is good preparation for dealing with agencies.

Letter Writing[13]

Many advocates don't hesitate to mobilize a letter-writing campaign to legislators or their governor but forget that the same tactic can be useful with agency officials. Letters such as this should be brief, stating the issue of concern and your request for specific action. Ask the official to respond. Consider sending copies of the letters to higher officials in the agency, the governor, or legislators. Sometimes when an influential person is copied on the letter, it gets more attention. If advocates feel they have been getting nowhere with an agency—after meetings and letters—it may be time to write letters to the newspaper (see chapter 7 for working with the media.)

Working with "Inside Advocates"

There are many helping professionals working for agencies who are advocates themselves, want the best for clients, and are frustrated by their agency's lack of responsiveness. Frequently, they have done all they can from inside the agency to change policies and procedures to be more proclient.[14] They have information on client outcomes, agency plans, or decisions that would be useful to outside advocates, and wish to work with other advocates by passing

---

13. This subsection about letter writing also applies to sending e-mails.
14. The NASW *Code of Ethics* (1996) indicates that "Social workers should work to improve employing agencies' policies and procedures and the efficiency and effectiveness of their services" (3.09b).

TABLE 4.2   PREDICTABLE AGENCY EXCUSES AND POSSIBLE RESPONSES[a]

Excuse	Response
• *No money.* "Yes, that's needed, but we are short of funds and are facing budget cuts already."	There are numerous ways to respond, because this excuse can mean so many different things. For example, it may mean that your issue is not a priority with the agency, and you will need to convince them of its importance. You may have to suggest cutting an outdated/ineffective program. You could also ask if there are other programs that are underspending or some federal or state funds that can be used. Ask if they plan to request funding for this issue in their next budget and with whom you should speak in order to improve the chances of approval.
• *We're the experts.* "We know best and must make these decisions. You do not understand all the complexities of the problem."	Remind the officials that you and your client(s) do know client needs. Agency staff are being paid by citizens to serve the needs of these clients and the community as a whole.
• *Denial of the problem.* "That is not a real problem. Do you have any proof?"	It may be the case that the agency is unaware of the problem or need and advocates are serving an important role by informing them. Bring your documented evidence to the meeting.
• *The exception.* "The examples you gave me are the exceptions. It may be happening to a few clients, but the problem is not widespread."	Point out that each client is important and put the burden on the agency to demonstrate that the problem is not widespread.
• *Blaming the victim.* "With this type of client, we really can't do that much."	The program should be designed to meet the needs of all clients and should definitely not exacerbate the problem.
• *Blaming the parents.* "We know it's a problem, but those parents don't seem to care about their own children."	Don't allow them to shift the blame. The agency should be held responsible for what happens in the programs it controls. The practice of labeling parents as "bad" should be avoided.
• *Delaying.* "Yes, I know the problem exists, but we need time to figure out the best thing to do." (Another version: "We have known all along about this, and we have plans to correct the situation, but our efforts must be given a chance.")	Ask specifically what is being done to solve the problems. Ask for their plans in writing with a timetable and the names of people responsible for implementing the plan.
• *An unimportant problem.* "Yes, it may be a problem, but there are so many more pressing issues at this agency."	Don't be sidetracked. You believe the problem is important and should be dealt with because it affects many clients directly.
• *We're not so bad.* "What you say is true, but other agencies like ours have similar problems; we are no worse than they are."	This doesn't excuse them from doing their job correctly. They should focus on meeting the needs of clients not how they compare to other (possibly mediocre) agencies.

TABLE

4.2

Excuse	Response
• *Further study.* "The problem needs further study and research before we can act wisely."	Ask who is doing the study, and when will it and implementation plans be completed. Ask the official(s) what can be done to help clients in need until the research is complete.
• *Community resistance.* "The community will not accept your solution. We would like to change, but the attitudes in the community would not let it work."	Remind the official that you live in the community too and might help garner support (or, at least, weaken/neutralize resistance).
• *Passing the buck.* "Yes, that is a problem, but I can't do anything because my hands are tied (by policy, contracts, higher officials in the administration, the computer system, etc.)." (Another version: "I understand the problem, but I feel it is not our responsibility; it is the task of the family and other institutions.")	Ask to see copies in writing of the policy, contracts, or memos that excuse the official from acting. If the official, in fact, is not accountable, then appeal to the official who is responsible.

ᵃThis material is an edited version of a previously published work; *The Child Advocacy Handbook*, H. C. Fernandez, 1980. Used by permission of The Pilgrim Press.

along this information. Richart and Bing (1989) talk about having "an informal network of trusted people who report . . . the 'initial rumblings' they hear or see" (p. 105).

Just like journalists, advocates need to verify the information they get from these sources to be sure the problems aren't isolated to a few cases that could most effectively be addressed by case advocacy. Further, Richart and Bing (1989) call these inside advocates "whistleblowers" and present good advice about protecting their identities and educating them about the consequences of their actions.

Joining Task Forces

A frequent outcome of agency advocacy is the creation of a task force to investigate the problem and propose solutions. Advocates are usually asked to be members of the task force, especially if they played a role in identifying the problem. There is an ongoing debate among advocates whether joining such task forces is a good idea. First, whether they join or not, advocates need to ask some hard questions. Is a task force really needed? Is there a more efficient way to develop solutions as opposed to several meetings with numerous people? Is this a delaying or co-optation tactic by the agency?

Those who advise advocates to join task forces think that this is a good way for advocates to contribute to positive solutions (instead of simply criticizing the agency), to develop working relationships with the agency, and to gain greater knowledge of agency operations. The other side of the coin is that by participating in the process, advocates are somewhat bound to support the solutions developed by the group. In some instances, the solutions may not be satisfactory for clients, and the advocates are somewhat constrained from pursuing better solutions. Those who question joining task forces wonder whether advocates aren't doing some of the work of the agency.

The author's bias is not to join, but there are situations when advocates might choose otherwise. Even if advocates are not official members of the task force, they may attend meetings and receive copies of all materials that are distributed. Advocates may request time on an agenda to make a presentation or submit a memo with suggestions. A particularly effective strategy is, instead of suggesting specific solutions, to outline the characteristics of a good solution. For example, if the task force proposed a new program, some desirable characteristics that advocates could highlight might be its low cost, that it is easily accessible, or that it is respectful of the client's family.

A similar dilemma advocates face is whether to get involved in decisions relating to the structure and organization of agencies. Task forces are frequently created to make recommendations on these issues. Questions such as the following frequently occur: Should there be a separate state agency for children, for example, or should that responsibility remain within the human services agency? Should the agency be decentralized? How much authority should regional directors have? Which specific programs should be administratively located in each department or division?

The danger of getting overly involved in these issues is that advocates tend to lose sight of the primary goal of advocacy, which is to ensure positive client outcomes. To the degree that an agency's administrative location or structure is thought to impact client outcomes, advocates may wish to comment. However, while many hold strong beliefs about the best arrangement of programs and agencies, there is little evidence one way or another (Ezell & Patti, 1990). The major point is that advocates shouldn't be sidetracked by these issues and should remain vigilant in their efforts to improve services and outcomes for their clients.

SUMMARY

Agency advocacy is one of the four major advocacy strategies discussed in this book. Many experienced advocates prefer the strategy of advocacy agency because agency decision makers have relatively wide authority over their operations. It is a critical oversight if advocates fail to influence agency processes used to develop budget requests.

The first section of this chapter described the kinds of agency problems that cause clients to be underserved or poorly served and the kinds of situations that might trigger advocates into action. The next section described the differences between rules, regulations, policies, and practices and the agency processes by which each is created. Understanding the distinctions helps advocates do better targeting and advocacy planning.

In order to use this strategy effectively, advocates need to be knowledgeable about how agencies operate, who makes decisions, targets and timing of intervention, and advocacy tactics. Key ingredients for successful agency advocacy are persuasiveness and credibility.

Advocates will be in a persuasive position if they closely monitor agencies' performance and remain in the heat of things. Tenacity and the countering of frequent excuses are excellent ingredients in this complex puzzle of how to bring about change for clients.

DISCUSSION QUESTIONS

1. Think about the group of clients that has your greatest interest. Describe a problem this client group has that is likely rooted in agency operations.
2. Does your state have an Administrative Procedures Act? How does it compare to the description in this chapter? Contact an agency of interest and request a copy of their rules and regulations.
3. Devise a series of tactics by which to replace an ineffective agency director.
4. Develop three other common agency excuses and arguments to counter them.

LEGISLATIVE ADVOCACY

CHAPTER OBJECTIVES

By the time you finish studying this chapter, you should

1. Know the type of information needed to understand and impact the legislative process.
2. Be able to engage in legislative monitoring, lobbying, and committee testimony.
3. Be familiar with the advantages of working with advocacy networks and coalitions.
4. Know whether and how to be involved in political campaigns.

The legislative advocacy strategy is used when the target for change is a state law, local ordinance, municipal code, or school board policy, or when the budget is being reviewed, changed, and approved by the legislative body. There are **legislative bodies** at the federal, state, and local levels, though the term is most often associated with state legislatures. Local legislative bodies are labeled county councils, city commissions, and school boards, for example. There is an abundance of writing on lobbying and influencing legislation, including numerous articles in professional journals, pamphlets, and several books. This chapter will provide a concise description of legislative advocacy by discussing advocacy tactics in three categories: (1) those to be used during a legislative session, (2) those to be used out of session, and (3) activities related to political campaigns.

UNDERSTANDING LEGISLATIVE PROCESS

Before gaining knowledge about legislative processes, advocates need to examine their beliefs, attitudes, and judgments about being involved in political activity. There are a number of human service practitioners who have negative opinions of politics and, therefore, activities associated with legislative advocacy, such as lobbying and participation in election campaigns. They think that politics is a dirty business and would prefer to steer clear of it (Ezell, 1993). Others have mixed feelings about the whole business, and they recognize that the political and legislative processes are central to the way society establishes policy and distributes resources. Dirty, squeaky clean, or somewhere in the middle, these processes create important opportunities to express client needs and influence change. The stark reality is that laws and budgets are going to be passed no matter what, and it's probably better to get involved and give proclient input than to sit on the sidelines. Melton (1983) puts it nicely when he explains, "To a large extent, the lobbyist is simply a provider of information on the effects of a particular piece of legislation, from the vantage point of the interest group that he or she represents" (pp. 138–139).

Advocates need to resolve and set these attitudes aside because they are detrimental to the task at hand. One study found that legislators perceive legislative advocates as condescending lobbyists and are reluctant to work with them (State Legislative Leaders Foundation, 1995): "They [legislators] perceive advocates as 'elitists' who view the legislative process and state legislators themselves with disdain or skepticism" (p. vii). Of course, it is impossible to determine the accuracy of these perceptions, and, while only a few lobbyists may be condescending and the remainder respectful, these perceptions are important to note.

Knowledge Is Power

After polishing up their attitudes, if necessary, advocates need to be fully informed about the legislative process they wish to impact. Even though there are differences from state to state, county to county, city to city, and school district to school district, each legislative body has a set of rules and procedures that govern how legislation is formally introduced, reviewed, and voted upon. Likewise, there are unrecorded, informal rules that determine how the process really works. The more advocates know about these processes, the greater the opportunity to influence the outcome. Knowledge such as this is power, because it tells the advocate whom to lobby, how, and when. Familiarity with the process will help advocates to know the key hurdles for legislation, which will then enable them to help get the bill over the hurdle, contribute to useful modifications, or influence its defeat. It is probably impossible to avoid partisan politics while engaged in legislative advocacy, and, therefore, knowledge of the political parties, their actors and agendas, and their relative numbers in relevant legislative bodies is critical.[15]

Table 5.1 is a list of the minimum information advocates need to know if they expect to influence the legislative process. For each item, an example has been included to elucidate the idea. Examples may not be applicable in every jurisdiction.

In their discussion of legislative advocacy, Dear and Patti (1987) pinpoint several "important realities or 'truths'" (p. 34) that advocates must face if they hope to be effective in their change efforts. One of the realities is that there are always more client needs to be met than resources to meet them. This being the case, advocates should remember that notwithstanding need or moral imperative, legislators' primary concern will be program costs. Therefore, knowledge of revenues, budget process, taxes, and the key actors in budget formulation is crucial to success.

Another key point Dear and Patti (1987) make is that only an average of 20% of the proposed bills are passed during a session, and those with the least chance of being passed are the following: expensive bills, those that involve major changes, and those that deal with unpopular issues. Unfortunately, this describes many human service bills. Consequently, advocates must develop multisession action plans in order to get legislation passed and to try to get their bill introduced as early in a session as possible. During the first session a bill is introduced, sponsors and advocates may only get as far as a brief committee hearing. During the second session, the bill may pass a substantive committee but get bogged down in the budget committee. It's possible that during the third session the proposal will make it all the way through one house but not another and, finally, get passed during the fourth session. This is not an uncommon scenario, and of course it can be shorter or longer, but it is clear that multiyear strategies are needed and that advocates should be realistic and tenacious about passing legislation.

It should almost go without saying that besides knowledge of the legislative process and the actors, advocates must be experts on the issue about which they seek legislative change. They need to know the nature, history, and causes of the problem as well as the current policy and programmatic responses. Expertise and credibility are very influential commodities in the legislative process.

To extend the example used earlier, when advocates sought to remove juveniles from adult jails, their knowledge of the issue was a major ingredient in their effectiveness. Advocates familiarized themselves with all state laws,

---

15. For the time being, the chief executive (e.g., president, governor, mayor) and his or her political party and how they relate to the legislative body and its politics won't be discussed. Understanding these dynamics, however, is important for successful legislative advocacy.

TABLE
5.1   **WHAT A LEGISLATIVE ADVOCATE NEEDS TO KNOW**

Item	Example
1. How to get your idea written into a bill and sponsored by a legislator	• Talk to the chairperson of the major legislative committee that will review the legislation. See if he or she is interested in sponsoring the legislation and, if so, ask if committee staff or legislative aides will draft the bill. It is advantageous to do this well before the legislative session.[a]
2. Whether a companion bill should be introduced in the other legislative house	• Seek the advice of the original bill sponsor on a companion bill in the house or senate and ask whom they'd recommend as a sponsor in that body. Sometimes the parallel committee chairperson is the best choice. For a variety of reasons, it may not be a good idea to work simultaneously in both houses.
3. How to get the support of the affected agency and the governor	• Conversations with relevant agency and gubernatorial staff should happen very early in the process, probably before finding a sponsor. Their opposition will not necessarily defeat the bill, but the probability of success diminishes greatly. Compromises may have to be made in the original idea, and, sometimes, the best you can get is an agreement that they will not take a position for or against the bill.
4. How to get the legislation referred to the "right" committee	• Advocates need to work with the leadership in the house to which the bill was introduced to be sure the proposal will be reviewed by the appropriate committee and is not referred to a large number of committees. If leadership is opposed to the bill, they may refer it to numerous committees, knowing that the legislative session is too short for it to make it through all committees. Advocates need to work in close partnership with the sponsor(s) during this and all stages of the process.
5. How to get the bill on a committee's agenda and then voted out of committee	• The committee chair must be lobbied to ensure that the bill is given a hearing and put up for vote. Advocates, the sponsor(s), supportive committee members, or all of these can do this. Advocates must organize supporters to testify for the bill in the committee and must lobby committee members to vote for it. The same is done for every committee to which the bill is referred.

(Continued)

TABLE 5.1	CONTINUED

Item	Example
6. How to get the bill to the floor of the legislative body for a vote	• Usually there is one committee controlled by the majority party that determines which bills will be voted on by the entire body. Advocates must lobby the chair and key members of this committee.
7. How to get a majority vote in favor of the bill on the floor	• Ideally, advocates would lobby each member of the house. Short of that, advocates should contact legislators who are known to be influential among their peers. Sometimes the caucus of each political party decides how its members should vote. Advocates should not leave this stone unturned.
8. How to get a satisfactory bill out of a conference committee	• When a similar bill passes both houses, it can be sent to a conference committee to work out differences. Advocates can seek to influence who is chosen to serve on the conference committee as well as the content of the conference committee report.
9. How to seek modifications to another piece of legislation	• Legislators can propose amendments at certain stages of committee work and floor debate. If advocates have specific language they'd like added or removed from a bill, they should attempt to discuss these proposals with the sponsors or other legislators to see if they are willing to propose the amendments.
10. How to seek modifications to a budget bill	• Sometimes legislative bodies have slightly different rules for budget bills than for substantive bills. It is best if advocates convince the executive who proposes the budget to include their item, and advocates can seek changes in subcommittees, full committees, on the floor, and in conference committee.

[a]Amidei (1991) recommends that when advocates look for legislators to sponsor their legislative idea, it is more effective to have multiple sponsors as a way to increase credibility, and it can also help to have bipartisan sponsors.

agency regulations and policies, and court cases related to the issue. Due to their extensive research, they knew which jails throughout the state were unable to comply with existing state law, and whether agencies were enforcing their rules, as well as how many youth had been commingled with adult inmates, for how long, and the circumstances of the commingling. They were prepared to offer solutions, and their knowledge of other states' and jurisdictions' successes and failures greatly contributed to this.

ADVOCACY ACTIVITIES DURING LEGISLATIVE SESSION

This section describes several tactics advocates can use while the legislative body is in session. They are relevant to legislative bodies at all levels of government—federal, state, and local, including school boards. Experienced legislative advocates can usually offer good advice on the potential of any given tactic. However, advocates should be careful about generalizing from one legislative body to another. For example, some congressional lobbyists think that committee testimony is a good way to draw public attention to an issue, but it rarely sways anyone's vote. On the other hand, state legislatures operate somewhat differently, and committee testimony has a greater likelihood of garnering votes (Dear, 1997).

Legislative Monitoring

Advocates should closely monitor the legislative process both within and between sessions. Depending on the focus and resources of advocates, this may mean reviewing every piece of proposed legislation to determine if it will help or hurt their clients. Legislation of interest should be tracked throughout the process to see how much support exists and to determine if modifications along the way are substantially changing it. Keeping track of the legislative progress of a bill allows advocates to voice their support or opposition (or do more focused lobbying) in a timely manner. Some bills never make it out of their first committee, and, while there is no absolute way to predict this, committee leadership and legislative staff can provide helpful information. Many experienced lobbyists advise not investing much time and energy in legislation that has no hope of moving. At the same time, advocates should watch to see if a legislator plans to amend their "dead bill" onto another piece of legislation later in the process. If advocates have established good working relations with legislators and staff, they can usually get advance warning about this type of situation.

Budget bills are more difficult to monitor because they include so much information. In Washington State, there is one budget bill that includes funding for all state agencies for a two-year period.[16] The governor proposes a state budget and delivers it to the legislature prior to the start of the session; then both houses (and usually both political parties, too) develop their versions of the state budget. Essentially, advocates must be aware of the governor's proposal and be able to track a senate and house budget; none of them are easily

---

16. In even numbered years, a small, supplemental budget bill is passed to adjust the biennial budget and deal with emerging issues. The House and Senate alternate responsibility for originating the budget bill. Some states separate operating budgets from capital budgets into different bills. Understanding all the details of this is critical.

decipherable, and experience and hard work really pay off in this area. Agency and legislative staff, as inside advocates, can be very helpful in explaining the format, jargon, and details of these budgets.

Legislative budget committees are usually broken down into subcommittees to do the budget work. Advocates need to know how this is done so they know whom to lobby and when. Budgets for health and human service agencies are frequently reviewed by one subcommittee, education agencies by another, and transportation and general government agencies by a third. Just like other bills, the budget must be approved by both houses and frequently is sent to a conference committee to iron out differences.

Richart and Bing (1989) argue that "policies affecting children are money-driven" (p. 78), and it is probably fair to generalize this to other client groups. They provide the following advice to advocates:

> Advocates must engage in all activities leading up to the development of the state budget, using all strategies to expand the amount of money available for children. Simply establishing a state policy which mandates that services be provided to children and their families is only the first part of the advocate's mission. (p. 79)

This underscores the importance of closely monitoring and influencing the provisions of the budget bill. It is very challenging; important work is rarely easy. Chapter 9 will present a detailed case study of impacting the state budget as a way to show how all advocacy strategies work together.

There are many different ways to monitor legislation. The two state legislatures with which the author has worked will mail copies of bills as they are filed to anyone requesting them. More and more legislatures have homepages on the World Wide Web, and bills can be downloaded from there. Advocates can review them to see which ones are of interest and should be tracked. Very few advocates have unlimited time to devote to this task, so it is wise to sort the relevant bills into categories such as high priority, medium priority, and low priority, and follow as many as time permits, starting with the high priority bills. The next piece of important information is to which committees the bills have been referred for consideration.

Once the committees of referral are known, there are a couple of ways to learn when a committee will hold a hearing and vote on the bill. Usually a weekly schedule of committee hearings and their agendas is published. Advocates can pick this up or have the schedule mailed to them. With the great technological advances of recent years, much of this information can be obtained over the Internet.[17] Many legislatures have designated phone num-

---

17. For example, the address (URL) for the Washington State Legislature is http://leginfo.leg.wa.gov/. The following information (and more) is included on this Web site and its links: members' names and addresses by district, lists of committees and membership, meeting schedules, and bill information. The information on individual bills includes copies of bills, brief digests of bills, amendments, and bill reports explaining both current law and proposed changes.

bers for citizens to call to get this information and request copies. Another way to learn about committee work on bills of interest is to call the staff of the committee. They can tell advocates if and when certain bills will be considered. It is important to remember that when legislatures are in session, action is fast and furious, and toward the end of the session this pace increases even more. Schedules and agendas change quickly, and this creates a challenge for advocates trying to keep up. Also, especially late in the session, phone and Internet systems cannot be updated fast enough, so there is a lag between what is really happening and what the posted information indicates. One of the great benefits of forming advocacy coalitions (to be discussed later) is that this labor can be divided and shared among coalition members.

Monitoring can continue once a particular legislative session ends and before the next session begins. Legislative staff frequently conduct interim studies that will inform legislative ideas during the following session, and advocates may be able to have input and be helpful at this point. This is also a time when legislators plan and draft their proposals for the upcoming session, and they might be open to advocates' suggestions. Legislators and staff frequently continue to refine legislation they proposed but didn't pass, and, again, input from advocates is generally well received at this point.

Lobbying and Testifying[18]

Lobbying consists of efforts made to persuade legislators to offer legislative proposals or amendments or to sway their votes for, against, or in favor of modifying a proposal. Lobbying involves persuasion, negotiation, and compromise; there are many different methods by which to persuade a person to vote in a way that will help clients. The best approach to use when trying to influence legislators may vary on different issues and on different days of the week. Many experienced lobbyists say that the basic approach is to pull on either heartstrings or purse strings. Some people are moved by evocative client stories, the predictable and disastrous negative consequences if problems go unaddressed, while others are swayed by instances of injustice. There are others, or the same people on other days, who are best convinced by money arguments, such as "This proposal is less expensive than existing practices," or "This small investment now will save the state millions down the road."

To say that these are the only types of arguments that persuade legislators or to imply that one or the other should be used is dangerous. There are other influential arguments, and, time permitting, multiple arguments should be

18. All advocates who lobby should become familiar with and follow their employing agency's rules on lobbying. Public agencies usually have policies on lobbying and who can speak for the agency. Advocates working for private nonprofit organizations need to be cognizant of the Internal Revenue Service's definitions and restrictions on lobbying. Also, legislative bodies have rules regarding who needs to register as a lobbyist.

advanced. Many legislators are very responsive to their constituents' preferences and may be strongly influenced by particularly powerful citizens
(Richan, 1991).

Legislators have the desire to remain in office and, therefore, will be motivated to do things that make them look good to voters and avoid things that
might make them look bad. Tapping into this mind-set can also create potential leverage. At other times political party leaders, committee chairs, or
respected legislative peers can help a legislator see the light or make a deal in
which votes are traded.

Position Papers

The approach used by many advocates is to present a rational, well documented analysis of the presenting problem, and to propose a solution (at a reasonable price) that has demonstrated effectiveness. The rational argument is
frequently encapsulated in a position paper that is given to legislators and staff.
It should be short (two pages at most, and one page is better) because legislators' time is at a premium and advocates can always provide more in-depth
information on request. There are many different effective formats; it is the
content that is essential. It is useful to summarize the background and extent
of the problem or need (e.g., estimates of the number of people affected, the
seriousness, and the costs and consequences), a synopsis of the proposal for
which you seek support, and contact information. Position papers are usually
printed on agency letterhead, and some people recommend using colored
paper to make them stand out.

One-on-One Lobbying

One form of legislative advocacy is one-on-one lobbying. This is when one or
more advocates meet with a legislator. This could occur while legislators are in
their district office, legislative office, in the hall or elevator on the way to a
meeting, on the phone, or over a meal. This type of lobbying can last a couple
of hours or be as brief as 30 seconds. During the legislative session, don't count
on having much time. What and how much you present depends on the
amount of time available, the legislator's prior knowledge of the issue, and
your prior relationship with the legislator. Legislators tend to specialize in certain areas, generally, but not always, consistent with their committee assignments. Don't make assumptions about what they know and don't know, simply
ask. Most legislators who are unfamiliar with an advocate's specific issue will
appreciate a briefing on the subject.

Although every advocate has to make a judgment call, experienced lobbyists have noted that focusing lobbying on legislators who are "on the fence" can
be of great benefit and is a wise application of advocates' limited resources.

Give positive reinforcement to legislators who are in favor of the advocates' legislation, and make brief courtesy calls to those who are known to be opposed.

Advocates should be specific and explicitly ask for what they want, such as (1) sponsorship of a bill or amendment, (2) support of a bill or amendment, or (3) opposition to a bill or amendment. Novice lobbyists occasionally fail to ask legislators for their decision, assuming their presentation was strongly persuasive and that polite head nodding meant agreement. Ask politely for the legislator's decision, and if he or she wants more time to consider the request, ask when you should followup to get an answer.

A study conducted by the State Legislative Leaders Foundation (1995) found that "State legislative leaders learn anecdotally about issues and not systematically, so their knowledge is often not national or statewide, but limited to what goes on in their districts and what others bring to their attention" (p. vi). Providing legislators with systematic, comprehensive information about clients is the primary objective of one-on-one lobbying, committee testimony, and district visits.

Legislators will ask questions and seek more information during these meetings, and advocates may not have the information at hand. Do not make something up; instead, indicate that you will find out and follow up as soon as possible. It's tempting for lobbyists to give undocumented answers when they think they might lose face for not knowing everything about the issue, but no one really expects advocates to be comprehensive sources of all information. It is more important to remember that credibility is crucial in these working relationships and, once lost, is nearly impossible to regain.

These exchanges require good judgment and strategy. Advocates may wish to have constituents contact their legislator before the one-on-one meeting, or have constituents attend meetings. Others may prefer to have constituents contact their legislator after the meeting. There are many effective approaches.

Committee Testimony

Testifying before a committee is a common legislative advocacy tactic. Usually committees establish a procedure for signing up to testify, but even though advocates may put their names on the list, there is no guarantee that they'll be called. In fact, even if the opportunity to testify comes up, it may not last more than 30 seconds. For example, I had a recent experience in which I woke up very early and drove 70 miles to Olympia, Washington, to testify at an 8:00 a.m. hearing. The hearing was scheduled to end at 10:00 a.m.; finally, at 9:55 a.m. the committee chair called my name to speak. I was well prepared, having stayed up late the night before to develop a couple pages of comments. After introducing myself and barely starting my remarks and sage advice, the committee chair asked me to sum up in 30 seconds. I was a bit flabbergasted, but recovered enough to make a couple comments before I crawled away.

This doesn't happen every time, but advocates should always be prepared to give very brief testimony. Advocates should introduce themselves clearly and identify the agency they represent, if applicable, and they should briefly thank the committee for the opportunity to give input. They should indicate whether they support or oppose the legislation and give specific reasons. Frequently, advocates are in the position of liking most of a bill but are opposed to one or two specific provisions. It is helpful if the advocate can indicate what changes he or she would like to see. Sometimes advocates don't testify for or against a bill but wish to testify for informational purposes or to share their concerns. In all cases, it is very useful to give the committee a copy of your remarks and changes you suggest, even providing specific wording, if possible.

It's a good idea if the person testifying knows the names and districts of committee members so that he or she can use data or give an example from one of these districts in his or her testimony. Also, committee members may ask questions of the testifier, and it's nice if advocates respond using legislators' names. As above, if advocates are asked questions to which they don't know the answer, they should indicate that they don't know but will find out and follow up with the committee.

Every now and then, a committee member may ask an aggressive or hostile question. These are not fun, and advocates should do their best to respond briefly and politely. It can be useful to pursue a private conversation later with the aggressive legislator to clear up any possible misunderstandings. One essential rule of lobbying is to avoid making enemies and not to burn any bridges. The legislator who opposes advocates' favorite bill may be a great ally on the next one. As is frequently said, Politics makes strange bedfellows, and maybe the same could be said for advocacy.

Who Should Testify?   An important issue regarding testifying is who and how many should testify. Advocates should coordinate their efforts with the sponsoring legislator(s) when trying to orchestrate testimony, and should try to get the committee chair to indicate how much time will be available. The following possibilities should be considered to offer testimony: clients; agency staff (usually directors); influential, high profile, or highly regarded citizens; or other advocates. Strategically, it can be wise to have one or more of the above be from the chairperson's legislative district or the districts of other members.

Many professional lobbyists advise that it is a mistake to push for a committee vote without knowing if there are enough votes to pass or defeat the bill, whichever is the goal. This isn't always possible, but advocates should do their best to poll committee members to see which way they'll vote. There are times when the committee chair, whether there are enough votes or not, won't allow a bill to be voted on in committee. This is a chair's province, and he or she may be doing this based on a personal decision or at the direction of his or her party leaders. Once again, persuasion is the tool advocates will need to use to get their bill voted on in (and, hopefully, out of) committee.

Alerting Constituents/Advocates

Activating a **network of advocates** is discussed in this subsection, whereas the activities necessary to create and organize this network are discussed in the next section. It is difficult to do the extensive, grassroots organizing needed to identify and enlist potential volunteer advocates while the legislative body is in session. Congress, with the exception of scheduled recesses, is in session practically year-round, while local legislative bodies and school boards hold their sessions weekly, biweekly, or monthly. In most cases, therefore, not all advocates have the luxury of organizing a network when the body is out of session.

Assuming that advocates—be they clients, volunteers, agency staff, or interested citizens—have been identified as willing to help pass or defeat legislation as needed, there are important times at which they need to be directed to contact their representatives in the legislative body. Generally, this is done when a bill is nearing a committee or floor vote. Accurate instructions need to be sent to the advocacy network so that participants know whom they should contact, when to do it, and what message to send (e.g., "please vote against Bill # 1234 because it hurts clients").

Traditionally, these networks are organized as "telephone trees" by which a relatively small number of alerting phone calls are made to advocates, and each of them makes calls to a few more advocates, and so on and so on until a large number of advocates have been activated. Another common method, although slower than phoning, is to mail periodic legislative updates that track the progress of relevant legislation to network participants and give them instructions for action. Copies of position papers may be included in the mailings.

Modern technology allows advocates to use e-mail and fax machines to alert advocacy networks very quickly, and to transmit input from constituents to legislators. These methods are mainly designed to get a large number of advocates to take action quickly, but they don't necessarily have to be used that way. At certain times, a more effective tactic is to alert a small number of influential citizens or individuals who have positive relationships with and easy access to the legislator(s) of interest. This doesn't have to be an either-or choice, both approaches can be used simultaneously. Advocates need to be careful, however, about overusing and burning out members of their network.

Another useful tool for alerting advocates is the World Wide Web. Many organizations operate Web sites that, among other things, include up-to-date tracking information on high-priority legislation. They also include instructions to advocates about what to do and, sometimes, which legislators need to be contacted. Position papers can be downloaded from these Web sites, too. Members of the advocacy network simply log onto the Web site periodically to get their information and instructions.

Generally, members of the network are asked to phone, visit, write, fax, or e-mail their representatives expressing their views on the legislation. Network participants need to know when legislative action is likely to occur so members can make decisions about which method of communication may be best. They should specifically refer to the legislation of interest (e.g., Senate Bill # 7899) and tell their legislators whether they should support or oppose it. If at all possible, they should provide reasons for doing so and indicate why they're concerned about the issue. This will solidify the message and may provide an anecdote or perspective that had not occurred to the legislator. It's not a good idea to make threats such as, "If you don't support this bill, I'll make sure you're never reelected." As always, be polite and keep the channels of communication open for the next issue. There is some consensus among professional lobbyists that legislators will ignore mass-produced letters or postcards. Finally, it's a good idea to followup with legislators and thank them for voting the "right" way and, if they didn't, to inquire about their reasons for voting as they did.

Working with Legislative Staff

There are generally two types of legislative staff: (1) staff assigned to assist specific legislators (referred to here as **aides**), and (2) staff assigned to assist specific committees (**committee staff**). Both are great resources for advocates. When advocates call their representatives, they frequently communicate with aides, because legislators can't take or return every call that comes in. Aides may pass on messages, tell callers how the legislator voted or is likely to vote, report on the progress of certain legislation, or make calls to pass on information as directed by their legislator. Obviously, maintaining a good relationship with aides facilitates better access to legislators.

Committee staff have expertise in the issue areas over which their committees have jurisdiction, such as health care, social services, corrections, and criminal justice. They are frequently the ones who transform a legislator's idea into legislative language. During this process, they frequently explain existing laws, policies, and programs to legislators and can persuade or dissuade legislators as they consider the idea. When a bill is to be considered by their committee, they prepare an analysis of it for the members.

In their roles as committee staff, these people are sources of endless information on bill scheduling, likely amendments, expressed and likely concerns of various groups and individuals, and potential costs and consequences. Occasionally they monitor executive agencies to determine if approved legislation is being implemented properly. They also conduct interim studies for their committees that frequently result in legislation. In a situation in which advocates are able to get a legislator to sponsor and file a bill that will help clients, the advocates can offer assistance to committee staff as they prepare their reports. They may have data on the nature, extent, and cost of the problem they're trying to solve, as well as studies that show their proposal to be cost effective.

Committee staff are hardworking professionals, but they can't be experts on absolutely everything. To get assistance, they will call on those whom they consider to be experts, who tend to be helpful and responsive, and with whom they are comfortable. Once again, maintaining good relationships with committee staff can be very beneficial. It almost goes without saying, but advocates should never ask staff to give out privileged information or do something unethical, surreptitious, or that could put their jobs at risk. That is not the purpose of maintaining positive working relations. The purpose is to nurture access points to legislators and legislative information, to increase receptivity to advocacy positions, and to develop a network of allies who wish to see improvements in services and conditions for clients.

Seeking Executive Veto or Signing

After legislative bodies pass bills, presidents, governors, mayors, and county executives may choose to approve or veto the legislation. This may occur during the session or slightly thereafter. Under certain circumstances, some jurisdictions permit the chief executive to veto parts of bills, such as the president's authority to line-item veto budget bills. Seeking the signing or veto is another instance of the use of persuasion and is an instance in which legislative and agency advocacy overlap. It is more likely that networks of advocates will be alerted and activated at this point than is usually the case when doing most agency advocacy.

As with agency advocacy, interested parties may wish to schedule a meeting with the chief executive to express their views. If this is the chosen tactic, the same issues arise: who will be able to gain access; who should attend; what preparations are needed; what should be said at the meeting; and so on. This is another opportunity to share the position paper on this subject, even if it has already been sent. There are times when these meetings could take place before the bill passes, if many different sources of legislative wisdom are predicting its passage. If a meeting occurs under these circumstances, and the chief executive is partially or totally persuaded to the advocates' position, the executive has some leverage (e.g., a threatened veto) and may be able to negotiate certain provisions in or out of the bill before final passage. In fact, as mentioned earlier, advocates' homework includes finding out where the executive stands on a proposal and teaming with him or her to the highest degree possible as early in the process as possible.

Aside from a face-to-face meeting, advocates may wish to persuade the chief executive by mobilizing some or all of the advocacy network and have them write, call, fax, or e-mail the executive to express their wishes on the bill. Advocates might also utilize the media to publicize the need for a bill or the problems that might occur if a bill is signed and implemented. They could call a press conference or issue a press release that informs media consumers about the issue. They might try to have an article written on the issue, write letters to the editor or op-ed pieces, or try to convince newspaper editorial boards to editorialize in a manner consistent with their position.

NONSESSION ACTIVITIES

There are four major nonsession activities that support legislative advocacy: organizing advocates into networks, coalition building, monitoring agencies as they implement policies and programs, and issue research. Some advocates are fortunate to have breaks between legislative sessions during which they can focus their energies on these activities, while others must do them while the legislative process is in progress. (Political campaigns can be considered nonsession advocacy work, and these will be discussed in the next section; the task of monitoring agencies was discussed in the last chapter as part of agency advocacy; and issue research will be covered in detail in chapter 8, "Doing Your Advocacy Homework.")

Organizing Networks

This work requires community organizing skills to identify individuals who are similarly concerned about the welfare of clients and want to do something about it.[19] Advocates have several objectives in mind as they do this work. First, they wish to recruit and organize a significant number of advocates who are willing to communicate their views to policymakers. The number of advocates is left undefined because there is no magical number. The idea is that the more advocates there are, the more policymakers will listen, and chances of influencing policy in favor of clients are increased. Advocates have recruited enough when they choose not to expend any more time or resources in this endeavor.

The second objective is to recruit and organize influential citizens who are willing to communicate with policymakers. As mentioned earlier, this objective does not necessarily contradict the first, because they both should be achieved. Which of the two is given higher priority and more energy depends

---

19. There are numerous, excellent textbooks on community and grassroots organizing if one seeks more information regarding these skills (for example, Homan, 1999; Rothman et al., 1995).

on the policy model to which one subscribes (see chapter 2 for a brief discussion of assumptions about policy models). The third and final objective is to educate, inform, and support networks and their members so that they are knowledgeable about high-priority advocacy issues, they are familiar enough with the policymaking process to know when to act and what to do, and, most of all, they remain motivated to advocate.

Identifying Potential Advocates   There are numerous ways to identify current or potential advocates. Many people are already doing advocacy and could greatly contribute to a network, and others want to do advocacy but don't know how to get started or haven't found a good outlet. The most effective technique is to talk to people, ask them if they want to participate, and ask if they know of other individuals or organizations who might be interested in advocating for clients. This way, everyone becomes a recruiter. A good place to start is with existing organizations, because these hold the possibility of recruiting large numbers of advocates.

Figure 5.1 lists numerous likely sources where advocates may be found. There have been many successful advocacy efforts that involved large numbers of clients (e.g., welfare rights movement), and others that are well known for recruiting family members of clients. Associations for people with mental retardation throughout the country are made up largely of the parents of these citizens, and they are highly respected and influential advocates. Other associations that come to mind are Mothers Against Drunk Driving (MADD) and Mothers Against Violence in America (MAVIA).

Sources of Advocates

✓ Clients

✓ Associations of professionals who serve client group(s) of concern

✓ Volunteer and civic organizations

✓ Employees of relevant agencies

✓ Family members and friends of clients

✓ Community leaders from various sectors (e.g., business, religion, health care, human services, education, labor, etc.)

FIGURE **5.1**

Where to look for potential advocacy network members.

Professionals who work with various types of clients frequently are members of associations at the national, state, or local levels. It is not uncommon for these associations to engage in advocacy for members of the profession as well as their clients, and many use paid or volunteer lobbyists. These associations might have organized their members into networks already, and they might allow advocates working on the same issues to tap into them. Many other volunteer and civic organizations are engaged in efforts, or would like to be, to help certain disadvantaged groups. There are far too many to name. It's important to remember that when approaching these organizations and associations, advocates are not seeking formal endorsements of their advocacy goals but are simply looking for access to a large number of likely advocates. (However, an endorsement would be icing on the cake.)

Other sources for network members are the organizations and agencies that deliver services to clients. It can almost be taken for granted that they will have numerous people who are interested in clients' best interests and who could be enlisted to participate in the advocacy network. They may be able to participate while at work or on their own time, but they should check to be sure that they are not violating agency policies. This is an important topic to cover when training network members.

Besides talking to lots of people, as mentioned above, there are numerous ways to approach an organization to get potential advocates' attention. Those who are putting together the advocacy network could ask to speak at one of the organization's regular meetings, or they could offer to conduct a workshop for the organization on the issue of interest and what can be done about it. Advocates could seek a copy of the organization's mailing list and send out announcements about trainings, issues, or other matters of interest. They could also offer to write a short article or place an announcement in the organization's newsletter.

Training Advocates   After recruiting willing individuals to be part of the network, it is very important to educate network members about the issues facing the client group for whom they will advocate and to train them about legislative advocacy. This should not be thought of as a one-shot affair; training should be repeated and enhanced periodically. There are usually some members who are experts at legislative advocacy or other high-priority issues and may be of great assistance, far beyond being a member of the growing network. There are dozens of ways to accomplish training, such as workshops, printed materials (e.g., position papers), and providing instructions on how to contact legislators by phone, letter, e-mail, or fax. If a telephone tree or something similar will be used, it can be very useful to conduct simulations as a teaching tool and utilize test runs to see if additional training needs to be conducted. Advocates participating in networks need to know how they will be alerted to act, and they need to be knowledgeable about the legislation they're supporting or opposing and its progress and modifications through the legislative process.

It is also important to remember that network members require care and nurturing. When training sessions, workshops, and materials are developed for members, they know that an investment is being made in them. When they don't hear from the organizers and leaders for a long time, they wonder if they're being taken for granted or if they misunderstood directions and are supposed to be doing something they are not. Positive reinforcement and simple gestures of appreciation go a long way, as does putting people's names in newsletters. Generally, people want to feel empowered, and showing them how their contributions fit into a larger effort to help clients is quite effective. Nurtured and highly motivated members will fulfill their role in the network and, frequently, will recruit new members.

Setting Priorities   Advocates have limited resources (especially time), to organize networks in all legislative districts, so they need to determine if some districts are higher priority than others. In the district of the legislator who has historically supported proclient legislation, a smaller network may be sufficient, whereas larger numbers may be needed to persuade more reluctant representatives. It is wise to organize networks in the districts of key legislators such as the chairpersons of committees that will consider legislation that impacts the client group of concern. Depending on the client group, this might include the chair of the human services or health care committee(s), the chair of the budget committee or relevant subcommittee, the leadership of each legislative house (e.g., speaker of the house, presiding officer in the senate, or the chairs of rules or calendar committees).

Every advocate has to learn to use his or her strategic judgment. Some argue that persuading the most resistant legislator will influence many other reluctant people to adopt that viewpoint or, at least, to give the issue greater attention. On the other hand, transforming a member of the opposition into an ally is very time consuming, and resources might be better spent working with legislators who are more ambivalent and are "on the fence" regarding the issue.

The tactic of organizing and mobilizing an advocacy network is not only important as advocates seek legislative change; the network can also be called upon to help with agency advocacy. There are times when top-level agency executives need to hear the preferences of consumers, constituents, and advocates. As time goes on, network members become agency monitors and identifiers of client problems and needs.

Coalitions

Coalitions differ slightly from networks in that coalitions consist of organizations and associations that have agreed to work jointly on certain issues. Certainly, employees, clients, and members of organizations participating in a coalition can and probably should become members of a network. There are many purposes behind forming coalitions, beginning with the need to increase the number of people and organizations working toward the same advocacy goal. Second, forming coalitions can bring expertise together that individual organizations may lack.

The term *organization* is being used quite broadly here to range from formally recognized organizations, such as public and private profit and nonprofit agencies, to informal groups of individuals who have banded together to accomplish an objective. For example, a large number of family members and clients may have organized to improve a law. They have firsthand knowledge of client problems and needs, but they lack experience as advocates and knowledge of the legislative process. The missing knowledge can be found within other organizations that would also like to see similar changes, have experience lobbying, but are few in number. Combining these two groups into a coalition will benefit both, for the whole is greater than the sum of its parts.

There are also political reasons for building coalitions. The people or organization leading the effort may not be well known, may be perceived by legislators as being politically extreme, or may have other political baggage. By finding other groups with which to form a coalition, an individual or organization can neutralize all of these challenges. For example, rightly or wrongly, many legislators perceive the goals and tactics of the American Civil Liberties Union (ACLU) to be somewhat extreme. If the ACLU identifies a problem that could be abated by changing a statute, its efforts might then be better received if it works in coalition with organizations that are typically perceived to be politically moderate, such as the League of Women Voters or the State Pediatrics Society.

Definition   Arguments are on going regarding the definition of **coalition** and how to form and maintain one, but most advocates agree that coalitions are most effective when organizations, groups, and agencies agree to work together informally for a short period of time toward a specific objective (Dluhy, 1990). Others argue that coalitions can be created around a broader goal (e.g., helping students with learning disabilities) and can be maintained for many years. There are instances when the latter approach is effective, and a closer look might reveal that the structure is more like a new organization rather than a coalition.

Sometimes organizations are brought together first, and then they jointly decide on their policy positions, but Melton (1983) indicates that those positions tend to be too watered-down to be effective. The author's practical experience leans toward the former; that is, after a specific advocacy change is identified, a coalition should be built around that, and the coalition should disband once the change is accomplished. If the coalition is successful, its members are very likely to work together again, and this can give the appearance of being members of a long-standing coalition. Organizing around broad, vague goals is tempting, because it's easier to get agreement when advocates recruit by saying, for example, "We want you to join our coalition to help prevent teenage pregnancy." If, on the other hand, the advocacy goal around which a coalition is built is to increase the availability of family planning information and services for teens (in order to reduce teen pregnancies), some organizations will be quick to join and others will not.

The author's former advocacy agency participated in many coalitions with other organizations. For example, Catholic Community Services was very active and helpful in a coalition to raise welfare benefits and another to remove children from adult jails, but they were not part of the coalition to increase family planning services for minors. Similarly, the advocacy agency chose not to join some coalitions because it was not comfortable with the change objectives. One of the strengths of this approach is that it is very respectful of each organization's agenda for change, its priorities, and its decision-making process.

Building Coalitions   Finding and recruiting other organizations to be members of a coalition is much like creating an advocacy network. In both cases, advocates have to talk to key people in each organization. This step in the process is similar to agency advocacy in that organizational leaders must be persuaded to join the coalition. It can be helpful to provide them with the advocacy research that has been completed, the change target, and an advocacy plan. Most organizations have a process they use to set their annual legislative goals and priorities, and frequently, for nonprofits, this includes seeking the approval of their boards of directors. For this reason, most organizational leaders are unable to give quick responses.

Another persuasive tactic is to explain that the probability of being successful is much greater when numerous organizations are involved, as compared to what might be accomplished by an individual organization. Also, while coalition membership does involve the investment of time, energy, and other resources, each group's investment is likely to be smaller when many are sharing the load.

One of the great benefits of coalitions is that the advocacy work can be divided and shared. One organization may work on the research while another drafts the needed legislative language, looks for a sponsor, or develops press releases. Consider the situation in which, due to prior advocacy work, Agency A has developed good relationships with

Representatives Curly, Moe, and Larry but has not been able to get very good access to Representatives Bear and Cuda. Another organization in the coalition may have good relations with them, however, and will take responsibility for talking to them about the coalition's proposal. It is very common for coalition members to share position papers or to jointly sign a letter to go to legislators.

Ground Rules   Many coalition experts recommend that participants sign an agreement or, at least, verbally commit to the coalition's goals and processes. It is strongly recommended that the coalition develop ground rules on how it will operate and make decisions. The following are examples of issues on which coalitions might develop ground rules: who can speak and negotiate for the coalition and when[20], how coalition decisions are made (e.g., by consensus or majority vote), how often members will meet, who is expected to attend, what is considered a conflict of interest, and what a member organization or the coalition as a whole should do when a conflict of interest arises or is suspected. Many advocates fail to reach these important agreements early in the process of solidifying the coalition. One of the main reasons these topics tend to be avoided is the fear that if the coalition organizers are specific about the coalition's operating policies, some agencies might be scared off. The author's experience shows that most, if not all, of these issues arise eventually as coalitions do their work, and they are less time consuming and far less disruptive if dealt with early. (Remember, never say "never," and always avoid saying "always.")

A paradoxical piece of advice on coalition ground rules is that they are important to have in place, but don't spend a lot of time on them. Try to avoid overinvesting in internal rules and procedures, because members' time and energy is best used when devoted to the accomplishment of the change objective. They should be looking ahead and outward, not inward. This is the reason for the recommendation that coalitions remain issue-specific, short-lived, and informal. Inevitably, it seems, the longer a coalition is around, the more likely it is to spend energy on itself (e.g., its structure, rules, and dues) as opposed to advocating for clients. Eventually, someone will suggest that officers be elected, bylaws written, a dues structure developed, or that nonprofit incorporation be pursued. These may be worthy ideas, but they are likely to distract members from the cause at hand, which is to push for a specific change to help clients. Coalitions, and, for that matter, organizations, always have organizational survival and maintenance as latent subgoals, but advocates need to worry when this gets out of balance with the primary, manifest goal of producing a specific change for clients. Finding the correct balance is a matter of judgment.

---

20. Designating a few leaders to have this authority is a good approach.

POLITICAL CAMPAIGNS AND ADVOCACY[21]

Many advocates and advocacy agencies devote time, money, and energy to assist office-seekers to be nominated and elected because they believe that certain representatives hold more promise for helping clients than others. When an incumbent seeks reelection, this person might not only hold good promise but may actually have a proclient voting record. Individuals seeking to become members of the various legislative bodies may receive support from advocates, and advocates should also remember that there are other important elected officials, such as sheriffs, school board members, superintendents, judges, prosecutors, and insurance commissioners. Besides electing public officials, there are frequently ballot measures that could have a major impact on clients (e.g., changing property taxes, spending limits on government, or policy issues such as gun control policies). Other reasons advocates may get involved in political campaigns are to establish potentially long-standing relationships with current or future office-holders, to influence candidates' campaign platforms or legislative agendas, or to increase the chance of having access to the person running for office.

There are many ways to be involved in election campaigns, and a few will be mentioned briefly. Certainly, candidates appreciate financial support or volunteer time from advocates. Making phone calls, stuffing envelopes, canvassing neighborhoods, or distributing signs are all time-intensive activities that play an important role in election efforts. A more high-profile election activity is for advocates, either as individuals or as organizations, to publicly endorse candidates or appear with them at certain speaking engagements. Many professional associations, such as the National Association of Social Workers, have sister organizations that are political action committees that go through an extensive process to decide which candidates to endorse and, if possible, to support financially. A more neutral activity is for advocates to sponsor a meeting during which panels of candidates are asked to address issues of interest to those advocates and the audience.

Whether to Get Involved   Like most advocacy tactics, there are reasonable arguments surrounding the issue of whether to get involved in election campaigns. Opinions abound and evidence is scarce regarding the effectiveness of this tactic to achieve advocacy objectives. The hoped-for benefits—electing proclient officials, improving their platform, and improved access—do result occasionally. The critical question is, "Can specific, proclient changes in policies be achieved more readily using these tactics as opposed to other types of approaches?"

---

21. Just like lobbying, advocates and agencies should be cautious about their involvement in election campaigns. There are federal and state laws governing public employees' campaign involvement (e.g., Hatch Act) and other policies, laws, and tax codes on organizational involvement.

Since there is no hard evidence one way or another, we can argue our opinions using philosophy, practical wisdom, and case anecdotes for support. Legislators have advised child advocates to become more involved in election campaigns by donating money to candidates who support their positions, by registering voters, or by sponsoring candidate forums (State Legislative Leaders Foundation, 1995). The author's (and others') recommendation is that advocates should definitely be involved in election campaigns in a neutral manner. That may sound rather contradictory, because one usually thinks that to be involved is to take sides, but if advocates engage in efforts to inform all candidates of issues facing clients, then they are involved without taking sides. The idea of sponsoring a candidate forum is neutral and will help voters who are interested in the client group gain insight on different candidates' views. Also, candidates will learn things they didn't know about the needs of a client group and the existence of a strong advocacy network.

There are numerous reasons why this is the preferred approach. First, while supporting a specific candidate holds promise, it also comes with the risk that the opponent will win. Opposition, or failure to endorse, is remembered just as well as support is remembered, and access to the elected leader may become a problem. Advocates need to be in a position in which they can lobby and persuade all legislators to make proclient votes. (Again, the study done by the State Legislative Leaders Foundation [1995] reported that legislators perceive child advocates to be too partisan). Second, involvement in election campaigns does not tend to be as cost-effective as other techniques. Campaigning for a candidate is rarely focused on a specific change objective, and it takes a long time for the investment to bear dividends. Advocacy works well when specific changes are targeted, such as adding a new section to the guardianship law, whereas supporting or opposing a candidate rarely translates into a specific change. Even if legislators supported by advocates eventually vote for this change, usually a significant amount of time will have passed between campaign work and the implementation of the needed change. This may be a good advocacy tactic, but it seems that more direct methods might bear fruit more quickly.

There are times when advocates might support particular candidates largely because of their political party. Their objective is to have a majority of the legislative body be members of Political Party X, a party traditionally more concerned with clients; they hope to create a positive context for change in their legislative body. Also, as might be the case with Congress and the president, advocates feel that if the same political party as the president's controls the House and Senate, there is a greater chance that proactive legislation will be passed.

Finally, and on a somewhat pessimistic note, extensive involvement by advocates in electoral politics is not recommended because they are not funded well enough to compete with large, expensive, and highly skilled campaign machines that political parties make available to most candidates. Whether society should be like this or not, advocates have limited resources and are advised to focus their energy and advocacy skills on more direct tactics, where it is likely that they'll get faster and better results with lower political costs.

SUMMARY

It is obvious that legislative advocacy is an important, time-consuming endeavor that has tremendous potential for helping clients. This chapter has introduced the basic information advocates need to use this advocacy strategy and suggested numerous specific tactics. For ease of presentation, legislative activities have been grouped into those that occur during a legislative session and those that are primarily implemented between sessions. This division is for presentation purposes and is useful as such, but it shouldn't be taken too far. Many of the specific tactics discussed need to happen at all times.

The chapter also discussed the strengths and challenges of political campaigns as advocacy. There are many highly regarded and effective advocates who place great emphasis on this, and others who think it's a good idea only if advocates have enough time. The bias in this book is not that any of these strategies or tactics are absolutely good or bad when individually assessed, but that their utility should be evaluated in a comparative fashion in light of the specific advocacy objective being sought and the resources available to achieve it. Advocates may choose different tactics for different advocacy efforts or even in different stages of a particular effort. Spend a little time wisely to assess, plan, and strategize, but, most important, get out there and work for change.

DISCUSSION QUESTIONS

1. Make a list of your local legislators, both representatives and senators, as well as their committee appointments. With which of these legislators and committees would you work on your particular advocacy effort? Why?
2. Think of other types of persuasive arguments besides those that pull either on heartstrings or purse strings.
3. Compare the skills needed to do legislative advocacy to those needed to do agency advocacy.

LEGAL ADVOCACY

CHAPTER

6

CHAPTER OBJECTIVES

By the time you finish studying this chapter, you should

1. Understand legal advocacy as a strategy to create change for clients and understand when it might be used.
2. Be familiar with several nonlitigious legal advocacy tactics.
3. Be able to discuss litigation, its purposes, techniques, strengths, and weaknesses.
4. Begin to anticipate when the legal advocacy strategy might be combined with other strategies.
5. Understand that courts, too, make public policy.

The primary purpose of this chapter is to acquaint human service practitioners with situations in which legal advocacy may be the best approach to help clients. It also describes the possible outcomes of this strategy so advocates can weigh the relative benefits of this strategy. The chapter separates the tactics associated with legal advocacy into two broad categories. The first category includes non-litigious tactics, those that are unrelated to the filing of lawsuits, and the second includes roles and tactics for advocates to use when involved in litigation. This presentation is being made with the assumption that human service practitioners are largely unfamiliar with concepts and procedures related to the practice of law and the courts. Legal jargon will be avoided to the greatest degree possible, as will many of the details associated with the practice of law. Attorneys can and do engage in many of the activities discussed here. Advocates can also engage in these activities, without having a license to practice law.

98

Legal advocacy is a strategy that is utilized for many different targets. Just as legislative advocacy takes place in the legislative branch of government, and agency advocacy in the executive branch, legal advocacy is primarily carried out in the judicial branch. When courts rule on cases, they are creating rights and, entitlements and establishing important social policies. As such, it behooves human service professionals to understand the power of the judicial branch (Lynch & Mitchell, 1995).

Legal advocacy is an important strategy by itself or in combination with other strategies, and it has the potential to solve terrible problems and produce dramatic change. This strategy is one of the four primary advocacy strategies presented in this book; as a result, this chapter deals with legal advocacy somewhat separately from the other three. Many attorneys, however, think of legal advocacy in a broader sense, in which legislative and agency advocacy are included, whatever arena necessary to help the client. There is absolutely no problem with this view, but, for the purposes of teaching advocacy within the context of this book, legal advocacy will be treated more narrowly.

Like all advocacy strategies, there are advantages and disadvantages associated with its use, situations when it is clearly the advocacy tool of choice, and other times when it is best left in an advocate's back pocket. Filing a lawsuit, a major and specific tactic under the category of legal advocacy, is commonly viewed as a last resort after other, and possibly less confrontational, tactics have been exhausted. According to Melton (1983), "The movement to the courts as instruments of change is apt to occur only when there is inaction by the other branches of government" (p. 164). Soler and Warboys (1990) also articulate the dilemma quite well when they say:

> Litigation can be expensive, difficult, time-consuming, unpredictable, and unpopular with legislators, executive officials, and even judges. Alternate strategies, such as lobbying the legislature or administrative advocacy, may be cheaper, easier, fast, and less controversial. But will they be as effective? (p. 112)

It is important for advocates to be knowledgeable about situations in which legal advocacy could be effective, to know the associated tactics, and to have a rudimentary understanding of relevant legal concepts. Many human service agencies have access to attorneys either on their board of directors or through other agencies. Attorneys can serve in a variety of roles, such as to educate advocates on opportunities for legal advocacy, serve as a consultant when relevant cases and situations arise, and provide advice about legal options.

There seems to be a general reluctance on the part of advocates to use legal tactics, probably because they are perceived to be confrontational. Rather than making conjectures as to why this is the case, it is far more important to remember that the avenues for relief being pursued with legal advocacy, such as filing lawsuits, are problem-solving mechanisms essential to the democratic form of government practiced in the United States. Access to the courts as a way to resolve disputes is an important feature of democracy, as is the use of the courts to maintain a balance of power between branches of government. It makes good sense to try other approaches if they have real potential to help clients. It doesn't make sense, and in fact raises ethical questions, if advocates fail to do what's best for clients because of a personal reluctance to use legal advocacy. Practical issues (such as being unable to recruit pro bono attorneys) and the lack of knowledge or experience with this strategy are much more pref-arable explanations for the underuse of this strategy rather than human service advocates' discomfort with conflict.

CASE EXAMPLES OF OPPORTUNITIES FOR LEGAL ADVOCACY

Most helping professionals are familiar with landmark U.S. Supreme Court cases that established specific client rights in a variety of fields. Litigation and court rulings have established or enforced a right to equal educational opportunity, prisoners' right to decent living conditions, the right to treatment and the right to refuse treatment in mental health settings, the insistence that many types of clients be placed in the least restrictive alternative for their needs, and the right to due process for juveniles accused of crimes, just to name a few.

An interesting legal action in which the author was involved can illustrate one type of situation that can be addressed by legal advocacy. This case example can also underscore how the use of legal advocacy both enhances and relies on other advocacy strategies. For many years, advocates were concerned about the poor conditions and treatment of youth at Florida's training schools for delinquents. Many of the problems seemed to stem from overcrowding, but underfunding, poor training, poor supervision, and out-dated practices were also to blame. The education and health care programs were deficient as well. One of the most stirring circumstances that brought attention to this institution was the "hog-tying" of youth, a disciplinary practice by which handcuffs and anklecuffs are used simultaneously.

The state's child advocacy organization had signed a contract with a public interest law firm so that egregious situations such as this could be addressed with legal advocacy. The advocacy organization had worked for several years using agency and legislative advocacy to address these issues, but no progress was being made. The attorney from the public interest law firm began to meet with attorneys from the American Civil Liberties Union's (ACLU) Children's Rights Project and the Youth Law Center in San Francisco to weigh the possibility of litigation. Eventually, a class action lawsuit was filed in federal court complaining that the constitutional rights of youth confined in these institutions had been violated. In this case, many administrators in the state agency responsible for operating these programs (helping professionals and advocates in their own right) welcomed the lawsuit, because they too felt frustrated with the lack of progress and felt that the legislature had been unresponsive to their efforts.

Eventually, the case was settled with a **consent decree**[22] calling for a reduction of the institutions' population to reduce overcrowding; a prohibition of cruel and unnecessary disciplinary practices; and an improvement in health, educational, and other programs. A great deal was accomplished with the lawsuit, but more was going on in other arenas as well, which is also important to note. While the lawsuit was in process, it was important that the media and members of the legislature understood the case, the problems that had been occurring in the institutions, and the proposed solutions. Community education tactics discussed in chapter 7 were used to get this information to the appropriate people.

The advocates delivered an important message to policymakers and agencies by their choice of strategies. The message was that the advocates were quite serious about making the state a better place for youth, that they would use whatever strategy was necessary to accomplish needed change, and that they were a force to be reckoned with. In the time period between filing and settling the lawsuit, the advocacy organization felt its influence in legislative and agency matters increase, and its exposure and credibility with the media improved greatly. Figure 6.1 summarizes several opportunities to use legal advocacy. Each of these will be expanded upon in this section.

Creating Rights

As an example of how legal advocacy can result in the creation of rights for a client group, imagine an everyday situation in which police stop a youth because he or she is suspected of a crime. In this scenario, the youth is handcuffed, taken to jail, and law enforcement officers neither contact the parents nor provide access to a lawyer. At a subsequent hearing with a juvenile court judge, it is decided that the youth will be rehabilitated best at one of the state's locked institutions for delinquents. Shortly thereafter, the youth is transported to the institution and serves an indeterminate sentence.

Readers might think this example is far-fetched, but it wasn't too long ago that these sorts of things were routine. Juveniles did not have the same rights as adults in criminal matters in the 1960s (and still don't, in fact). As a result of a series of lawsuits, the courts decided that law enforcement officers must

---

22. *Black's Law Dictionary* (1990) defines *consent decree* as "a judgment entered by consent of the parties whereby the defendant agrees to stop alleged illegal activity without admitting guilt or wrongdoing."

OPPORTUNITIES FOR LEGAL ADVOCACY[a]

✓ *To protect or create rights* A federal, state, or local law, or agency rule or practice may violate a person's established or perceived rights. The result of litigation could be to articulate a new right for clients or reinforce existing rights.

✓ *To change court rules* Advocates can seek changes in court operating procedures by following a process dictated by their state.

✓ *To change agency rules* Under state Administrative Procedures Acts, changes in agency rules can be sought.

✓ *To support or oppose a legal brief* amicus curiae ("friend of the court") briefs can be filed to support one of the sides in a lawsuit.

✓ *To create or improve services* Creating services is a result of lawsuits that show clients' rights are being violated when their service needs are neglected or when agencies are not fulfilling their statutory responsibilities.

✓ *To eliminate detrimental agency practices* Agencies might be treating clients in a discriminatory, punitive, or disrespectful manner, and legal advocacy can bring these practices to a halt and replace them with more effective ones.

✓ *To raise public consciousness* One objective of many lawsuits is to draw the attention of the public and policymakers to the client problems being addressed (e.g., deplorable living conditions or maltreatment of clients). Rarely, if ever, is this the primary objective of litigation.

✓ *To fund services* There have been instances when a president or other chief executive refused to spend funds appropriated by the legislature, and lawsuits were necessary to have the funding released. Other instances have occurred in which a state was not adequately funding services until a lawsuit facilitated larger appropriations.

✓ *To clarify an interpretation/application of laws or constitutions* Separate laws on the same subject may contradict each other to some degree, or the implementation of a law may be perceived as inconsistent with legislative intent.

---

[a]It is important to note that just because legal advocacy *can* be used in these situations does not mean that it *has* to be used. Many advocacy tactics are relevant for these situations, and legal advocacy, especially litigation, is generally used as a last resort.

FIGURE **6.1**

Opportunities and targets for legal advocacy.

read juveniles their rights, and that they are entitled to lawyers and to due process hearings at which the evidence can be weighed and confronted.

Changing Court Rules

Courts, like agencies, have formal rules of procedure that dictate how they operate. There are rules of procedure for both criminal and civil court matters. How cases are to proceed through court—such as how much time is allowed between various legal steps, what kind of information will be exchanged between parties, or how expert witnesses are handled—is dictated by court rules. Advocates may feel that the way the court operates is detrimental to their client group, such as the absence of interpreters for clients who don't speak English or of signers for people who are hearing impaired, and they may seek to change court rules. In most cases, it is possible for advocates to seek changes in court rules. The exact process for doing this differs from state to state but may involve the filing of a petition. It is similar to the process used in the Administrative Procedures Act discussed earlier.

For example, the author's advocacy organization sought a change in court rules when they proposed a new rule calling for a hearing to determine if adult jails could safely house juveniles accused of crimes. One section of state law indicated that certain juveniles in specific situations *may*[23] be placed in adult jails; another section required that adult jails have the ability to keep juvenile inmates separate from adult inmates. The proposed court rule required a hearing to be held when adult jailing was being considered, to ascertain whether the jail could handle the juvenile properly and maintain separation from adult inmates. This is an example of legal advocacy being used to create or change a court rule and of how substantive policy can be realized by tightening procedures.

Changing Agency Rules

A similar example of legal advocacy is associated with states' Administrative Procedures Acts (see chapter 4, "Agency Advocacy"). These laws allow the filing of petitions (or a similar process) to call for changes to agency rules and regulations. Petitions don't necessarily have to be prepared by attorneys, but consulting with an attorney in these situations is highly recommended. Many examples of the need for changes in agency rules and regulations were discussed in chapter 4.

---

23. *May* is emphasized for very important reasons. Previously, state law said that certain juveniles *shall* be held in adult jails. Advocates worked extensively to prohibit the housing of any juvenile in adult jails and were successful getting the word *shall* changed to *may* so that placement in adult jails was not mandatory.

Friend of the Court

Another opportunity for legal advocacy occurs when advocates and organizations not party to a lawsuit file **amicus curiae briefs,**[24] which are also known as friend-of-the-court briefs. This is usually done when a case is filed in or reaches higher level courts. The legal briefs filed by plaintiffs' attorneys articulate complaints and the legal reasoning behind them. The attorneys for the defendants respond to the complaints and argue that the complaints are unfounded, the legal arguments weak or faulty, or both. There are other relevant issues that come to bear on a case besides those introduced by attorneys. For example, an amicus curiae brief filed by advocates could present relevant research findings on the effectiveness of services like those involved in the lawsuit, or they can explain the psychological damage that is likely to occur if clients continue to be treated in a certain manner.

For example, the September 1997 issue of *NASW News* includes an article with the headline "NASW Joins Court Battles: Legal Briefs Back the Rights of a Gay Father and a Student with Disabilities" ("NASW Joins Court Battles," 1997). In the first case, a gay father lost custody of his son because of his sexual orientation. When the case was appealed to a higher court, the NASW joined several other organizations to file an amicus curiae brief arguing for equal treatment of parents notwithstanding sexual orientation. The second case involved a student ("Jones") with developmental disabilities who was allegedly assaulted by another student; the assaulter ("Doe") was known to have behavioral problems. A lawsuit was filed arguing that the school district had violated Jones's rights under federal law, but the court dismissed the case. This decision was appealed, with the NASW (informed by their School Social Work Section) arguing that the school allowed a hostile environment and detrimental student conduct, thereby denying Jones the benefits of education. These two examples are meant only to illustrate how friend-of-the-court briefs can be filed. There is not enough space here, nor is it the purpose of this book, to present enough facts for the reader to analyze the cases.

Stopping Detrimental Practices

The hog-tying case discussed briefly above is a good example of several opportunities for legal advocacy, and the interdependencies between this and other advocacy strategies. Better services were created for delinquent youth as a result of this lawsuit and the resulting consent decree, and improved medical, social, and educational services were implemented to correct the gross defi-

---

24. Black (1990) supplies the following definition of the term *amicus curiae*: "Means, literally, friend of the court. A person with strong interest in or views on the subject matter of an action [lawsuit], but not a party to the action, may petition the court for permission to file a brief, ostensibly on behalf of a party but actually to suggest a rationale consistent with its own views."

ciencies highlighted by the litigation. Also, the detrimental agency practices were stopped. The case served as an effective vehicle by which to raise public consciousness about the operation and ineffectiveness of large institutions for delinquent youth.

Increasing Funding

A good example of a lawsuit that resulted in increased funding for services is one that occurred in Pennsylvania in the early 1990s. The basis of the lawsuit was that "the state would not provide funding to the county agencies [who are responsible for services] commensurate with the needs of the growing number of dependent and delinquent children" (Richart, 1993, p. 38). As a result of the lawsuit, the state began a needs-based budget process that committed the state to funding the county service providers at a level comparable to the established needs. Those involved in the lawsuit believe that many millions of dollars in new state funding have resulted from it. Usually advocates employ legislative and agency advocacy to increase budgets, but this example shows that legal advocacy may be used if other strategies come up short.

NONLITIGIOUS TACTICS

There are a number of tactics advocates may use that do not involve direct involvement in litigation. Some of the tactics are intended to facilitate litigation by others. A key factor in the success of these tactics is the advocates' expertise about services, the systems that deliver them, policies, funding, and regulations. They are able to identify situations in which clients' rights may have been violated in the denial of services or during the delivery of services, when agency rules are not in clients' best interests, or when agencies are perceived to be misinterpreting laws and regulations. They can identify instances that call for legal tactics. Not only can well-informed advocates assist clients, parents, organizations, and other advocates to identify the need for legal advocacy, but, most important, they may help locate and secure the needed legal help.

Accessing Attorneys

If advocates and clients don't have immediate access to attorneys for whatever reason (money, lack of familiarity, etc.), there are many other sources for assistance. At the local level, advocates might consult with public defenders,[25]

---

25. Not all communities use the term *public defender* to refer to the attorneys who represent people who cannot afford a private attorney in proceedings that require court-appointed counsel. While this is probably the most common title, some jurisdictions refer to them as "legal aid attorneys," or use another title.

legal services attorneys, representatives of the American Civil Liberties Union (ACLU), or the local bar association. The ACLU has local chapters in many cities as well as state chapters and a national office. Clients and their advocates shouldn't hesitate to call for assistance. There are usually local and state bar associations that will be able to help locate attorneys who have expertise on the issues in question. Certainly, there are other lawyer referral programs that one might consult. Organizations with an interest in certain social issues could also help advocates and clients find attorneys. For example, if advocates were to identify instances of discrimination against women in the delivery of benefits or services, they could contact the local chapter of the National Organization for Women (NOW).

Legal Services

The types and amount of assistance available through legal services is very difficult to summarize. The funding for legal services attorneys continues to go through major changes, both at the state and federal levels, by which funding levels are being greatly reduced or eliminated, and more and more restrictions are being placed on what they can do. However, these attorneys can be a great resource to advocates and should be members of advocacy teams and networks whenever possible.

Notwithstanding funding and policy shifts, local legal services organizations are using a wide variety of approaches to continue their legal advocacy for people who are poor. They have a history of helping on consumer issues (e.g., unfair sales practices and consumer fraud), a wide range of family matters (e.g., adoption, custody, visitation, divorce, separation, annulment, guardianship, termination of parental rights, domestic violence, paternity, and child support), health issues (e.g., Medicaid and Medicare eligibility and payments), housing (e.g., landlord rights, tenants rights, and foreclosure), income maintenance (e.g., TANF, food stamps, social security, SSI, and veterans benefits), individuals' rights (e.g., mental health, rights in long-term care facilities, abuse of older people, immigration, prisoners' rights, rights of people with disabilities, and the rights of people who are institutionalized), employment issues (e.g., discrimination, sexual harassment, and wage claims), as well as many others. In most circumstances they can offer legal help for individual cases. Some may also provide assistance if class actions are contemplated, or individual attorneys may be willing to volunteer their expertise after hours.

The author's experiences with legal services organizations and with individual attorneys have been very positive. Not only have they been great legal advocates for indigent clients, they are very helpful in working with other advocates to solve client problems.

NLADA

Another valuable resource in legal advocacy is the National Legal Aid and Defender Association (NLADA). Its purpose is to provide technical assistance and support to advocates for people who are poor or have a low income. They maintain a database of individuals and organizations who can provide legal assistance to people who are poor. Their biannual directory, *The Directory of Legal Aid and Defender Offices in the United States and Territories*, is a very useful document and may be found in law libraries or purchased. Figure 6.2 is a list of legal organizations from the directory that could assist advocates as they confront various legal barriers.

Advocates should not be shy about contacting any of the organizations listed (see p. 108). Even if a particular organization can't help directly with the immediate issue, they will be able to provide suggestions as to who would be better to contact.

Raising Funds for Litigation

Organizations involved in litigation incur substantial expenses as they initiate and carry out the case. Advocates involved in a case or with an interest in the case could make financial contributions or help raise funds for the litigation. If they win the case, there might be an award of attorney's fees, but these may not cover all the expenses, and they can't offset the fact that financial outlays occur much earlier in the litigation process. To repeat the sentiment of Soler and Warboys (1990), litigation is expensive.

Expert Witnesses

A major expense in lawsuits can sometimes be expert witnesses.[26] Having quality, well-credentialed, experienced, and convincing experts can be critical to a lawsuit. The people with these qualifications are in high demand and will expect to be paid at a rate commensurate with their status. Many human service practitioners have served as expert witnesses, another role advocates can play in a legal advocacy strategy.

In the training school case described earlier, experts who had extensive experience operating institutions for delinquents testified as experts. They needed to convince the judge of their in-depth, practical knowledge of similar programs and issues. They had to explain not only that disciplinary practices such as hog-tying were extreme, but that alternative practices are available, in use, and as effective. They had to be able to point out the deficiencies in the

---

26. Black (1990) defines an expert witness as "One who by reason of education or specialized experience possesses superior knowledge respecting a subject about which persons having no particular training are incapable of forming an accurate opinion or deducing correct conclusions."

Name	Phone
ACLU National Prison Project	(202) 234-4830
ACLU Reproductive Freedom Project	(212) 944-9800
Center for Law & Education	(202) 986-6648
Center for Law & Social Policy	(202) 328-5140
Center for Reproductive Law & Policy	(212) 514-5534
Center on Social Welfare Policy & Law	(212) 633-6967
Children's Defense Fund	(202) 628-8787
Education Law Center	(201) 624-1815
Food Research & Action Center	(202) 986-2200
Indian Law Support Center	(303) 447-8760
Judge David L. Bazelon Center for Mental Health Law	(202) 467-5730
Legal Counsel for the Elderly	(202) 434-2120
Migrant Legal Action Program	(202) 462-7744
National Association of the Deaf Legal Defense Fund	(202) 651-5373
National Center for Youth Law	(415) 543-3307
National Center on Women & Family Law	(212) 674-8200
National Clearinghouse for the Defense of Battered Women	(800) 903-0111
National Consumer Law Center	(202) 986-6060
National Employment Law Project	(212) 764-2204
National Health Law Program	(202) 887-5310
National Housing Law Project	(202) 783-5140
National Immigration Law Center	(213) 938-6452
National Senior Citizens Law Center	(202) 887-5280
National Veterans Legal Services Project	(202) 265-8305

Note. Information for this figure came from *The 1995/96 Directory of Legal Aid and Defender Offices in the United States and Territories* of the NLDA. The NLDA may be reached by phone at (202) 452-0620.

FIGURE **6.2**

Legal organizations for indigent clients.

school and health care programs, the consequences of these problems, and that improvements could and should be made.

Consulting

The author has served as a consultant to attorneys involved in litigation, often providing them with summaries of relevant research, reviewing studies conducted by expert witnesses, discussing experts' observations of programs, and serving as a member of strategizing teams. Practitioners bring many valuable skills and much knowledge to the litigation team, which will be well-received by the attorneys. It can be the case that helping professionals are expert at considering whether the likely outcomes of the case will be good for the clients. Advocates can also help attorneys find clients to represent in order to seek change in a systemic problem or policy question. Practitioners know the specifics of all their clients, both past and present, like no one else. They know who was denied services, who was treated poorly, and who got less than they deserved. This case-specific knowledge, provided within ethical bounds of course, is priceless.

Individuals with legal training can help advocates analyze proposed legislation, existing law, agency rules and regulations, court cases, and **case law**[27] as they relate to an advocacy effort. These activities are important support work for legislative and agency advocacy and possible future legal advocacy efforts. The important thing to remember is that attorneys are excellent advocates and strong members of advocacy teams.

Monitoring Court Orders

Moss and Zurcher (1983) wrote an excellent article describing the function of social workers when institutional reform litigation is occurring or has been settled. Other types of practitioners can serve in these roles as well. They can play an important role monitoring the implementation of the court order, consent decree, or settlement agreement. Moss and Zurcher point out that one of the many enforcement procedures used by judges to implement, monitor, and enforce their orders in a case is to appoint committees made up of citizens, experts, advocates, or attorneys to ensure compliance. Nonlitigious roles and tactics for advocates are summarized in Figure 6.3.

LITIGATION

In their study of child advocacy organizations, the American Institutes for Research (1983) found that litigation was underutilized as an advocacy tool, but that litigation and advocacy to revise state statutes were the most successful of all activities (p. 176). This underutilization may be a result of overly cautious interpretations of the "last resort" guideline on litigation. It may be that advocates steer clear of confrontational tactics, preferring more collaborative or less costly approaches. Clearly, if advocates do not understand the potential

---

27. The term *case law* refers to "The aggregate of reported cases as forming a body of jurisprudence, or the law of a particular subject as evidenced or formed by the adjudged cases, in distinction to statutes and other sources of law" (Black, 1990).

> ROLES AND TACTICS
>
> - Identify clients in need of legal advocacy
> - Locate legal help for clients
> - Raise funds for litigation
> - Serve as expert witness
> - Provide consultation to the litigation team
> - Participate in the strategy team
> - Monitor the enforcement of court orders and settlements
> - Engage in complementary legislative advocacy
> - Conduct community education efforts regarding cases

FIGURE **6.3**

Nonlitigious roles and tactics for advocates.

of litigation, are not experienced or confident identifying circumstances when it is relevant, or they do not know how to mobilize legal and other advocacy supports, this powerful advocacy tool might not be used. Sadly, the clients who are being ignored, underserved, or mistreated may have a longer wait for relief.

There are not many human service practitioners who work in organizations that employ attorneys whose job is to engage in litigation on behalf of clients. The same is true of advocacy organizations. Therefore, most advocates will be in the position of having to locate qualified and willing legal counsel. Even if the organization has attorneys or has a contract with attorneys, as did the author's advocacy organization, once a client or class of clients is secured and an agreement reached between the clients and the attorney, the attorney is ethically bound to represent the clients, not the advocate or advocacy organization.

In this book, **litigation** refers to filing a lawsuit with and on behalf of clients in an effort to achieve policy reform. More often than not, this objective is difficult to achieve by representing an individual client at the trial level.[28] It may be possible to accomplish this through an appeal of the trial court's decision, however. It is likely that broad policy reform will involve class action litigation, in which a lawsuit is filed in the name of one or more clients who are representative of a similarly situated group of clients. The validity of the class of individuals being represented must be asserted by their attorney and approved by the court; the establishment of class is not automatic.

It is beyond the purposes of this book to discuss such things as whether to file cases in state or federal courts, how to make the case, discovery, and other

---

28. A very important advocacy objective could be to make sure that funding and statutory provisions are adequate to ensure that clients have legal representation when needed, especially if they are people with a low income.

technical legal matters. Advocates involved in litigation and other advocacy strategies should discuss these matters with attorneys on their advocacy teams.

When to Litigate

Certainly, it is important for advocates to know what kinds of issues should be given consideration when contemplating litigation. Figure 6.4 has been reprinted from Richart and Bing's (1989) book on child advocacy, in which they outline the issues to consider before litigating. Children are their frame of reference, but the ideas are easily applied to other client groups. The questions on this list shouldn't be viewed as having determinate answers. Once advocates think about the specific items, they should step back and consider the issues as a whole, in balance, weighing the trade-offs and compromises, and doing their best to calculate risks. Gains for clients are rarely achieved without a great deal of investment and risk.

Advantages of Litigation

In order to balance the argument a little and not leave the impression that advocates should steer clear of litigation, it would be helpful to list the advantages litigation has over other advocacy strategies. Mnookin (1985) lists several advantages of litigation over legislative advocacy. First of all, as a matter of one's rights, courts are open and complainants must be heard as long as their complaint can be put in proper legal terms. Also, frequently as a matter of right, parties can appeal rulings. Certainly, the court's rules of accessibility are much more clearly delineated than those of legislatures; and, as Mnookin points out, when a court rules against a party, it has to explain its reasoning, whereas legislatures don't. He doesn't say this, but it seems that courts are a more level playing field than the legislature. Formally, it doesn't matter that one party is an individual and the other a big state agency. They both have to operate by the same procedures to make their cases. In legislative action, however, state agencies can employ numerous lobbyists, and even the governor will speak for them. The connections between those on the side of the state agency and the legislators who shape public policy may be very political and based on campaign contributions. Although arguable, this is not so in court.

Next, Mnookin explains that courts may be swayed by principled arguments and the costs of their alternative decisions are not generally considered. Legislators are almost always concerned with costs and are reluctant to approve expensive policies and programs, notwithstanding their rationality.

Much is said, even here, about the cost of litigation in both time and money, and Mnookin doesn't pretend that litigation is cheap. Advocates usually underestimate the cost of legislative lobbying, however. To engage in legislative advocacy, coalitions need to be formed and nurtured, lobbyists paid,

WHEN TO LITIGATE: SOME SELECTIVE CRITERIA[a]

Because litigation is a last-resort solution, the appropriate time to litigate should be calculated carefully. In deciding whether to litigate, advocates should assess the following:

The seriousness of the issue: Are there clean and specific injuries to children which can be identified and documented? How many children are affected?

Other prior strategies: Have other strategies been thoroughly exhausted? Are there other ways short of litigation to generate public support for systemic changes in the treatment of children?

Public and legal support: Is there an organization or a constituency which can be called upon or organized to support the litigation over a period of years? Is there financial support for court costs which will be incurred? Does the organization have the resources to monitor the implementation of a consent decree, out-of-court settlement, or court decision?

Forum: Is there reason to believe that the state or federal court will grant relief? Do these courts have a record of understanding the plaintiffs' claims?

Precedent: Has some other advocacy group in some other state previously litigated this issue? Did this litigation result in an out-of-court settlement or consent decree? Or did a court ruling establish a precedent?

Outcomes: What are the advocate's expectations of this litigation? Can the case be won? Might something unintended result?

Choice of counsel: Does the advocacy group plan to use its own in-house counsel to litigate? Have attorneys agreed to litigate this issue pro bono publico (without compensation "for the public good") and dedicate sufficient time to assure aggressive representation of children's interests? What prior experience do these attorneys have with the advocacy group? Will the advocacy group have any control over the lawsuit? What prior experience have these attorneys had with class action litigation?

---

[a]Reprinted with permission of the authors (Richart & Bing, 1989).

FIGURE **6.4**

When to litigate.

and position papers researched, written, and mailed, just to name a few of the costs. Also, major legislative victories are many years in the making. As Mnookin points out:

> Recent statutory changes give successful plaintiffs the right to recover fees from the losing government defendant. Legislatures are not in the habit of reimbursing the lobbying expenses of a group that successfully presses for a new bill. Finally, while the Internal Revenue Service limits the ability of charitable foundations [and not-for-profit organizations] to fund lobbying activities, no similar constraints exist with respect to litigation. (p. 524)

He also describes the advantages a court victory can have for advocates and their clients. Increased publicity about previously unnoticed people and circumstances can be a positive result. Did the public and policymakers know about children lost and lingering in foster care—especially poor and minority children—prior to several major child welfare lawsuits? This publicity may motivate allies and potential coalition members to step forward. The filing of a lawsuit against a public agency must receive a response, and that response is almost always a public response. Administrators and legislators may be less likely to avoid some of these issues and relatively powerless clients when the spotlight is on them.

SUMMARY

This chapter has included discussions about the importance and positive potential of the legal advocacy strategy and its related tactics. An effort was made to describe situations in which various forms of legal advocacy could be used, from violations of clients' rights to changing agency and court rules, from the filing of amicus curiae briefs to the filing of lawsuits to remedy the underfunding of essential services. A wide variety of legal tactics were also presented, including the following: consulting with clients, practitioners, and other advocates as to whether a given situation might call for legal tactics; locating legal assistance; raising funds for legal advocacy; serving as an expert witness; serving on committees to oversee the implementation of court orders; and engaging in legislative advocacy as a follow-up to litigation.

Throughout the chapter, practitioners have been encouraged to use litigation and also cautioned about its costs and consequences, a seemingly mixed message. The intended message is that litigation is a forceful advocacy tool that deserves special respect relative to other approaches.

Some advocates are quick to threaten lawsuits, but unless litigation has already been used successfully, it is likely that the threat will be ignored and the advocates' credibility tarnished. If successful litigation has been accomplished, most administrators and policymakers will heed the potential exercise of that tactic without anything being said. It may be best to allow attorneys to threaten litigation as they confer with the opposing party prior to taking action. These conferences can, by themselves, produce positive results for clients and eliminate the need for litigation. Litigation is not only expensive for advocates but the defendants too, as they counter the complaints made against them. They are well aware of the costs, the time, and the energy necessary to defend against a lawsuit, and they may be willing to negotiate in order to avoid all of this.

DISCUSSION QUESTIONS

1. Contact your local legal services office and interview an attorney about what kinds of clients the office serves and how to refer clients to the office.
2. Identify a significant Supreme Court ruling that has influenced public policy and service delivery in one area of human service. Conduct research on that case to find out what event triggered the litigation and who was involved.
3. Describe a client's situation with which you are familiar and explain why legal advocacy may be needed.

COMMUNITY ADVOCACY

CHAPTER OBJECTIVES

By the time you finish studying this chapter, you should

1. Understand that ideas and attitudes are major forces that shape public policy and that those ideas need to be altered while advocating for policy change.
2. Understand how and why community education is used as a strategy for changing ideas and attitudes.
3. Be familiar with different types of media and be able to utilize several specific media tactics.
4. Be able to use community education tactics to promote advocacy goals.

The critical point of this chapter is that ideas and attitudes need to be changed and new ones created in order to change public policies and programs. The assertion that public policies are based on ideas, beliefs, attitudes, myths, philosophies, and ideologies is not a new one. While other factors drive policy, ideas and attitudes are the major shapers of policies and programs and their implementation. For example, notice how many public policies, programs, and agency regulations are in place because of widely and deeply held beliefs about welfare mothers, many of which are unfounded and largely untrue. Notice too how racism and sexism are reflected in many public policies. If there is to be any hope for changing welfare policies and improving the programs, inaccurate beliefs have to be neutralized, at least, and reversed if possible.

With this issue in mind, Brawley (1997) points out that "media depictions of poverty, crime, mental illness, and drug abuse are all problematic, with negative consequences for public opinion and social policy" (p. 447). Brawley goes on to describe a relevant study by Wahl (1995) regarding media portrayals of people with mental illnesses. The content of media messages illustrates the dangerousness of people with mental illness and their unwillingness to seek or receive treatment. This coverage also implies that the public needs to be protected from these individuals and that confinement is the policy of choice. The public, therefore, has come to believe this about all people with mental challenges, and the fear generated by this belief contributes to regressive policies and underfunded programs.

As another demonstration of this important point, ask yourself what images and feelings come to mind when you think of juvenile delinquents or young offenders? I suspect that most people visualize teenage boys engaging in violent crimes, such as rape, strong-armed robbery, assault, or murder. In many people's minds, these youth are members of ethnic minorities. The media significantly reinforces these images and "provokes unnecessary fear of victimization among the public" (Brawley, 1997, p. 448). If policymakers and agency leaders are thinking this way when new policies and programs are being planned, don't you think these will take on a tone consistent with the surrounding imagery and attitudes?

In order to advocate successfully for more progressive programs for delinquents, these powerful attitudes and ideas have to be countered. Policymakers need to be constantly reminded that significantly less than 10% of juvenile arrests are for violent crimes (Snyder & Sickmund, 1995, p. iv), and, therefore, policies and programs for delinquents need to provide options for dealing with nonviolent offenders. The mental imagery is accurate in that most juvenile offenders are males, although crimes by female juveniles seem to be on the rise, but policies entirely focused on male offenders won't be effective. Another important fact of which to be aware is that more white youth are arrested than youth of color.

These examples and the ensuing discussion include many controversial issues, and there may be reasonable differences of opinion about them among practitioners as well as between practitioners and the author. The point is that advocates must remain vigilant at community advocacy. They need to remain aware of inaccurate or incomplete information that is being used to create new policy or defend the status quo. They should be sensitive to the attitudes and beliefs reinforcing existing programs and those inherent in new proposals. This is a major advocacy challenge, and successful, long-term advocacy in the best interest of clients depends on it.

Practitioners should be careful not to conclude that totally false information is being distributed or that sinister plots and bad attitudes abound. Much of the power of the imagery that supports the status quo comes from the fact that there is a little truth in the advertising. Oversimplifications and generalizations of a partial truth can be misleading.

It is easy to fall into the trap of feeling as if no one cares about oppressed people or persons with the various challenges our clients face, and, therefore, feel hopeless about implementing change. All of us have days when we think that the public not only is ambivalent toward our cause, but that it has a negative attitude toward helping professionals. Brawley (1997) directly touches on these feelings:

> Although the term "welfare" is viewed negatively by the public, they are, in fact, very supportive of specific services intended to help a wide range of vulnerable groups. . . . Therefore, there is reason to believe that the public will be supportive of human service professionals who identify themselves as persons who care for vulnerable groups in society—older persons, people with disabilities, poor children, or anyone who might need assistance during difficult times. (pp. 452–453)

This chapter discusses community education as an advocacy strategy and explains the logic behind it and the steps necessary to carry it out. Tactics associated with this strategy are categorized as either media tactics or other tactics.

COMMUNITY EDUCATION AS AN ADVOCACY STRATEGY

Community education as an advocacy strategy involves choosing between numerous approaches and tactics. As has been emphasized throughout this book, for every advocacy strategy there are several specific change targets, and the same is true for the community education strategy (see Figure 7.1). The phrase "ideas and attitudes" will be used as shorthand to refer to all the specific targets listed in Figure 7.1. If inaccurate information on an issue or client

Targets
• Counterproductive Philosophies
• Dubious Ideologies
• Erroneous Myths
• Inaccurate Information
• Incomplete Information
• Insidious Attitudes
• Lack of Information
• Misleading Imagery
• Unfounded Beliefs

FIGURE **7.1**

Targets for change of community education.

group is prevalent, it needs to be corrected and replaced by accurate information. Insidious attitudes, beliefs, myths, and ideas are sometimes based on inaccurate and incomplete information; and there are other personal, political, and social forces that hold them in place, such as economic self-interest, maintenance of power, or personal investment. These, too, are change targets for community education. These attitudes, which frequently operate on an unconscious level, are dysfunctional in the sense that they buttress ineffective and inequitable social policies.

There are two critical steps to community advocacy. The first is to identify the beliefs, attitudes, misinformation, and imagery that underlie status quo policies and programs. The second step is to neutralize and counter the status quo ideas by replacing them with new or slightly altered ideas. When advocates talk about framing the issue, they are referring to the different ways it may be packaged and presented. Much of framing involves persuading the intended audience to set aside its existing ideas on an issue to see the issue in a new way.

Uncovering Prevalent Ideas and Attitudes

Identifying the underlying beliefs that support the status quo is not research that can be done in the library. Whether advocates are trying to alter the status quo or defeat others' unsatisfactory policy proposals, the first step is learning to listen. As hard as it is, because you generally want to start arguing, go with the flow. There's a little intentional light-heartedness here, but allowing yourself to meditate on the status quo, and noticing what images come to mind when you do, will help you focus on the prevalent ideas and attitudes that defend the status quo.

A frequent source of misinformation is the ignorance about other cultures that pervades American society. Negative stereotypes of some client groups derive from racism, and negative evaluations are frequently based on comparisons to the behaviors and values of members of the dominant culture.

In addition to mulling over the status quo, one should also brainstorm with a team of advocates. Go through the list of questions included in Figure 7.2 and reach a consensus among the team. In most cases, the first task for the team will be to gather and study available materials defending the status quo or materials that propose changes. Sometimes it's easy to spot inaccurate or incomplete information, making the target of advocates' community education efforts obvious.

Policies are built on assumptions. Reversing or eliminating a policy often depends upon discovering these assumptions. Assumptions that are more subtle can be very powerful because they play on the subconscious minds of the audience. They need to be identified and raised to the conscious mind in

---

Brainstorming Questions

✓ What information is being presented in defense of existing policies or in favor of disempowering proposals?

✓ What do these policies assume about clients and their behaviors?

✓ What do existing policies assume is the best way to change undesirable client behaviors?

✓ What images are being promoted by those who advocate for the status quo or for policies contrary to the best interests of clients? Do they present case examples that contribute to the image?

✓ Do the ideas and imagery tap into peoples' deep fears and prejudices? What are those fears and prejudices?

✓ How would a political cartoon representing the status quo policy look?

FIGURE **7.2**

Brainstorming questions to identify status quo ideas and attitudes.

---

order to be countered. Examples of probing questions by which to identify assumptions include the following: Do the policies assume that the clients in question are self-motivated or lazy? Do the policies paint clients as greedy, smart, violent, lacking in self-control, disrespectful, law-abiding, weak-willed, or inferior?

Most policies and programs take one of the following two approaches to changing or maintaining human behavior: they provide incentives to produce desirable behaviors; or they create disincentives, and even punishments, to deter undesirable behaviors. A concerned advocate must evaluate what is known about the effectiveness of the approach embodied in the policy and whether there is an implicit or explicit image that represents the policies and programs of the status quo. Case exemplars are frequently used to explain, defend, or market the wisdom of an existing program, and the advocacy team should analyze those if possible. The exemplars are notorious for being simplistic, incomplete, and deceptive, and they are loaded with the assumptions being made about clients and preferred approaches.

The author has long been amazed at the genius of political and editorial cartoonists and the power of their work. A small picture can portray a great deal of information, numerous ideas, attitudes, beliefs, and myths. These cartoonists can represent the status quo or burst its bubble with a relatively straightforward picture. With that in mind, it could be useful for the advocacy team to try to imagine a political cartoon representing the status quo policy. If that's possible, it may be easier to begin dividing it into its component beliefs, ideas, and misinformation.

Developing New Messages

After identifying the ideas and attitudes underpinning the status quo, the next step is to produce counter-intelligence, more complete and accurate information about clients and about proposed approaches. Decide what ideas, information, and imagery would best counter and replace those of the status quo or of the opposing advocates. The material produced in this step should then be disseminated to particular audiences with specific techniques. Much of it can appear in position papers, briefing notes, or other communications sent to advocacy networks involved in legislative advocacy.

Intended Audience(s)

When engaged in community education, who is the intended audience? If engaged in state-level advocacy, should every citizen in the state be targeted for receiving information? Do the attitudes and beliefs of every person have to be changed in order for advocacy objectives to be accomplished? If it were an ideal world and advocates had unlimited resources, the answer to each of these questions would be "Yes." Since this isn't the case, priorities on how to use advocates' time, skills, and money must be set. It makes sense for community advocates to focus their limited resources first on those who are most closely associated with the policy. Are some individuals more likely to be involved in making and implementing the policy than others? If so, who are those individuals? Which individuals are closest to the decision advocates want made, and which ones will be responsible for changing or operating the programs of interest? Frequently, the answers to these questions lead us to the legislators and agency leaders who are responsible for policy implementation. It is also the case that legislators' ideas can be changed if large numbers of their constituents educate them; however, as is readily evident, this approach will take longer and require more resources. Advocates should not view this choice of tactics as an either-or proposition, but rather a way to prioritize the use of time, energy, volunteers, and money. An approach that uses a little of both is recommended, by which energy is invested in the education of policymakers and in the education of those constituents who are most likely to communicate with policy leaders.

Just as advocates must set priorities regarding whom to educate first in a community, they also need to prioritize the communities they will target. Again, referring back to the chapter on legislative advocacy, not all legislators have equal influence over the outcome of a policy proposal. When deciding where to engage in community education first, one way to set priorities is to start in the communities where the chairs of the relevant legislative committees reside.

Reminder About the Definition of Advocacy Community advocacy is a strategy of a different sort than that of the other three—agency advocacy, legislative advocacy, and legal advocacy. Recall the definition of advocacy used in this book: **Advocacy consists of those purposive efforts to change specific existing or proposed policies or practices on behalf of or with a specific client or group of clients.** Community education, although purposive, does not aim to change a specific policy or practice in an immediate and direct manner. The strategy instead aims to alter attitudes and beliefs that support particular policies and practices.

When to Engage in Community Advocacy

Community education, therefore, is not a strategy advocates would use singularly; it is always used with other strategies. With that in mind, readers could reasonably ask why it is elevated as one of the four major advocacy strategies. There are two reasons for its prominence in this book, both of which touch on its importance. First, the author's experience indicates that it is *always* called for when using other strategies. Effective advocates should always think about framing their issue, influencing public opinion (Richan, 1991), developing supportive information and imagery, and do so in a manner that counters prevailing ideas. Second, experience demonstrates that advocates frequently ignore or underinvest in this strategy, and this could be one explanation for their lack of success or the limited application of their short-range accomplishments. Therefore, the comprehensive approach to advocacy described in this book gives great prominence to tactics intended to change ideas and attitudes.

There are many skilled and experienced advocates and practitioners who make a reasonable argument that community education should be implemented to create a climate for change. They assert that the more informed and knowledgeable citizens are about clients and effective service approaches, the more supportive they will be of human services and proposals for progressive change. They will also be more inclined to elect leaders who are better informed and more receptive to change. Likewise, the more public dialogue there is about human services issues, programs, budgets, and the people who use the services, the better off we are and the greater the likelihood for progressive change. Those who assert this viewpoint may be absolutely right, but we must consider the fact that implementing this approach will take massive amounts of resources and a very long time to transform society in this very desirable way. Advocates need to learn patience because change can be slow, and many clients will suffer while waiting for broad, grassroots, community education efforts to take effect. Also, advocates simply do not currently have the resources to pull this off, nor is it likely they can muster them. Therefore, advocates who engage in community education as a strategy to change ideas and attitudes should always have specific policy and programmatic change in mind.

Challenges of Community Education

A major question with which advocates will have to struggle is whether accurate and complete information alters people's attitudes and beliefs. Unfortunately, the answer is conditional. It depends on how strongly and how long individuals have held their beliefs, and how personally invested they are in the beliefs. There is little doubt that information that is well organized and persuasively presented can change people's attitudes and beliefs. At the same time, advocates shouldn't expect this to work all the time with all people. As advocates gain experience, they will become better and better at framing their issues and presenting their case in different ways to different audiences.

It's also important to remember that as long as a policymaker votes for advocates' proposals, whether their ideas and attitudes are consistent with those of the advocates is of little import. It can be dangerous to insist that not only should people do the right thing, but that they also should do it for the right reasons. In the short run, we just want them to do the right thing, notwithstanding their philosophy; in the long run, it is unlikely that a person will consistently support advocates' proposals if their beliefs are contrary to those conducive to proclient policies.

MEDIA TACTICS

One of the best ways to get images and information disseminated is through the media. Television is so dominant in our lives it is easy to forget the other types of media that exist. Table 7.1 lists numerous examples of two types of media, electronic and print. With most types of media, multiple aspects can be used. For example, newspapers have news articles, editorials, op-ed pieces, letters to the editors, and feature articles. There is no guaranteed method to help advocates choose which types of media and what aspects are best when undertaking community advocacy. On the list of factors to be considered are such things as the following: how much it costs, how much time advocates have to prepare the message, how long it takes for the media to distribute it, and whether advocates have the knowledge and skills necessary to take advantage of a particular type of media.

Before advocates begin to strategize and debate about how to get their message out to the intended audiences, they need to be clear about the message content. Much of the advice provided in the next chapter will help with

TABLE 7.1	DIFFERENT TYPES OF MEDIA

Print Media	Electronic Media
✓ Daily Newspapers	✓ Television
⇨ News Articles	⇨ News
⇨ Feature/Human Interest Articles	⇨ Talk shows
⇨ Editorials	⇨ Public Service Announcements
⇨ Op-ed pieces	⇨ Documentaries
⇨ Letters to the editor	⇨ Advertisements
⇨ Advertisements	⇨ Public Access Channels
✓ Weekly/Community Newspapers	✓ Commercial Radio
⇨ Articles	⇨ News
⇨ Editorials	⇨ Talk shows
⇨ Advertisements	
✓ Magazines	✓ Public Television
✓ Agency and Association Newsletters	✓ Public Radio

this, but essentially advocates need to know what client problem their advocacy effort seeks to address, the nature and extent of the problem, their proposed solution, and estimates of its costs. Do not assume that every message must contain all of these elements. That would be a big mistake, for electronic media has taught us to think in sound bites, a little at a time. Advocates may choose to draw media attention to the existence of a problem without proposing a solution at that time. Later, the same or different media might be useful to disseminate the proposal. The strategic question here is the following: Which part(s) of the message goes to which members of the intended audience, when, and in what order?

In strategizing before discussing how to use different types of media, remember that the purpose of community education is to neutralize the ideas and attitudes that support the unsatisfactory status quo and to replace them with information and beliefs conducive to the change advocates are proposing. We wish to disseminate accurate and complete information as well as images that capture the ideas and assumptions implicit in the proposal. There are more ways to do this than can be counted, for images are created both by pictures and by words. Some audiences are persuaded by hearing case studies of clients, while others are impressed with a more systematic approach including statistics and cost-benefit analyses. Frequently, both approaches are needed. Case studies can help to create empathy, concern, desire for change, and hopefulness, while statistical presentations systematically demonstrate the extent of the problem to persuade listeners that the case study is not a rare event but, rather, happens with regularity.

As all instructors who teach writing and speaking tell their students, you must first know your audience. This is a difficult challenge, and trying to meet it should slow advocates down long enough for them to contemplate what persuasive approach will be appropriate for the audience. It is a hard line to walk, but advocates should be careful neither to under- or overestimate the knowledge of their audiences. Certainly, avoid the use of jargon and abbreviations.

One of the unfortunate realities of disseminating information through any mechanism is that once you share information, you have very little, if any, control over how recipients will interpret and use it. With media, one cannot always predict when or if the message will be transmitted. Since timing is usually an important consideration, as in publishing a newspaper editorial just prior to a major vote on legislation, lack of control can lead advocates to the brink of pulling their hair out. This is very much a part of being an advocate—feeling frustrated and moving ahead anyway. Do as much as time permits to influence the content and transmittal of the message, and then move on to other tactics that need to be accomplished to produce desired change.

The following suggestions about how to use different types of media are a fairly general overview based on the author's experience. There are numerous individuals in every community who have extensive knowledge and experience with different types of media and would be good members of advocacy teams, either in an ongoing or occasional role. Often these individuals are expected to and like to provide consultations pro bono. Marketing and advertising firms are a good place to look for individuals with this expertise, as are media companies. The author was fortunate to persuade a local editorial cartoonist to donate some of his time to a particular advocacy effort. He produced a fabulous cartoon that was subsequently distributed quite widely, and a copy was put on every legislator's desk.

Newspapers

There are at least seven ways by which newspapers may be used in advocacy efforts: articles on your advocacy issue, personal interest articles, in-depth investigations, editorials, op-ed pieces, letters to the editor, and advertising space. These approaches are described in the subsections that follow.

News Stories   Problems faced by client groups can make for good news stories if they get journalists' attention and are framed appropriately. Journalists will not find these stories automatically, however, so advocates should contact the paper with suggestions about pressing issues. It is even better if the specific journalist who covers the relevant beat is contacted.

No two newspapers make assignments in the same way, so advocates need to check to see who usually covers the following areas: local news, statewide news, education news, human services news, health care reporting, and state capital news. Not only are there differences between newspapers but between individual journalists. Each has a unique work style, personality, and interests. While an advocacy issue may not click for one journalist, two others may jump at it. Keep trying and don't burn any bridges, because the next issue may click even if this one did not.

Personal Interest Articles   Besides news articles, newspapers frequently include feature or personal interest articles. These can draw attention to the good work of an agency, the dedication of a group of advocates working to improve service delivery, or even one or more clients who have overcome obstacles and found success. Profiling a few clients creates an opportunity to educate citizens regarding the extent and nature of challenges faced by community members and the types of supportive policies and programs that facilitated their growth. Articles such as these frequently include photographs that can become prevalent images.

In-Depth Investigations   From time to time, newspapers assign reporters to more in-depth investigative projects. Editors should be willing to listen to advocates' suggestions on topics that warrant this approach or allow advocates to assist reporters as they do their research. Several years ago the author worked extensively (and behind the scenes) with a reporter doing research on juveniles who commit murders. Inevitably, these articles include the opinions of experts, policymakers, agency leaders, and advocates. They usually provide some assessment of how well or how poorly current policies and programs work, and they conclude by making recommendations. These investigative reports usually get a lot of attention and can stir policymakers into action.

Advocates can play multiple, important roles in this process. They will be trying to persuade reporters of the magnitude and severity of client challenges and to convince them of the wisdom of suggested solutions. Well-honed communication skills and persuasiveness are important, but the author's bias is that nothing is more important than being well prepared in terms of having done one's advocacy homework.

Editorials   The editorials published in daily newspapers are sometimes the first things that policymakers read in order to keep a finger on the pulse of the public, so having editorial support for advocates' proposals can be very helpful. Papers have editorial boards that discuss which issues to editorialize about and what the editorials will say. Usually one of the editors on the board will write the piece. After sending a letter explaining the issue, advocates should request meetings with the editorial boards in order to make their case.

A technique the author has found to be effective is to have well-placed members of the board of directors—individuals who are well known in the community—seek appointments with editors. This could be a supportive legislator or community leader who can pave the way. In the author's experience, once the meeting with the editorial board began, after a brief introduction by the community leader, the author made his case about the problem of concern and proposed solutions.

After making a presentation, advocates may leave an information packet with the editors providing them with more detailed background information. In addition, papers may be willing to editorialize or give space to client issues. For example, one of the Seattle daily newspapers publishes a short report on children on a monthly basis as part of an editorial.

When meeting with the editorial board, be prepared for the editors to ask insightful questions that may be tough to answer. While this can be nerve-racking, don't automatically assume that the tough questions mean the editors disagree with you. They may be supportive of your point of view but wish to shore up a potential weakness in your argument. It may be a question they know they'll be asked, and they want an expert's help on it. It is their editorial that will be printed and widely distributed, so they have to feel confident of their ability to defend the position they take. The editors also know each other quite well, and one who is on your side may ask a question that seems oppositional but actually is intended to get you to address certain concerns or approach the issue in a way that will convince more skeptical editors.

Keep in mind that even the most supportive editors may take a while to write their editorials if they do not think your issue is a very high priority. Unfortunately that's the way the world works. Sometimes they assign someone to look into the issue to verify advocates' information or to look for another angle. A news article might result, and *then* the editorial will be published.

One thing advocates should always do at these meetings is to ask the editors what they think, whether they agree or disagree with the ideas, and whether they will write a supportive editorial. Stay in touch via phone, fax, or e-mail to update editors, clarify a discussion, or follow-up with information that wasn't available at the time of the meeting. A thank you note is a common courtesy and will help you get another meeting with the board on the next advocacy effort.

Op-ed Pieces   Another way to get advocacy issues into the consciousness of policymakers and community members is to write an op-ed for the paper. The op-ed page is the page opposite the editorial page and can include writings by syndicated columnists, editorials from special editors, letters to the editor, and the views of community members. Special editors contribute columns periodically, and many of these editors specialize in certain topics or offer a particular slant on the world. For example, one of Seattle's papers features a contributing editor who writes about race and ethnicity in the community and how certain issues impact people of color. Advocates should certainly consider connecting with these editors to see if they're interested in the advocacy issue and could use some ideas and information for their column. Generally, it is their job to stay in touch with what's going on in the community, so unless they have a tight deadline, they'll welcome your calls. There are a number of helping professionals throughout the country who have an agreement with their paper to publish a weekly column on a human service issue (see Brawley, 1997, for several examples), so there is good reason for advocates to pursue this option.

Advocates also can submit their own op-ed pieces presenting their views on a problem or policy debate. Advocates can call the editor and discuss their ideas for a column as well as their credentials for writing on the topic, but editors are usually (and understandably) noncommittal prior to seeing a draft of the piece. They also will have fairly strict length limitations of which advocates should be aware.

The author had an op-ed piece published recently that differed from the paper's recent editorial. (It was submitted, and the editor said he wanted to publish it but the number of words had to be reduced drastically.) The state legislature was considering the creation of a separate children's department instead of keeping programs for children and youth in the existing state human services agency, and the paper published an editorial supporting this (an idea which has merit). Meanwhile, the author of this text had conducted national research on the topic, and his op-ed systematically weighed the pros and cons of such a move. It also weighed the costs to employees and to clients, financial and otherwise. The conclusion stated in the op-ed was that while there were problems with the way the state agency delivered services and managed programs, those could be corrected more quickly if children's programs were left in the umbrella agency. Also, with federal law and funding changes in progress, the timing was bad for such massive change at the state level. Child advocates came down on both sides of this issue, but a persuasive case was made to leave well enough alone for the present. A copy of the published op-ed was widely distributed to legislators and others by the child advocacy agency.

Letters to the Editor   Letters to the editor are another good tactic to use as advocates try to neutralize nonprogressive ideas and to frame and present their proposals. Many people, including policymakers, read these letters. The letters have to be short and succinct, and this can be challenging (especially for academics like the author whose inclinations run in the opposite direction). Most of the challenges confronted by human service advocates are very complex and resist simplistic descriptions. One way to manage this dilemma is to coordinate the writing of several letters to the editor, each one commenting on a slightly different aspect of the topic.

Again, there is no guarantee that the paper will use the letter; but even if it doesn't, advocates have now produced a succinct version of their message that can be used for a number of other purposes. Writing succinctly is an important skill to learn, because many lobbyists insist that information handed to legislators must fit on one page or they won't read it.

When writing op-eds or letters to the editor, avoid the use of sarcasm and use humor sparingly and very carefully. It is best to avoid name-calling (e.g., "Senator Cromagnon is a Neanderthal!") or personalizing policy debates. Be respectful toward the individuals who support a particular point of view, and don't question their intentions. However, don't hesitate to criticize their policy proposal and point out the false assumptions on which it is built as well as the negative repercussions of implementing such a proposal. Hit proposals hard, not people. You never know whose support or vote you might need next week.

It is very common for advocates to be perceived by policymakers and the public to be naysayers or pests who are always criticizing agencies and policymakers. While there are many shortcomings in our service systems about which to be concerned, it is smart to publicly comment on positive developments, success cases, promising starts, silver linings, and potential. This is where the old adage, "Praise in public, criticize in private," really pans out. Applaud the work of an innovative program, the efforts of particular policymakers and agency leaders to be responsive to client needs, and pat editors and reporters on the back for a job well done. This approach makes friends and allies, builds bridges, and provides positive reinforcement. Most of the "newspaper tactics" already discussed can be used for this purpose.

Advertising   The last and very underutilized tactic involving newspapers is to purchase advertising space just as politicians and political action committees do. The ads could contain many things such as a position paper, a political cartoon that captures the issue, photos with brief explanations, relevant quotes from community leaders, or announcements of meetings, community forums, and opportunities to volunteer. This tactic comes with cost considerations, of course, but advocates should inquire as to the price of a quarter page ad, for example, before rejecting this option.

Weekly Newspapers

The larger the city, the more types of newspapers they are likely to have in addition to the dailies. There are many weekly or monthly publications that are targeted to particular audiences. Neighborhoods frequently publish newspapers that include news reports and editorials of interest to those particular residents. These newspapers generally publish letters to the editor as well. Many of these have large readerships, and advocates should consider using them when engaged in community education, especially if a key legislator lives in that community. Neighborhood papers are also an excellent way to reach ethnic minorities.

As mentioned earlier, if the paper publishes a supportive editorial, or advocates' op-eds, letters to the editor, or advertisements, make copies of these and send them to allies, members of networks, coalitions, policymakers and agency leaders. Attach them to a one-page position paper if that is appropriate for a particular audience. The fact that a newspaper chose to publish advocates' work lends credibility to the advocacy effort.

Magazines

More and more magazines are becoming localized. Major cities have magazines devoted to them and many take a statewide or regional focus. They don't tend to be news oriented, but they certainly will have articles about challenges facing the city or state. These can be in the human service arena and can be suggested or even written by advocates. Advocates, as important community leaders, might be profiled and interviewed in an article, giving the advocate an opportunity to express concerns, ideas, and proposals. Some of these magazines also welcome editorials or articles written by advocates.

Newsletters

Thousands of agencies, professional and civic organizations, religious groups, societies, leagues, unions, and clubs publish periodic newsletters that are distributed to members, potential members, and clients. Advocates should find out which newsletters are read by legislators, for example, and how advocates can get their messages printed in them. Usually, these are low-budget operations and the editors will warmly welcome a submission by advocates. It is not uncommon for organizations participating in an advocacy coalition to publish each other's position papers and background research. Some newsletter editors want articles and editorials to be penned by a member of the group, and, in these cases, advocates need to work with one or more members to develop the contribution.

Television

As the late Andy Warhol said, "In the future everyone will be world-famous for fifteen minutes" (Bartlett, 1992). This certainly can apply to advocates, and television is a quick way to get notoriety and have at least a sound byte of fame. Most practitioners are well aware of the different types of shows on television, including those listed in Table 7.1 on page 123. That there is a difference between commercial television and public television is old news, but with dozens of channels now available to subscribers, it's getting hard to distinguish one from another. Now there are channels devoted entirely to news, sports, weather, old movies, and other specialized subjects. Wouldn't it be great if some well-to-do philanthropist or foundation funded an "advocacy channel?" Until that happens, advocates need to strategize about how best to access existing channels and their programming formats to conduct effective community education campaigns.

TV News   News segments of local broadcasts include no more than 10 to 15 minutes of on-air time, making the competition for those minutes quite fierce. Certainly, advocates can be very helpful to television journalists by giving them leads about newsworthy issues and situations relating to their client group or advocacy effort. When advocates go public with their concerns about a social problem and announce ameliorating proposals, television journalists may be interested.

Both as part of regular news broadcasts and special news programs (e.g., *60 Minutes, 20-20*), in-depth stories are presented. Again, advocates can bring story ideas to the attention of reporters and assist them in their coverage. Advocates, as experts, will be sought out for either on- or off-air interviews. A number of years ago, *60 Minutes* broadcast a segment on the deplorable conditions in juvenile training schools. Dr. Jerome Miller, a well-known advocate for human service change, was interviewed at length. The videotape of this program was used extensively with community groups to familiarize them with these issues. Likewise, when the author was working with his advocacy agency, he received at least a call or two a month from producers of various news programs seeking a story or information on one they were investigating. Advocates should proceed cautiously, however, with programs that tend to use a tabloid approach.

News broadcasts sometimes include opinion pieces by commentators, executive producers, and broadcast company executives. As advocates become familiar with the individuals who usually write and present these editorial statements, they should contact them with issues that need attention and ideas on what direction to take. If the station presents an editorial in opposition to the position advocates are pursuing on an issue, advocates may ask the station for equal time to present their views.

Talk Shows   Talk shows and public affairs programs are produced both nationally and locally, and advocates can appear on these to present information about clients, challenges they face, and what changes need to take place. Media tend to prefer case studies of real people so that the issues are more tangible than when presented with statistics, bar graphs, and pie charts. When advocates appear on television or radio, it's a good idea to share stories about people in the community who have personal challenges. Talking about our neighbors helps neutralize the idea that a particular problem would never affect us or occur in our community.

Public Television   Public television is a great resource for advocates because the absence of advertisements allows for different types of shows aimed at different audiences. News broadcasts tend to be more in-depth and special reports more frequent. If a program on public television agrees to broadcast a segment related to the advocacy effort, this can be announced in a press release or an advertisement, which may bring more coverage from different types of media. Similarly, as part of cable industry regulation, public access channels are available for which advocates can easily develop a program. Of course, work such as advertising and announcements in newsletters will have to be done to create a larger audience. Advocates should also consider hosting their own shows from time to time. Many human service agencies have arrangements with their local public television (and radio) stations to use 30 minutes of program space periodically. The opportunities are endless if advocates are creative and persistent.

PSAs   In addition to all the different types of shows, commercial television and radio frequently broadcast public service announcements (PSAs) for all kinds of groups and organizations. These can be used to educate the community on a social problem or solicit support for advocacy proposals as well as to recruit volunteer advocates or raise money for an advocacy effort. Like commercial advertisements, PSAs last between 30 and 60 seconds, and, as mentioned in the discussion on letters to the editor, it is a challenge to get an attractive, noticeable, and effective message across in that brief period of time. For example, in the late 1980s, the National Association of Social Workers began an advocacy effort on homelessness. They developed a PSA for radio and television in which Dorothy from *The Wizard of Oz* said her famous line, "There's no place like home." This attention-grabber lead to information on homelessness and selected photographs (Brawley, 1997).

Radio

Radio, both commercial and public, has many things in common with television in terms of the different types of programming available throughout the day, night, and week. There are brief news reports, longer news shows, traffic and weather reports, public affairs programs, and entertainment. One feature that television doesn't have is talk or call-in shows. Talk radio has become extremely popular in recent years, and this format creates huge opportunities for advocates to present new ideas and shape public opinion. Advocates might host a call-in show or just a segment of one. They can suggest topical ideas to producers and hosts or appear on these shows as experts.

The author did just that several years ago. His research and academic position give him some credibility on the topic of juvenile crime, and his advocacy work in this area gets him some attention (usually far more than he wants or is useful). He was invited to come to the studio of the radio station and be on the air with the host of the program and a legislator (a committee chair) who was sponsoring a juvenile crime bill. They held a discussion on the strengths and weaknesses of the proposal, and the author took the opportunity to dispel myths and correct misinformation on the subject, reinforcing parts of the legislator's proposal and making suggestions to change other parts. After the legislator signed off, the author and the host took on-air phone calls from the listening audience. Responding to these questions mostly involved correcting misperceptions and false assumptions about the extent and nature of juvenile crime, what interventions show promise, and what types of programs have proven to be expensive time wasters. It was amazing how many people told the author that they had heard him on the radio.

Radio stations, both public and commercial, broadcast numerous PSAs, and the advertising time is more reasonably priced than that for television. Public radio has many programming formats that are ripe for advocates. Hosts of public affairs or call-in shows frequently invite guests who are familiar with particular community issues or are proponents for new policies and programs to participate in discussions. Public radio listenership is very high in general, but it can be higher or lower at different times of day and for different types of programs. When advocates successfully arrange a personal appearance or coverage of their advocacy issue, they should consider ways not only to increase the size of the audience but also to get targeted audiences to listen. With both with television and radio, tapes of shows, segments, or interviews can be distributed and played at meetings.

News Releases, Press Conferences, and Interviews

No one needs to apply for a license to issue news releases or to hold press conferences. Advocates' lack of experience or their perceived lack of standing shouldn't hold them back. The bigger question of concern will be whether any of the media will use the information in the news release, follow up on it, or attend the press conference. This is where advocacy homework pays off, as do media and marketing skills. News releases can contain advocates' policy proposals and statements on recent events and proposals at the state and local levels, or they may announce a press conference, the availability of a report on service inadequacies, or the scheduling of a community forum on client needs. These are instruments designed to get the attention of media. Richan (1991) provides several tips about news releases as well as an example (pp. 207–210). Word processing software (e.g., Microsoft Word) has built-in news release templates that can be used as is or may be modified.

Press conferences can be held for a number of reasons and the print and electronic media should be notified when one is scheduled. Frequently such events are used to release advocates' findings and assessments of unmet client needs, the initiation of a lawsuit, or the announcement of advocacy proposals or legislative agendas. The limited selection of examples here shouldn't limit advocates' creativity, however. When the author's child advocacy organization finished its report on children in adult jails and was prepared to publicize the findings and recommendations, a news release was issued announcing that a press conference would be held to deliver the report. Not only was the news release distributed to all media statewide, specific journalists who had covered similar issues in the past or who would be expected to cover similar events were contacted personally. The release included just enough information to attract journalists' attention and let them know the topic, who would be present, and that more specific information would be available at the conference. The press conference was scheduled at a time of day and day of week that increased the chances of getting attention, not having to compete for reporters' time, and giving reporters time to prepare their articles for the next issue of the paper or broadcast of the news.

A great deal of energy was expended to prepare for the press conference. The president of the organization's board of directors came to town to make opening remarks, and other board members also attended and were introduced. This lends credibility to the advocacy effort when the inevitable question arises about advocates' credentials and experience. After introductory remarks describing the purpose of the advocacy organization and the study, the author was introduced to give more specific findings. A short question and answer period was permitted before concluding the press conference, at which point board members and staff were made available for interviews.

A very effective technique was used to insure media coverage in all parts of the state. Even though the report and advocacy effort were statewide in nature, specific information packets for different media markets had been prepared for distribution. For example, we made general remarks as to the number of youth held in adult jails in the state and how many were commingled in cells with adults. A television station is more likely to include this news in their broadcast if they can announce that their local jail in particular was (or was not) one of those commingling juveniles and adults. This technique successfully attracted attention, but it is risky. We had to be absolutely certain that our research was accurate if we were going public and essentially pointing fingers.

This example raises a useful reminder that advocates should carefully consider who will appear at the press conference. Just as was discussed in chapter 4, "Agency Advocacy," and chapter 5, "Legislative Advocacy," advocates and community leaders can play different roles, both visible and invisible, when meeting with legislators, agency leaders, and the media. The considerations are similar in these situations. If advocates have a prior history with the media or particular reporters and are viewed as knowledgeable and credible, then less emphasis will need to be placed on the presence of a high-profile community leader. As in the case of visiting editorial boards, certain individuals are better known to editors than others, and they can gain entrée and generate interest more easily.

Interviews   If a news release is distributed, a reporter will frequently call to do a follow-up interview in person or over the phone, depending on the type of media and the nature of coverage desired. Try to decide in advance which one or two major points you'd like to make. Decide which key phrases you want to use and repeat, and, if applicable, be prepared to be very specific about what listeners or readers can do to help (e.g., "Call Senators Salt and Pepper to thank them for their willingness to file this important legislation."). Think in terms of a few sound bytes that could be used.

OTHER COMMUNITY ADVOCACY TACTICS

There are hundreds of ways to conduct community education and to influence public opinion that do not involve the use of newspapers, television, or radio. This section will briefly discuss a few of these tactics, but advocates should rely on their experience and creativity to add to, adapt, or combine these tactics. This will involve either attracting community members to educational meetings or taking the education to the audiences.

Direct Education

Direct education of citizens, policymakers, and other advocates is one of the most effective approaches available. Lobbying itself can be construed as direct education of legislators. The challenge is to figure out how to gain access to the people you wish to educate. Non-media tactics you may use are summarized in Figure 7.3.

As you may know from experience, a popular method is to mail information to people whose ideas, attitudes, and behaviors are important to alter. Advocates use the mail to deliver information in many different formats, ranging from **reports** and **position papers** to **newsletters** and solicitations. Of course, there's more than one way to mail items (first class, bulk rate, and private carriers), which is another detail advocates need to consider. Mailing is easy, however, when compared to getting the recipient to read the materials. Again, advocates need to consider length, style of presentation, and layout, as well as a number of different techniques, to engage the recipient.

Action alerts asking individuals to contact their legislators are usually distributed to select audiences such as advocacy networks or coalitions, but there

Ways to Educate, Inform, and Influence the Community
✓ Mail (reports, position papers, newsletters, legislative alerts)
✓ Telephone
✓ Door-to-door canvassing
✓ Community forum (debates, presentations, panels, hearings, awards)
✓ Presentations at meetings of groups and organizations
✓ Educational workshops
✓ Distribution of pamphlets and flyers
✓ Internet, e-mail, and newsgroups

FIGURE **7.3**

Community education tactics (non-media).

are instances in which broader distribution might pay off (after having dealt with cost considerations). We have all seen **legislative alerts** published in daily newspapers: "Paid for by the Committee to . . ." They use a variety of techniques to catch our attention, hoping we'll take action.

Many individuals' primary learning styles involve listening more than reading. On a one-to-one basis, the **telephone** is a good way to get people's attention and have them listen to your message. Face-to-face encounters are also very useful, so advocates should consider using the election technique of **door-to-door canvassing**. Political campaigners are convinced that this is a good method to get the word out about candidates and their positions on important issues. Canvassers usually leave information with the resident in the form of pamphlets or short position papers. Many of their conversations with voters involve correcting misperceptions. If no one is home, an information leaflet can be left on the doorstep.

Presentations to Groups

Obviously, it is far more efficient to meet with groups than one person at a time. Civic organizations, clubs, professional associations, unions, churches, and other groups hold regular **membership meetings** at which advocates could seek an audience. They may ask to make a brief presentation, to conduct a lengthier training session, or just to have information distributed. These groups frequently are searching for speakers.

Advocates can organize a variety of different meetings, either inviting selected audiences or the whole community. Organizations whose members are likely to be sympathetic to the advocacy issue are sometimes willing to give advocates their mailing lists for distributing invitations. **Workshops** can be designed using numerous teaching and participative techniques that convey information about the issue at hand and proposed new policies. This is important for members of both the local advocacy network as well as the public at large. Sometimes advocates can sponsor community forums at which an **expert panel** discusses or **debates** an issue of concern. Also gaining popularity are techniques such as simulations and dramatizations.

Another technique is for advocates to conduct **hearings** at which community members can present their concerns about the problem of child abuse, for example, or the impact of a new law on the investigation of child abuse. These events, like all of those suggested, must be carefully planned and well focused. It is a good idea for one of the advocates to make introductory remarks to establish the focus and boundaries of the discussion and establish ground rules. Introductory remarks also give participants a few specific ideas or proposals to which they may react. Planners shouldn't assume that lots of people will read about the forum in the paper and show up ready to speak. They should ask specific organizations and individuals to make remarks. They also should ensure that the information they've collected on the issue and their solutions are presented, as well as have fact sheets and other handouts available.

Internet

The last community education tactic to be mentioned stems from technological advances and the increasing number of people using computers every day. The **Internet, e-mail,** and **homepages** are exceptional tools by which advocates may provide information for community members to access. Designing homepages that present background research on an advocacy issue and policy proposal in an attractive, easy-to-follow manner, is a relatively straightforward task. It is very likely that someone on the advocacy team can do this or knows someone who can. The homepage could be arranged with links to various aspects of the issue, such as one that gives background information on the client problem(s), another that outlines policy and program proposals and includes information from other states on the effectiveness of similar programs, another that describes a family facing the particular challenges of concern, and one that tells browsers where they can get more information or what they can do to help. The sky's the limit on how creative advocates can be with the Internet. Once again, the challenge will be to get various audiences, from those closest to the policy decision point to those more removed, to read the advocates' homepage and its links.

Many advocates are using e-mail to distribute information and alerts to their networks and coalitions. Speed is one of the great benefits of e-mail, and the ease of responding is another. For example, if an advocate e-mails a position paper to someone who either disagrees or who has a misperception of the problem, that person can respond immediately to the sender with questions and concerns. The advocate can quickly and easily respond by passing on more information, or clarifying a fuzzy or complex part of the argument. Even if the recipient is not persuaded to the advocates' point of view, the advocates are now aware of an objection to their proposal and can prepare counter arguments. There are also ways to distribute information to a larger number of individuals by using special e-mail addresses that distribute the message more widely.

SUMMARY

In this chapter the emphasis has been on changing ideas and attitudes by using community advocacy. Readers should notice that similar events are discussed here as in chapter 5, "Legislative Advocacy." In that chapter, attention was given to mobilizing and nurturing advocacy networks and coalitions by using some of the same tactics discussed here. Both can (but don't necessarily) occur at the same time. As advocates engage in community education, regardless of their specific tactic, they should always be cognizant of the need to recruit volunteer advocates and members of networks and coalitions. One or two individuals almost always identify themselves during these various meetings as being interested in giving more of their time. Experienced advocates usually have a special handout with contact information in their back pockets to use in the case of such serendipitous events.

DISCUSSION QUESTIONS

1. Describe a common misconception about the client group in which you are interested. What specific techniques would you use to change this misconception and what new image do you wish to reinforce?
2. Write a letter to the editor describing a policy change that needs to occur in your community.
3. Identify and describe several ways community and agency advocacy can be used together.

DOING YOUR ADVOCACY HOMEWORK

CHAPTER OBJECTIVES

By the time you finish studying this chapter, you should

1. Understand the value of and steps involved in doing advocacy homework.
2. Be aware of several techniques for identifying advocacy issues.
3. Be able to collect the necessary information to gain an in-depth understanding of the clients' problem or need selected for an advocacy effort.
4. Be able to identify advocacy targets and map the decision system(s) whereby those targets can be changed.

Knowledge is power. Getting and using information is the basis for effective action. Fact finding is a must. (Fernandez, 1980, p. 74)

The key to successful advocacy is the background investigation that leads to precise targeting of change efforts and, eventually, it leads to the selection of advocacy strategies. Richan (1991) refers to this as one of his cardinal principles of advocacy. The materials developed during this stage of advocacy are indispensable when constructing persuasive arguments expressing the need for change and when presenting the attractiveness of the proposed policy or program. This chapter discusses the preparatory work that must be done to practice advocacy effectively.

The chapter is divided into three major sections, each of which discusses a slightly different purpose for advocacy homework. The first section delves into the background research needed to understand fully the needs of a client group. Techniques that advocates can use to locate the primary targets of the advocacy effort will be covered next. The last section identifies methods by which to understand the decision system through which advocates will seek to have their proposals approved. Preceding these sections is a brief discussion of various techniques for identifying the need for change. Following these sections is a discussion selecting strategies and tactics.

Many scholars and practitioners have written about the preparation and planning stages and their work greatly contributed to the development of this chapter. For example, Kettner, Daley, and Nichols (1985) discuss identifying and analyzing the change opportunity, setting goals and objectives, and designing the change effort (see also Taylor, 1987, pp. 90–104; Richan, 1991, pp. 34–117; and Coates, 1989, pp. 265–274).

Three things are important to keep in mind throughout this chapter. In general, we are talking about the homework necessary to engage in effective class advocacy. Many of the same techniques are useful when engaging in case advocacy too. Taylor (1987) has written very helpful guidelines on how agencies can take case situations that need advocacy and develop class advocacy efforts. Second, as stated previously, community advocacy is always called for in conjunction with one or more of the other advocacy strategies. Advocates must always explore what beliefs undergird current practices and policies and how to make their proposals persuasive. Those techniques were discussed in chapter 7. Finally, advocacy is not a linear process by which practitioners can complete the steps in consecutive order without circling back to earlier steps. As mentioned earlier, the advocacy process and the organizations and systems it tries to change are constantly in flux.

An important warning needs to be stated. Several delicate balancing acts need to be done during the homework stage. The first is based on the assumption that advocates have limited resources, including time, energy, and funding. Even though the homework is crucial, it is important to avoid putting too much time and energy into it to a point where nothing, or very little, is left for the action stage of advocacy. Unfortunately there is no clear demarcation as to when homework is using too many resources, but experience helps. The author's experience is that advocates rarely overinvest in research and planning, and because of this they tend to expend resources inefficiently during the action phase.

Sometimes advocates are predisposed to use a particular strategy regardless of their research findings. For example, many advocates enjoy and feel most confident doing legislative advocacy. When determining possible solutions to client troubles, they inevitably see legislative targets. Many times their analysis is correct, but all too often they ignore the possibility that clients would be helped more quickly and effectively if advocates engaged in agency advocacy and tried to get the agency to shift some of its funding or alter a rule or policy. Richan (1991) explains advocates' overall preference for legislative advocacy in the following way, "We are most aware of the legislative phase of policymaking because it is most exposed to public scrutiny and lends high drama to the process" (p. 51).

One reason for the inattention to thorough homework is that advocates tend to take on too many issues and causes. They deserve kudos for their willingness to work hard, but to be effective advocates in the long run, they also need to work smartly. This means setting priorities and not tackling more issues than time, energy, and funding allow. The importance of setting priorities and establishing a limited advocacy agenda cannot be overstated.

As mentioned in the introduction to part 2, in terms of a chronological approach to advocacy this chapter is out of order. Obviously, most of the homework should be done before implementing any advocacy strategy. The chapters were organized in this way because it is easier to explain the tasks involved in the homework stage after readers develop an understanding of the basic advocacy strategies. Building on knowledge of the advocacy tactics simplifies the process of explaining how to make the necessary preparations for them.

While it is true that most of the background research is done before the action stage, a very important point to remember is that as each strategy or tactic is implemented, new information arises that advocates should evaluate to determine whether they should alter their tactics. The change process itself, including the people and organizations involved (both for and against the change), is very fluid. It isn't that earlier decisions were wrong, but that new insights indicate the value of a different set of tactics. Try as they might as they do their homework, there is always going to be information that is impossible for advocates to acquire until they start their effort. Once the new information arises and tactics are adjusted, advocates are advised against second-guessing themselves and encouraged to accept these events as inevitable and move on.

Advocacy Needs Assessments

Many practitioners conduct **advocacy needs assessments** everyday as they work with clients. As they listen to their clients' needs and identify barriers that prevent them from getting what they need, human service practitioners are determining if advocacy is needed, who or what is the target, and which strategies and tactics to use. If advocates are not in direct service roles, such as staff or volunteers of advocacy agencies, they may be able to gain access to clients and inquire about pressing needs and unresolved problems. This kind of information can be collected from clients one-on-one, in group interviews with clients, or by talking to clients' parents or guardians. Many agencies have developed a variety of internal techniques for the direct service staff to notify advocates about client problems that need to be addressed by class advocacy.

If advocates are well networked in a particular service system, they will begin to hear what Richart and Bing (1989) refer to as "initial rumblings" of a problem. These are reports from trusted informants indicating that clients' needs aren't being met adequately, that rights are being violated, or that access to services is limited, among other things. One report or rumor of this kind is not enough information on which to act, however. Advocates, like journalists, should verify their information with more than one source. Almost all direct service providers are very interested in and committed to their clients' well being and will point out inadequacies in the service delivery system, but every now and then the person tipping off advocates is misinformed or is a disgruntled employee trying to make trouble.

Advocates should use informal methods to collect information about clients and the effectiveness of services, such as periodic phone calls or visits to agencies and reviews of agency annual reports and other statistical documents. In chapter 4, "Agency Advocacy," many agency monitoring approaches were discussed. All of those are valuable ways to learn what issues are problematic for clients. Also discussed in chapter 4 were a number of agency problems that advocates might target for change. Figure 8.1 repeats that list (but see chapter 4 to refresh your memory of the discussion) because these are the sorts of issues to monitor, for they form the basis for questions to be asked of clients and workers.

Chapter 5 discussed legislative advocacy and among the numerous advocacy techniques explained, legislative monitoring was described in some detail. Just like agency monitoring will identify client problems, legislative bodies need to be monitored to determine if proposals have been made that will help or hurt clients.

Problems
1. Ineffective agencies
2. Inappropriate behavior by worker(s)
3. Ineffective intervention/service approach
4. Failure to coordinate program with other services
5. Inaccessibility of program/services
6. Outreach inadequate or misdirected
7. Program implementation inconsistent with legislative intent
8. Plans to scale back or eliminate a program
9. New program/service(s)
10. Lack of accountability on service use and outcomes

FIGURE **8.1**

Agency problems to monitor.

Setting Priorities

When multiple issues need advocacy, advocates, whether they are operating as a coalition or as an advocacy organization, need to set realistic priorities. This is one of the most challenging aspects of doing your advocacy homework. Advocates do not have the resources to address all the problems at once, which requires that tough choices be made.

The author's former advocacy organization used networking, key informants, reviews of agency reports, and original research to identify potential advocacy issues. The board of directors was responsible for selecting the high-priority issues to be addressed. Several advisory committees were formed to identify advocacy issues such as children's mental health, education, and child welfare. The members of these committees were key agency staff and volunteers who were knowledgeable, experienced, and interested in these areas. As a group they were familiar with clients' needs, agency operations, pending legislative proposals, and prior legislation. Each of the advisory committees submitted prioritized lists of needed advocacy efforts to the board of directors.

The board, which was composed of citizens and professionals unaffiliated with any child-serving agencies, discussed and decided on the following four categories of issues: (1) items on which to provide advocacy leadership; (2) items on which they would be part of an advocacy coaliton but not be the lead organization; (3) items they would continue to monitor for possible action; and (4) items on which they would not get involved. Frequently, advocacy strategies would be discussed and suggestions made. The board sought staff recommendations to be careful not to overstretch the agency's resources.

This section discussed many of the ways that human services staff can identify possible advocacy issues. The truth of the matter is (and it's a sad truth) advocates will never be at a loss for issues on which to advocate. The bigger problem is deciding on which one, among many, to work. The next section discusses how advocates can gain an in-depth understanding of an issue.

UNDERSTANDING THE PROBLEM OR NEED

Whatever method is used to identify issues, advocates' next step is to become thoroughly familiar with all aspects of the problem they wish to solve on behalf of and with their clients. In the end, they must be able to present information that makes a persuasive case that a significant problem exists for a substantial number of people and that the proposed solution is reasonable and will work without wasting resources. This is a big order *and* it can be done. Frequently, as mentioned before, this stage of the process requires an advocacy team.

Early in this stage of doing your homework, advocates need to make a preliminary estimate of how many clients are affected by the identified issue. If an initial investigation shows that the problem is experienced by a very small number of clients, whose cases appear to be anomalies, it might be best to consider case advocacy with or on behalf of those individuals rather than a class advocacy effort. This is a difficult judgment for advocates to make. If possible, they should confer with the clients and heed their preferences.

Guiding Questions

This homework stage involves answering a series of questions. The questions are summarized in Figure 8.2 and discussed in detail below. The intent of these questions is to help advocates focus on the problems and needs of clients. This is a problem-solving process, and, as such, you start with the problem, not the solution. It is much easier to develop solutions and advocacy strategies when issues have been clearly specified. For example, saying that agency staff members who investigate reports of child abuse and neglect need additional expertise to conduct medical and psychological assessments of alleged victims is far more helpful than just saying that child abuse and neglect are problems we must solve. The former implies the need for medical and psychological training or the availability of expert consultants, whereas the latter doesn't offer any readily identifiable solution. The following suggested questions are overlapping and may not be relevant in every case; similar questions asked in different ways may click for some people and not others.

With what client group are you concerned?   Are abused children the group of interest, or single mothers, pregnant teens, or homeless veterans,

---

Questions

✓ With what client group are you concerned?

✓ What is the specific client problem or need of concern?

✓ In what geographic jurisdiction does the client group reside?

✓ How many people have the problem and who are they?

✓ How long has the specific need existed?

✓ What are the consequences of the problem for individuals, families, communities, and society?

✓ Why is this issue undesirable?

✓ What ideas, beliefs, attitudes, values, or myths support the existence of the problem or get in the way of change?

✓ Have any communities found ways to prevent the problem effectively?

✓ Are there successful interventions to help people with the problem or need?

FIGURE **8.2**

Questions to ask to understand the problem.

for example? Define the client group as specifically as possible because, eventually, you will want to be able to say how many there are. As you can see, the term *client group* refers to both a category of people (e.g., teens) and a condition they experience (e.g., pregnancy). This leads to the next question.

What is the specific client problem or need of concern?   Identify the problem, condition, issue, or need the clients face. Taylor (1987) recommends asking the question "Who is hurting?" (p. 95). Collect as much supporting data to justify the existence of the problem or need as is possible given the constraints of time, people, and energy.

In what geographic jurisdiction does this client group reside?   Are you interested in advocacy with and on behalf of substance abusers in your county, state, particular communities or neighborhoods, or the entire country? Delimiting this helps advocates to know which governmental or legislative bodies they will approach.

How many people have the problem and who are they?   Is the problem or need increasing over time? Of those with the problem, what proportion are male and female? What age range, ethnicity, and social class do they tend to be? Are there other important demographic characteristics that should be pointed out?

How long has the specific need existed?   What is the history of the problem? How long does the problem last? Has the nature of the problem changed over time?

What are the consequences of this problem?   This is very important information because being able to describe what will happen if the problem is not addressed, its consequences for individuals and communities, can be very persuasive and can move people toward action. Sometimes advocates will need to consult with experts or read the professional literature in order to answer this question. A similar question is why is the condition that you've identified undesirable? This is the point at which you want to mount the evidence that the problem you've identified is a bad thing in need of our attention. Just because advocates documented that hundreds of youth are commingled in jails with adults doesn't mean that it's a problem. Just because advocates are concerned about the situation doesn't mean others will be. This is the "So what?" question. *So what* if kids are commingled with adults in jails? What bad things are likely to happen in the short run and the long run? What's so harmful? What is it about your problem that is likely to make people feel angry, uncomfortable, guilty, impassioned, discontent, and irritated? It's easy to leave out this information because it seems so obvious to members of the helping professions, but the human and social costs are not always obvious to decision makers.

Research and Critical Thinking

Part of this task involves the pulling together of information and statistics, while another part involves clear, analytical thinking. It's hard to say which is more difficult. Experience shows that advocates rarely find the exact data they want. Frequently, advocates have to make do with incomplete information, statistics that may be a little out of date, data that was not collected in a systematic manner, or estimates. In these cases, advocates are advised to use multiple sources of information. Also, when relevant statistics can't be found, seek estimates from well-known community experts. Quoting key informants can be a very useful technique.

Identifying the lack of funding (or underfunding) as the problem is frequently done but not advised. First, the lack of resources is so universal in human services it doesn't tend to capture policymakers' attention. Everyone is seeking more funding. Second, advocates seek funding for their proposed solution, but the identification and description of the solution should be addressed first. Third, identifying a lack of resources does not really tell policymakers what needs to be done to solve the problem.

Statement of the Problem

At this point, advocates should develop a problem statement. It is wise to develop the problem statement in at least two forms. One would be a well-organized statement that includes all the information gathered above, a research paper. The second should be a short, crisp, hard-hitting paragraph or two that captures the essence of the problem. The latter is recommended because when lobbying, advocates sometimes have only 30 seconds to explain their issue. Brief statements are also useful when dealing with the media. The draft of the problem statement, in both forms, can be used to start building a coalition to work on this issue.

Prevalent Beliefs

The second set of questions to be addressed in this stage involves analyzing how policymakers and the public think about the issue. What ideas, beliefs, attitudes, values, or myths support the existence of the problem or get in the way of change? What is the attitude of the general public toward the problem? What is the attitude toward the problem in the system where the problem occurs? As discussed in chapter 7, "Community Advocacy," answering these questions will help prepare advocates to combat the status quo.

Solutions

The final set of questions in this stage involves learning what can be done about the problem or need. Have any communities found ways to prevent the problem effectively or to address the need? Are there successful interventions to help people resolve the problem or need?

Private foundations and the federal government frequently fund pilot or demonstration projects to develop innovative programs. When these are found to be effective, advocates will often attempt to have that program replicated in their area. It is often the case that other states have confronted the issue of concern to advocates and have created policies and programs that are meeting with success. Advocates need to research these and understand the circumstances under which they work and the costs. When advocates eventually propose new policies or programs they'll need to be ready to answer the usual first question "How much does it cost?"

The World Wide Web can provide great assistance to advocates during the homework stage. Annual reports and service statistics are frequently a part of an agency's homepage, as well as demographic information. The Web can be particularly useful when researching possible solutions to the identified problem. Federal agencies often include information on their Web sites about model programs they have funded, along with evaluation and outcome studies. This is also an excellent tool for finding out what other states have been doing to address similar client needs.

Prevention or Remediation?   At this point, advocates may need to make a strategic decision. They may need to choose whether they will seek solutions to prevent the problem of concern, remediate it, or attempt to advocate for both prevention and remediation. This is a perplexing challenge because in most situations, and without intending to be cynical, even if effective preventive measures are taken, some people will still have the problem and will need remediation. For example, effective drug abuse prevention and awareness programs could proliferate the land, but, unfortunately, some people would still abuse drugs and need treatment.

So, both approaches are necessary. Advocates will need to make a somewhat political assessment of what's possible given the problem and solution they've identified, their time and resources, and the agency and legislative context within which they'll work.

ESTABLISHING ADVOCACY TARGETS

After doing the homework that enables an in-depth understanding of the specific client problem, looking for preventive and remedial approaches, and deciding on the goal solution, the next stage involves deciding on the specific targets for change. According to Richan (1991), "Knowing what one wants sounds simple, but it is a step which is all too frequently ignored in advocacy" (p. 36). Advocates must ask themselves what needs to change to resolve this problem or meet this need. Taylor's (1987) particular framing of the question is also helpful, "Where will the advocacy group intervene in the system?" (p. 100). Obviously, there are a large number of answers to this question, but what advocates are looking for here are the targets that advocacy can impact.

Advocacy is an intervention that is capable of altering policies, practices, programs, and funding. Advocates must be familiar with the advocacy strategies outlined in chapters 4 through 7 to complete this stage of homework (which is why this chapter comes after those). Again, a series of questions will help to narrow the search. This stage of homework, just like the one above, requires some digging. The answers produced during this stage put advocates in the position of being able to decide whether they'll use agency, legislative, or legal advocacy strategies.

One of the first things to establish in narrowing the list of possible targets is which agency has (or should have) responsibility for the problem or need. Most agencies are set up to deal with particular issues or client populations (e.g., mental health, elderly services). Once advocates can focus in on one or two agencies, they should ask a series of questions. Will a change or addition to the laws governing the agency and its programs solve the problem? If so, it is very important to identify the specific statutory language that needs to be deleted, added, or changed. According to Kettner, Daley, and Nichols (1985), "Lack of precision in defining the target can set up almost insurmountable odds and can lead to defeat" (p. 69). Whether the answer is "yes" or "no," the next question should be whether a change in the agency's funding will solve the problem or meet the need. Certainly, if advocates seek to implement a new program for their clients or wish to expand an existing program, the advocacy target will be the agency's budget or the process that develops and approves its budget. With the implementation of new programs, it is frequently the case that both funding and statutory change are necessary.

The problem of concern may not derive from statutes or funding but agency regulations and practices. Advocates who determine this to be the case will pursue change either through formal rule-making processes or by persuading agency executives to alter their practices. As mentioned above, once regulations or practices are pinpointed as points of intervention, advocates need to be very clear about the changes they desire in existing regulations, programs, and agency practices.

In summary, advocacy can be directed effectively toward numerous targets. Chapters 4 through 7 covering the four major advocacy strategies discussed in detail the types of targets each strategy could change effectively. Knowing all of these will help advocates as they investigate where to intervene and at which targets to aim their change efforts.

MAPPING THE DECISION SYSTEM

The next phase of homework involves gathering information regarding the decision system in which the change effort will play out. For example, if advocates decide that a change in a law is needed to help clients, this stage focuses on the process for changing a law. On the other hand, if an agency's program needs to be modified to fit client needs better, the focus is on the process for getting an agency to change a program. This involves gathering information to "map" the decision system. The concept of mapping the system is borrowed from Fernandez (1980), in which she raises the question, "Who controls the decision making?" (p. 75).

One question with multiple parts leads advocates to the necessary information: What tasks need to occur to change the advocacy target, when, and by whom? The first part of the question asks what needs to happen. In the example of changing a law, the answer would be that proposed legislation needs to be drafted, introduced, and passed by the legislative body. In this example alone, one can see that there may be several tasks associated with each step of the decision-making process, and for advocates to be successful they need to understand the steps in detail. When seeking a change in a program, what needs to happen is that program staff needs to be convinced to make the desired changes. This will probably involve meeting with them, sharing concerns, and proposing a solution. Advocates need to find out with which staff to meet to document the issues and develop one or more solutions.

The next question is critical: When do the tasks and all subsequent tasks need to be completed? Advocates must have in-depth understanding of when certain actions need to occur, because timing is critical in advocacy. Strategies and tactics are designed around this information. With proposed legislation, bills can be introduced after specified dates but before an agreed-upon cutoff date. When a bill is referred to a legislative committee for review, there is usually a deadline by which the bill has to be voted out of committee. All of these different deadlines create opportunities for advocates to intervene with and on behalf of their clients. The next chapter will discuss a hypothetical case example of an advocacy campaign that seeks to secure funding for a new program. As will be shown, the budget development, approval, and implementation process has numerous steps at which advocates can intervene to accomplish their objectives.

When should advocates meet with agency staff to seek programmatic changes? This is a more difficult question to answer. It may depend on how substantial or controversial the changes are and whether they have budgetary implications. If the proposed changes will require additional funding, it may be wise to meet with staff while they are planning next year's budget. In other cases, the problems advocates are trying to eradicate may be so harmful to clients that efforts to meet with staff should begin immediately.

Determining who makes and contributes to the critical decisons is the fourth question to address. To continue the above example, legislators sponsor proposed changes, but as we know, the drafting of the proposal, as well as a lot of the work involved in getting it passed, may be carried out by advocates. Depending on the decision system, advocates themselves can carry out certain tasks (e.g., make an appointment with an agency executive, file a lawsuit), while in other cases only specific individuals can accomplish the task. In the latter case, these individuals will notify advocates with whom they need to work and who they need to influence. When public officials carry out the task, advocates need to do background research on the person and learn a good way to gain access to him or her. Questions such as the following might be pursued: what are this person's goals and priorities; what is the person's background; do any advocates know the person; and has the person made any public statement on the issue of concern?

The final question to ask in order to map the decision system is to determine who and what are the sources of resistance or opposition to the proposed changes. By asking this question, advocates can ascertain how much opposition they'll encounter and from where it will come, placing them in a better position to plan accordingly.

SELECTING STRATEGIES AND TACTICS

Strong consensus among advocates advises that collaborative, nonconfrontational strategies should be attempted first before advocates resort to other, more confrontational approaches. There are many good reasons to heed this advice. One reason is that success through collaboration makes everyone involved look good, and advocates make allies for future efforts. This is the approach by which everyone wins. Conversely, confrontational strategies rarely win friends because distinct lines are drawn and someone loses. A second reason to exhaust collaborative tactics first is that they usually require fewer resources to implement. Since advocates tend to spread their resources too thinly, the most prudent use of time, energy, funds, and volunteers is highly recommended. The third reason is related to the second in that collaborative tactics tend to get faster results than confrontational tactics. This is because confrontational tactics are applied when advocates meet with resistance, and any time proposed changes are being resisted, the advocacy effort is a longer, uphill battle. Kettner, Daley, and Nichols (1985) further suggest that confrontational strategies frequently become an issue themselves and will draw attention away from the real issues. They also point out that solutions achieved collaboratively tend to last.

The process of identifying advocacy targets discussed above makes the selection of the overall strategy somewhat straightforward. If a law needs to be changed, created, or repealed, or if funding needs to be increased or shifted, legislative and community advocacy are the strategies of choice. If agency rules, practices, or programs need to be changed, created, or repealed, agency and community advocacy are the strategies to use. Legal advocacy should be chosen largely when the needed change must take place in the judicial arena. Complementary community education tactics should also be used.

Compromise

As advocates debate the strategies that might be used, it is also a good time to discuss compromise. Are we willing to compromise, and if so on which details? This discussion, although very challenging, needs to occur before advocates are in a position in which they might have to make very quick decisions. As Coates (1989) aptly points out:

> The act of compromise, a much maligned art, has a place in advocacy. It is often said, "Why settle for half a loaf?" The question is "Would you settle for three quarters?" And even half a loaf may be far better than a crumb. (p. 271)

Many advocates don't even like to whisper the word *compromise*. Another way to approach this is to consider optimal and acceptable short-term, mid-term, and long-term outcomes. Besides the decision about whether to compromise, it is also important to think about when to compromise. Advice easily given but hard to define and implement is to try not to compromise too early in the change process. The longer advocates can go without giving up something they want, the greater their chances are of getting it. Compromising takes aspects of the proposed solution off the table of negotiations and, once this has occurred, it is very difficult to put them back on.

SUMMARY

This chapter has taken advocates through several of the steps involved in doing advocacy homework. Techniques to conduct advocacy needs assessments were discussed, as were a series of questions advocates can use to understand clients' needs. The next section of the chapter presented methods of establishing advocacy targets, or the specific change objective.

The latter part of the chapter discussed the process of mapping the decision system, whereby advocates gain an understanding of how the decisions they need to influence are made. Understanding the decision system leads advocates to the points of intervention, the tactics needed to intervene and influence decisions, and the appropriate timing for those tactics. The chapter concluded with a discussion of how to choose strategies and the reasons for which we generally lean toward collaborative approaches.

Discussion Questions

1. Make four lists of possible advocacy targets. One list should include those targets for which agency advocacy is recommended, one for legislative advocacy, one for legal advocacy, and the last for community advocacy.
2. List three possible sources for information regarding client needs in your community. Where might a list of such sources be available?
3. If you identified three pressing, unmet needs of clients in your community, what factors would you examine and how would you decide on which to focus?

ISSUES, DILEMMAS, AND CHALLENGES

CHAPTER 9   PUTTING THE ADVOCACY PIECES TOGETHER
CHAPTER 10   ADVOCACY SKILLS, CHALLENGES, AND PRACTICE
             GUIDELINES

Chapter 9 presents a case study that includes three advocacy strategies and numerous tactics. In order to create a new program, advocates follow and impact the state budget process from the time state agencies prepare their proposals through the legislative session and back to agency implementation.

Chapter 10 discusses critical advocacy skills and attitudes needed with all strategies and tactics. Knowledgeable and skillful advocates will be less than effective, however, unless they maintain certain attitudes regarding their work. There are many challenges advocates will face as they promote change for their clients. Those are discussed here, and methods to avoid these stumbling blocks are described as well. Finally, a set of advocacy practice guidelines is proposed.

CHAPTER 9

PUTTING THE ADVOCACY PIECES TOGETHER

CHAPTER OBJECTIVES

By the time you finish studying this chapter, you should
1. Grasp the critical nature of the homework stage.
2. Understand how the process of the decision system impacts the timing of tactics.
3. Be familiar with the overlap and interdependency of advocacy strategies.
4. Appreciate the significance and centrality of funding to help clients.

The centerpiece of this chapter is a case study in which advocates see the need for a new program and want to advocate for funding in the state budget. The process will start with the identification of the issue and move on to the use of agency advocacy to persuade the relevant state agency to include the new program in its funding request. The case study will follow the funding process to the governor's office and through the legislative process. Opportunities for community advocacy tactics and legislative advocacy will also be identified throughout the study. Tactics used to avoid a gubernatorial veto are described, and, finally, advocacy measures needed to monitor agency implementation of the new program are discussed.

The case will be as realistic as possible, but to avoid repetitiveness and excessive length, it will lack detail in certain spots. For example, it would be nearly impossible to reproduce all the nuances and relationships of the legislative process. Advocates have existing relationships with certain legislators and other policymakers, both good and bad, which influence tactics. Advocates are usually working on more than one issue during a legislative session and tactics on one issue influence other efforts. For example, it may not be wise to ask the same legislator repeatedly to offer the advocates' amendments or points of view. Those sorts of details won't be included in the case study. Also, the discussion of planning the advocacy effort is kept brief in order to maintain an emphasis on action.

The purpose of this chapter is to show how all of the advocacy strategies discussed in this book might fit together in a change effort. The case study also illuminates how critical timing is in an advocacy campaign.

Doing Their Advocacy Homework

Several separate pieces of information have made advocates aware that child protective services is not functioning as effectively as possible. The Department of Social Services' (DSS) quarterly statistical summaries report the number of child abuse and neglect reports for all of the state's service regions as well as the number that were validated once investigations were completed. With these two numbers, a validation rate can be calculated. Advocates notice that in several regions, including Region 5, in which there is a large and active group of child advocates, the percentage of validated cases has been declining over the last two years. When informal questions are raised with workers, many of them talk about how the increasing abuse of drugs and alcohol, as well as other societal factors, is causing cases to be more complex. The statistical summaries also show that a low percentage of cases are referred for criminal prosecution and, of those, the conviction rate is low.

There had also been a couple of recent, unfortunate, and widely publicized cases in Region 5 that came to the attention of advocates. Investigative journalists found that in several cases regarding badly abused children, incidents had been reported to the DSS early on, but little or nothing had been done. The earlier incidents were not considered serious enough by themselves to remove the children from the home. Different staff from different agencies conducted the investigations of later incidents and were unaware of the previous reports or investigations. Advocates also found that training was inadequate, and very little social service experience or knowledge was required for a child protection job. Expert social workers consulted about these cases observed that several of the alleged child victims appeared to be somewhat traumatized by the experience of numerous investigatory interviews from child protection, law enforcement, medical personnel, and investigators from the prosecutor's office.

Advocacy Ideals Contradicted

This unfortunate situation seems to be inconsistent with several advocacy ideals. Certainly, every child has a right to live and develop in nonabusive circumstances. Children will have a difficult time pursuing their potential if they continue to be subjected to abuse and neglect. Clearly, the failure of social service programs to coordinate their efforts to investigate and intervene in abusive or neglectful families is having negative ramifications for children.

Creating a Core Team of Advocates

The publication of a series of articles in the local newspaper caught the attention of many individuals including teachers, social workers, nurses, pediatricians, assistant prosecutors, a juvenile judge, and numerous volunteers active in children's issues. Two social workers who work for a local nonprofit children's agency decided that something needs to be improved in order to avoid more of these situations. They seek an appointment with the juvenile judge who was quoted in one of the articles as having said that she's very concerned. They hope she'll lend her name to an organizing effort to look for and advocate for solutions. Initially, they'd like her to help identify a few others who could serve as the core leadership group for this effort. Eventually, they hope she'll be willing to sponsor a community forum to familiarize concerned citizens (both directly and through the media) with the problem and potential solutions and to energize and mobilize an advocacy effort. They have one more item on the agenda for the judge. They want her to call their supervisor, the executive director of the agency, to request that these two social workers' caseloads be temporarily reduced while they work on this issue.

The social workers meet with the judge and are totally successful with their agenda, including being released from regular duties to work on this issue. A meeting of the core group is scheduled, and, in the meantime, the social workers pull together the quarterly data from the DSS and other relevant materials in order to develop a problem statement. They work on a meeting agenda that has very clear outcome objectives. The judge volunteered to meet with the Region 5 administrator to find out if the DSS is concerned and if they have any plans to address this issue. The judge told the social workers that she didn't want the regional administrator to feel ambushed by the core group, and that the best case scenario would be for the regional administrator to be part of the coalition that works on this issue.

Preliminary Agency Advocacy

When the judge meets with the regional administrator, she takes one of the social workers with her because the social worker is very familiar with child protective services and recent statistics. The regional administrator brings the coordinator of child welfare services to the meeting. The discussion is very constructive, and the judge learns that the regional administrator is aware of the problem of declining validation and prosecution rates and that investigations are not well coordinated. The administrator hopes to request funding for solutions in next year's budget but does not know what form those will take. Certainly, an increase in training funds will be requested. The judge thanks the regional administrator for his time and openness and expresses her optimism that they can work together on a solution. The regional administrator volunteers the coordinator to work with the two social workers to look for solutions; he suggests that other states may have faced similar problems and their solutions could be useful in this state.

Drafting a Problem Statement

The judge asks the social workers to draft a problem statement in preparation for the meeting of the core group. She thinks this will focus the discussion and facilitate consensus among the different leaders on the nature and extent of the problem. She says that this is an essential first step. The draft problem statement is shown in Figure 9.1. The problem statement indicates that the population of concern is children in Region 5 who are alleged or actual victims

---

DRAFT

Cases of alleged child abuse and neglect are becoming more complex to investigate and validate. The validation and prosecution rates in Region 5 have declined significantly over the last two years. In the first quarter of 1996, there were 1,500 reports of child abuse and 61.5% eventually were validated. In the first quarter of 1998, there were 1,683 reports and 47% were validated, a very significant decline.

The decline of validation rate creates situations in which children are unprotected, some children remain in abusive and neglecting families, needed services are not made available to the family, or perpetrators may go unpunished.

Due to the lack of coordination and communication among investigators, they are left unaware of earlier reports and incidents in many families. Children needlessly are interviewed multiple times because the various agencies are not communicating with each other. In addition, it does not appear that the caseworkers who investigate reports of abuse have substantial, relevant experience and knowledge of all the sequela of abuse and neglect.

DRAFT

FIGURE **9.1**

Draft problem statement.

of child abuse or neglect and their families. The potential consequences if this problem continues to be unaddressed and unsolved are that these children may be subject to more abuse, services to support the family will not be made available, and the most serious perpetrators will remain unprosecuted.

The judge, the two social workers, the assistant prosecutor for juvenile matters, a pediatrician, and two citizen volunteers attend the meeting of the core group. The judge facilitates the meeting, and after introductions are made, they start to discuss the newspaper articles and the statistics gathered by the social workers. Lots of questions are asked, and each person is given a chance to tell his or her stories. The judge distributes the draft problem statement and asks if it seems to summarize the problem that has been identified in Region 5. In order to avoid writing by committee, the judge announces that this will be considered a working document and that the social workers will make notes of the discussion, but they should also be contacted after the meeting regarding suggested changes. Everyone agrees that the statement will suffice for the time being but may need to be updated after more information is collected.

Case or Class Advocacy?

The assistant prosecutor offers, and the judge agrees, that the problem is not restricted to a case here and there but is, instead, systemic. She also observes that there isn't anything in the relevant state laws to account for the declines in validation rates, so the group will need to look elsewhere for a solution. The group makes one immediate decision and plans the next two steps. First, they all agree that the problem is too large to use a case advocacy approach. Second, there is consensus that if the problem is to be solved, they must propose a concrete solution, which will require more homework. Third, they need to mobilize concerned professionals and citizens about the problem. They decide to hold a community forum at which information about the problem will be presented and discussed. In addition, the social workers are asked to do research on potential solutions and to be in touch with the Region 5 coordinator of child welfare services for assistance.

Researching Solutions

The social workers have a brief meeting with the coordinator and then begin talking to local and national child welfare experts, from whom they learn that many communities throughout the country have had similar problems. One very common and effective response is to organize a multidisciplinary team to investigate reports of child abuse and neglect. The teams frequently include physicians, social workers, nurses, psychologists, and law enforcement officers.

All of these professionals work together to investigate reports; collectively, they have the specific professional training necessary to sort through the complexities of families and incidents of abuse and neglect. Not only do the teams conduct investigations, but many of them also have taken on the responsibility of interagency coordination so resources are used efficiently, agencies know what each other agency is doing, and children are not traumatized by excessive interviewing. The social workers gather as much information as they can on multidisciplinary teams, how they work, how much they cost, as well as evaluation studies. All of this information is compiled and delivered to the juvenile judge.

Selecting Advocacy Targets

The juvenile judge is persuaded that the creation of a multidisciplinary team in Region 5 is the way to address the problems they are documenting, and she calls another meeting of the core group of advocates to discuss this. The group is very pleased to support this solution. The judge and assistant prosecutor contribute that they don't think state statutes need to be changed, because multidisciplinary teams can be created and operated at the discretion of the DSS. They have the program design in hand; all they need is the funding. They have estimated, based on the experiences of other communities, that it will cost approximately $300,000 per year to operate a multidisciplinary team in Region 5. Now they need to understand how the decision-making process works so they can influence it.

Mapping the Decision System

Knowing that the regional office of the DSS needs funding to implement the new program and that no funds are currently available, the advocates study the state's budget process and decision-making structure. This informs them about who makes decisions related to social service funding and when those decisions are made. If the region requests the funds for this new program, the central office and secretary of the DSS will have to be in agreement to send this new program request to the governor. Figure 9.2 shows, step-by-step, the process of getting funding approved for a new state program.

As shown on the left side of Figure 9.2, the region begins to plan its budget for the following fiscal year (FY 2002—July 1, 2001 to June 30, 2002) in the beginning of the current fiscal year (FY 2001—July 1, 2000 to June 30, 2001). They might use a variety of techniques to assess needs, get input, and project funding needs for the following year, and they know that their budget request is due in the central office of agency headquarters by September 1, 2000. The central office will provide the regions with planning guidelines,

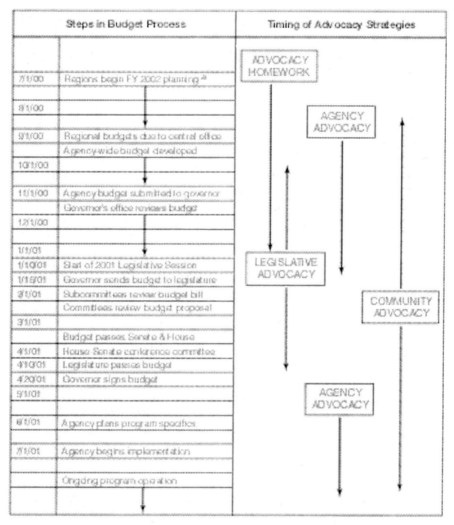

ª The Agency is planning for FY 2002 that begins on July 1, 2001 and ends on June 30, 2002. The planning for FY 2002 takes place during FY 2001 (July 1, 2000 through June 30, 2001).

FIGURE **9.2**

Timeline for agency budget development, approval, and implementation.

including priorities, caseload projections, and budget targets. In addition, the regional administrator will present a draft of the proposed budget to the Citizen Advisory Board in mid-August for their feedback. The social workers obtain a list of the members from the regional office.

During the next step, staff at DSS headquarters review all the requests from the regions, prioritize, and prepare the budget that will be forwarded for the governor's consideration. The highest ranking child welfare person at headquarters will have a lot of input regarding whether to include funding for the multidisciplinary team, and, finally, the secretary of the DSS will decide on the agency's proposed budget. That proposed budget is due to the governor by November 1, 2000. The secretary of the DSS does not plan for any formal public input.

The governor's Office of Financial Management (OFM) reviews all the state agency budgets to see what may or may not be consistent with the governor's priorities and policy directives. Just like the central office of the DSS, the OFM sends budget guidelines and priorities to all state agencies. This staff will begin to see if the sum total of all departmental budgets will exceed the revenue projections for the next fiscal year. This is almost always the case, and they will begin recommending reductions in proposed budgets. There is a time when the staff of OFM are in frequent contact with DSS staff, clarifying and refining budget requests, solving problems, revising projections, and, in some cases, negotiating.

As part of the budget preparation process, the governor schedules hearings at which each agency director has an opportunity to present his or her agency's budget proposals and priorities, but no formal public hearings are scheduled. The governor's recommended budget for FY 2002 is due to the legislature on January 15th, 2001, and he will hold a press conference on that day to announce his budget proposals.

Upon receipt of the governor's budget, the House and Senate send it to their budget committees for analysis and consideration. Both of these committees are further divided into subcommittees. In the House, the Subcommittee on Social Services does the initial work on the budget for the DSS. In the Senate, the Subcommittee on Corrections and Human Services has similar responsibilities and is responsible for the budget for the Department of Corrections. Both subcommittees will hold hearings and will report their recommendations to the full Budget Committees by their deadlines. The House and Senate Budget Committees will also hold hearings to review the budgets. By this point in time, the budgets will be in the form of draft legislation.

The House and Senate committees and subcommittees may be working on different time lines, and it may also be the case that the respective subcommittees will make different recommendations regarding the funding of the multidisciplinary team. This could range from one house recommending full funding to the other house deleting this proposal from the bill. It could also mean that both subcommittees have deleted it, or both have included it, but at different funding levels.

Once one or both Budget Committees vote these bills out, they are officially filed as proposed legislation and are given bill numbers. It usually does not take long before at least one of the bills will go to the floor of its respective house for a vote. When a bill is on the floor for consideration, there will be extensive debate, many amendments will be offered, and, eventually, one house will pass its budget.[29] Given the politics and diversity of interests and priorities, it should not be a surprise to learn that House and Senate budgets are never the same, and some items are excluded or funded at a very low level as part of strategies to compromise and trade for other items. Inevitably, when nearing the end of the session, a budget conference committee of a few senators and representatives will be named to negotiate the differences between the House and Senate budgets. The governor's original budget recommendations will be reflected differently in each version, and lobbyists from the governor's office, among others, will be working hard to influence the conference committee. Once the conference committee completes its compromise budget bill, the bill will go to each house for a vote. Usually, no amendments are allowed and the bill will be approved.

During this process, legislative staff usually produce documents that compare the governor's budget to that of the House and Senate. These are very helpful, and advocates should study them closely. Note, however, that the process moves very quickly in the late stages of the legislative session, and documents can be out of date by the time they're printed.

Once approved by both the House and Senate, the bill becomes the Budget Act and goes to the governor for review and approval. The governor has three options, which must be exercised within 10 days of receiving the approved legislation: (1) sign the bill as is; (2) veto the bill in total; or (3) use a line-item veto to delete certain items and then sign the bill. The governor does not have the authority to add anything to the Budget Act, but under certain circumstances, an agency may use its funds to pay for items not included in the Budget Act. If the governor vetoes the Budget Act, the legislature will either override the veto or compromise with the governor and send him a new Budget Act to review. If the governor signs the new Budget Act, with or without line-item vetoes, it becomes law, and state agencies are expected to implement it.

Planning the Advocacy Effort

The core group of advocacy leaders meets several times to discuss the strategies available to them, and how and by whom they'll be implemented. They do not view legal advocacy as a viable approach at this point but they don't rule it out as a future possibility. They draft Plan A as best they can given the information available to them at the moment and the numerous uncertainties with which they must struggle. They discuss alternative action plans in case their

---

29. A common scenario in the author's experience is the following: one of the houses passes its budget and sends it to the other house for consideration; that house, whose budget is done or almost done, amends its budget onto the bill, approves it, and sends it back to the first house for approval; the first house does not approve it, and a conference committee is appointed to work out compromises.

initial efforts are blocked at critical points, and they discuss whether and how much they might be willing to compromise. They decide that the multidisciplinary team can't operate on less than $150,000 per year and maintain an acceptable level of service quality. All too often, they have seen the legislature tell the DSS to start a new program with existing funds, only to witness these efforts stall and fail. On the one hand, they agree that this isn't acceptable. On the other hand, they know that the effort to get funding for a multidisciplinary team in Region 5 might take on a life of its own, and these decisions will be out of their hands. For example, if they find a legislator to champion their cause, he or she will likely be in a position to negotiate the amount of funding, and the advocates may not be able to influence their champion.

AGENCY ADVOCACY

The core group thinks that the judge, the assistant prosecutor, and one of the social workers should visit the regional administrator in mid-July and propose that he include a funding request for a multidisciplinary team in the next state budget. They know that the coordinator of child welfare services likes the idea because she and the social workers have been working together on the background research. When the judge requests the meeting, she suggests that the regional administrator include the coordinator.

The meeting begins with the judge thanking the regional administrator for taking time to meet and, also, for all the cooperation and good work of the coordinator. The judge briefly reviews the problem statement and supporting statistics with the regional administrator and adds that they have done a great deal of research and have found an excellent solution, one that has been successfully implemented in many other communities. The social worker has prepared a handout on multidisciplinary teams that is explained and reviewed. The regional administrator seems impressed, but his remarks are cautious. Finally, the judge very specifically states, "We would like you to include funding for a Region 5 multidisciplinary team in your proposed FY 2002 budget. We have begun to develop a network of advocates who have agreed to support such a request with the secretary of the DSS, the governor, and the legislature. Do you think we can work together on this to do a better job protecting children and supporting families in our community?"

The regional administrator, ever the politician, said he was impressed by all the background work that had been done and, as he had previously, acknowledged the problem of declining validation rates and what he referred to as "the seemingly uncoordinated investigations of alleged abuse and neglect." He indicated that he would like to work together to solve the problem, but it was too early in the region's budget planning process for him to commit to including this proposal. He said, "We are gathering necessary data to project caseloads and identify major gaps in services. After that we will set priorities for funding and align them with the priorities given to us by the central office. There are so many high-priority needs, it will be difficult to address them all, and other interest groups will also be pressuring us for funding. We'll just have to wait and see."

More Planning

The core group holds a meeting after the conference with the regional administrator to debrief and plan their next steps. Everyone agrees that the meeting turned out as expected. They would have been surprised if the regional administrator had committed himself to the proposal after hearing it for the first time. They decide that the regional administrator needs to know that there is wide support for the idea in the community. They also decide on several other actions to take. They realize that they need the support of the secretary and central office of the DSS as well as the governor, whether the funding is included in the region's budget or not, and they should start working on that. They also decide to begin their legislative advocacy at the same time they are doing agency advocacy by scheduling meetings with their state representatives and senator. If any or all of their local legislative delegation is supportive, they will ask them to call the regional administrator to voice their support and to encourage him to include funding in his budget request. (More legislative advocacy tactics will be discussed in that subsection.)

Advocacy Network

The group agrees on several new action steps. First, they need to increase the number of people in the network of advocates who are concerned about child abuse and are supportive of the multidisciplinary team approach. They especially need to expand the membership to include others besides those traditionally thought of as involved in human service issues. The group brainstorms the names of influential businesspersons in the community who might be willing to participate. A phone call or letter at the right time from a bank president, for example, would be extremely helpful.

Coalition

Second, the core advocacy group decides to proceed with the formation of a coalition that will work together to gain the necessary funding. The coalition should be comprised of organizations that will lend their name to the cause, contribute time and money to the effort, and cover all aspects of the political spectrum—from conservative to liberal. They especially want to involve organizations that employ lobbyists. Again, the group spends some time thinking of potential coalition members. They prioritize the list and determine who in the group has a contact in the organization. That person is expected to initiate a conversation with his or her contact person, which, hopefully, will lead to coalition membership.

The judge worried out loud about a challenge the group will face in the future. The legislative subcommittees that will review the budgets are comprised of legislators who do not live in Region 5. Of course, it can work well for citizens in Region 5 to contact these legislators, because as public officials they serve the entire state, but she feels their chances might be better if some of these legislators' own constituents would lobby for the proposal. This group, however, doesn't have the means to organize networks in these other districts. Several ideas were suggested. The judge, prosecutor, and social workers all have colleagues in these other areas who could be contacted and whose help could be solicited. They are all members of state associations that have lobbyists, whose support could be sought. The pediatrician volunteered to find out if any of these legislators received campaign contributions from a pediatricians' political action committee and, also, to locate the chair of each relevant district's legislative committee. Every member of the core group was asked to think of people they know in the districts of those legislators serving on relevant subcommittees. Also, everyone who will be attending a state conference was asked to seek out colleagues from these districts to add to their growing mailing list.

As soon as possible, the core group wants members of the network and organizations in the coalition to write letters and make phone calls of support to the regional administrator, the secretary of the DSS, the governor, and local legislators. It is important to let these policymakers know early in the budget process that broad concern about child abuse exists in the region and strong support for funding of a multidisciplinary team is present. The judge serves on the region's advisory group and agrees to call the chairperson and lobby her to support the proposal. With the chair's permission, they will send materials to all the members of the advisory group.

The highest priority at this time is getting the funding proposal in the regional budget. In order to lay some groundwork but not inundate the secretary and the governor too early in the process, only a few letters will be sent at this time. The core group thinks it is a good idea to meet with the governor as soon as possible, so they'll be looking for possible times to do this. It's not easy to get an appointment with the governor, even a very short one, so they need to think about who they know that might be able to help them gain access.

More Action

The judge has a productive conversation with the chairperson of the advisory group and mails the other members the problem statement and proposal for a multidisciplinary team. Numerous letters have been sent to the regional administrator encouraging him to include funding for a multidisciplinary team in the region's budget proposal. One of the local legislators, Representative Jones, is particularly interested and agrees to be supportive. She calls the regional administrator to discuss the matter and further encourages him to include funds for a team.

At the meeting of the advisory group, the regional administrator presents the nearly finished budget. It is divided into three parts: (1) ongoing programs, which includes existing programs budgeted for projected increases in case-loads; (2) improved programs, which includes funds for certain program expansions and modifications; and (3) new programs, which includes, among other things, the $300,000 proposal for a mulitidisciplinary team. Members of the advisory group ask numerous questions and express their support for the proposed budget. They ask the regional administrator what they can do to help support his budget in general and the multidisciplinary team in particular. He gives them several ideas and shares his concerns about the prospects of getting the team funded. He explains that when revenues are tight, the first part of the proposed budget to be reduced or eliminated will be new programs. He thinks that it is essential for the central office to reframe the request and present it as an improved program. The governor has, in the past, directed that proposed budgets include no new programs but hasn't indicated whether this is neces-sary this year. Based on current state revenue projections, the regional admin-istrator thinks that is a likely scenario.

The regional administrator's second concern is that the secretary of the DSS usually doesn't like one region to have a program that other regions don't have. He says that he will speak with the secretary directly and propose a strat-egy that includes pilot testing three multidisciplinary teams in the state and evaluating them before implementing the program on a statewide basis. Besides Region 5, he thinks it would be smart to propose a team for the respective regions of the legislators who chair the budget subcommittees, Regions 8 and 12. This way, they might become advocates for the proposal and protect the funding. He estimates that approximately $1 million will be need-ed to establish teams in the three regions and for the evaluation.

Letter Writing

The advocates in Region 5 quickly mobilize for letter writing. They are now focusing on the secretary of the DSS. They emphasize two things in their let-ters: (1) the problems documented in Region 5; and (2) their support for pilot testing multidisciplinary teams in three regions of the state. Copies of the let-ters are sent to the state director of child welfare services as well as the head-quarters' budget analyst responsible for child welfare. Representative Jones calls the secretary to inquire about the possibility that $1 million could be ear-marked in the DSS's budget for this purpose.

All of the feedback from the secretary indicates an openness to consider this idea. The Region 5 advocates continue to make phone calls, write letters, and visit as many policymakers as possible. (See the Legislative Advocacy subsection for parallel activities.) They are also spending time building and training a network of advocates and contacting organizations that might wish to join the coalition. They feel lucky to have the regional administrator as an ally, for he is being somewhat of an inside advocate as he lobbies departmental officials and provides the core group with strategic information. The advocates' efforts seem to be paying off. The secretary includes $1 million of funding for the pilot test in three regions; $300,000 for each of the three regions and $100,000 for the evaluation.

The focus now shifts to the governor. The letter writing and phone calling continue. Several influential individuals from Region 5 try to make appointments with the governor. None of them get in to see him, but they do receive phone calls from the governor's chief of staff to find out the purpose for the meeting. In separate calls, they explain their concern about decreasing validation rates and the need for funding improved programs. The chief asks a few questions about the DSS's position on the issue and whether there is any documentation. Luckily, the DSS has already included the funding in its budget, and the problem statement is faxed to the chief of staff. The chief of staff promises to relay the messages to the governor, confer with the budget analyst in charge of the DSS's budget, and offers the governor apologies for not being able to meet due to his busy schedule.

The core group of advocates in Region 5 discusses whether to seek a meeting with the appropriate budget analyst as well as the governor's policy adviser for social services. They decide that a few phone calls will suffice because these individuals are extremely busy, and the director of child welfare will be working with them. The judge and the prosecutor volunteer to inquire about the status of this funding request for improved programs and to make themselves available to answer questions about the problem and how the team will work. They are aware that Representative Jones is working on a bill and that the draft will have been circulated among the governor's staff for review, and they will ask the budget analyst's opinion of it (see below regarding this legislation).

As January 15th approaches—the date the governor submits his proposed budget—the advocates nervously await the news. They know they have the support of the DSS and that Representative Jones has filed legislation to secure the funding. All will not be lost if the governor doesn't include this proposal in his budget, but it will be very helpful if he does. The day before the governor releases his budget, the regional administer calls the judge to inform her of the mixed news. The governor is requesting $750,000 for the pilot programs—$200,000 is for Region 5; $250,000 is for Region 8; $300,000 is for Region 12; and the evaluation is to be conducted out of existing funds. They both label this a partial success and are well aware that the advocacy challenge is far from over.

The core group holds another planning session. They want to thank the secretary and the governor and pledge their support. Since both the DSS and the governor have lobbyists who will be working the budget legislation through the process, the core group decides to contact them so that all lobbying efforts can be coordinated. (Agency Advocacy will continue after Legislative Advocacy.)

COMMUNITY ADVOCACY

Early in the effort, the core group of advocates hold a meeting to discuss how to frame their issue of concern and what ideas they want to stress as they deliver their message. Also, they identify inaccurate stereotypes and misinformation they want to reverse. They examine the ideas, attitudes, misinformation, and imagery that underlie the current situation and how they can be neutralized or reversed. They decide that until the investigative journalists published the findings of their work, it was not well known that validation rates were declining, that the system for investigating reports of abuse and neglect was not well coordinated, and that children, alleged victims of abuse or neglect, could be traumatized by repeated investigatory interviews. The public is unaware of the consequences this malfunctioning system can have on children, families, and communities. By and large, the advocates cannot identify a strong ideology supporting this status quo. They are well aware that there is long-standing controversy surrounding state investigations of child abuse and neglect and an outspoken group protests that the state has no right to judge parenting practices. The advocates agree that they hope to steer clear of this controversy if possible and will monitor their messages carefully. In the main, they agree that the low validation rate is not widely known, and that finding a solution to this problem has not been a priority of the DSS.

Framing the Issues

As they prepare their position paper, train advocates, lobby policymakers, and contact the media, there is a set of ideas they agree they'll try to communicate. First is the fact that many forms of child abuse and neglect are hard to diagnose. Psychologists are needed to assess emotional abuse or neglect, and well-trained physicians are needed to examine alleged victims of abuse and neglect. Further, it is important that these cases are investigated systematically and that evidence is gathered in a manner that will hold up in court. They want to underscore the fact that neglect is more frequent than abuse so they don't create any inaccurate images of the social problem.

Another message they want to convey is that child abuse and neglect frequently occur in families that lack the necessary resources to raise children, and it is often the case that inadequate knowledge about child development and child care are at the root of the family's troubles. Certainly there are cases in which disturbed, predatory individuals abuse children. Multidisciplinary teams should be able to sort out the nature of the situation in each case, which will be of great assistance to the court and social service agencies in deciding how to respond appropriately.

The advocates also want to underscore the efficiency and effectiveness of their proposed approach. Multidisciplinary teams have been operating in many communities throughout the country, and there is substantial evaluative data on the results, costs, and cost savings. In addition, all the significant players at the local level are involved, have endorsed the proposal, and have pledged their support, including the juvenile judge, the prosecutor, several law enforcement agencies, hospitals, local chapters of pediatricians, social workers, psychologists, and nurses.

Editorial Support

The judge volunteered to write an op-ed for the local newspaper but first wants to see if the advocates can meet with the editorial board. If that meeting goes well, they might not need an op-ed. The judge, therefore, proceeds to contact the editor of the editorial page to see if a meeting can be arranged. The call is made, and it turns out that the editor is pleased to have an opportunity to sit down with the juvenile judge and discuss issues of concern. The group's position paper is shared and discussed, and copies of other resources are passed out (e.g., a copy of one of the evaluation studies, names and phone numbers of local and national experts). The advocates attending the meeting respond to several questions, such as "Why is it necessary to spend more money to get these various agencies better coordinated when they should be doing that within existing budgets?" The social worker who attended the meeting explained that it doesn't come naturally for individuals from different agencies to work as a team with a shared philosophy and agreed-upon protocols. A coordinator will facilitate the team and provide training as needed.

The meeting with the editorial board goes well, and the editor indicates that their initial reaction is positive, but they will need to do some research and discuss the matter further. They want to talk to the reporters who wrote the recent articles focusing on the declining validation rates. About a week later, the editor calls the judge to indicate that the paper is willing to help by publishing a supportive editorial. The editor is experienced in these matters and wonders about the best timing for the editorial. Should the paper offer its endorsement while the governor is preparing his budget or wait until the legislature is in session? The judge, thankful for the support, suggests that the paper run the editorial soon and include language that encourages both the govenor and legislature to fund the regional multidisciplinary team.

News Conference

One media tactic the advocates decide to use is to issue a press release the same day the governor holds his news conference to announce his budget proposal. They will prepare two versions, one in case he includes the funding for a multidisciplinary team and one in case he doesn't. They anticipate that reporters will be looking for various groups and individuals to react to the governor's proposal, and by issuing a press release, advocates can notify reporters of their interest in and reaction to the governor's budget proposal. The press release is a very brief statement and includes the names and phone numbers of people the media may contact for more information. The advocates will attempt to find out the details of the budget before it is officially released. If they can get some advance warning that funding will not be included in the governor's budget, their press release will announce a news conference at which they will make their case for funding.

Prior to the legislative session, the advocates will seek out opportunities to appear on public affairs television and radio shows to discuss the issue and their proposal. They will coordinate these efforts with Representative Jones, who is interested in increasing her public exposure and garnering support for this bill.

Workshops

The advocates also plan to offer several workshops for new advocates who have joined their network as well as those contemplating participation. The workshops will focus on several objectives: (1) to increase participants' knowledge of the problem of investigating child abuse and neglect in Region 5; (2) to familiarize advocates with multidisciplinary teams and the specifics of the Region 5 budget proposal; and (3) to teach advocates about the budget and legislative process and how to impact it. Besides these workshops for advocates in Region 5, other members of the core team volunteer to conduct similar workshops at statewide meetings of organizations and associations to which they belong.

LEGISLATIVE ADVOCACY

As is obvious from the subsection on agency advocacy, not only do advocates have to plan ahead for legislative advocacy while doing agency advocacy, but the two overlap considerably. As mentioned above, the core group of advocacy leaders decided to meet with members of the legislative delegation to gain support for funding the multidisciplinary team. They wanted to do this, knowing that the funding request would eventually need legislative approval whether the agency and governor included it in their budgets or not. Another goal of the meeting was to see if one of these legislators might be willing to sponsor a bill to establish and fund a multidisciplinary team in Region 5 on the chance that the governor and secretary did not include it in their budget.

They decide that two people would go to the meetings, someone who has a prior positive relationship with the legislator and a member of the core group, if possible. The judge said she could not attend, but she volunteered her assistant to make the calls requesting appointments, under the assumption that the judge's name and status would help gain entrée and lend credibility to the effort. The social workers prepared an updated problem statement and brief position paper explaining the proposal. They hoped to complete all these appointments by mid- or late August. Part of their reasoning was that if one or more legislators agreed to file a bill with the funding request, and it was filed before the governor completed his budget, this could influence the governor to include the funding.

Meet with Legislators

All of the meetings with legislators went well. Having read the newspaper articles, they all expressed concern about child abuse and appropriate responses to it. Representative Jones, an insurance agent, was especially interested and mentioned that she was very concerned when she read the articles in the paper. She already asked her staff to follow up on it to see what might be done. She does not serve on any of the committees that will review the budgets (which would have been very strategic) but volunteers to provide leadership on this issue. She will explore filing legislation that includes the funding request.

She calls local Senator Smith, a former school board member, to see if he will file a bill in the Senate. He says that he's overcommitted but that a companion bill in the Senate may not be the best strategy. If Representative Jones has success in the House, her bill will eventually be amended into the overall budget bill and won't stand alone. Senator Smith, who serves on the Education subcommittee of the Budget Committee, says that he will help, but his specific strategy will depend on what the governor recommends, and his help will be strictly behind the scenes.

Bill Drafting

In early August, Representative Jones asks one of the staff of the Human Services Committee to draft a bill that directs the DSS to pilot test multidisciplinary teams in three regions (i.e., 5, 8, and 12) and appropriates $1 million of funding for this purpose.[30] After she reviews the first draft—with the assistance of the judge and regional administrator—she requests a few changes, and she specifically asks the staffperson to send the draft to the governor's office and the secretary of the DSS asking them for feedback and their respective positions on such a proposal. In the cover letter, she asks that they include funding in their respective budget requests. She is timing this work so that the secretary and governor know of her interest in this proposal and to increase the chance that they will include funding in their budgets. Although there are risks in this strategy (e.g., if they are opposed, they are given more time to develop reasons to oppose), she opts for this collaborative approach knowing that if the funding is approved over the objections of the DSS, program implementation would suffer.

The secretary sent word to Representative Jones of the DSS's support and the governor's office indicated that it wishes to remain neutral until they are further along in the preparation of their budget.[31] With this news, Representative Jones formally files the legislation and is advised that her bill is HB (House Bill) 555. Shortly thereafter, the Speaker's Office refers HB 555 to the Committee on Children and Youth. If that committee approves it, the bill will go to the Budget Committee.

Monitoring

The advocates have their work cut out for them. They need to monitor and influence three pieces of legislation: (1) the House budget (yet to have a bill number); (2) the Senate budget; and (3) Representative Jones' HB 555. This is where a coalition really pays off. Not only do the governor and the Department of Social Services have lobbyists who will be working this issue, but so do the State Association of Juvenile Court Judges, the State Nurses Association, the Association of Juvenile Prosecutors, and the State Chapter of Social Workers. There is also a statewide child advocacy organization whose assistance will be sought. Representative Jones schedules a meeting of these lobbyists and other involved advocates in early December, at a time when most will be in the state capital for meetings. The purpose of this meeting is to plan and coordinate the lobbying effort.

In late November Representative Jones is informally notified that the governor is likely to include funding for the multidisciplinary teams in the new

---

30. This is a frequently used strategy that draws attention to a specific funding request. Even though the governor's budget proposal may include funding for this purpose, as well as the House and Senate appropriation bills, this is a backup plan. If they don't, and Representative Jones' bill receives positive review, it will eventually be amended into the overall appropriations bill.

31. Frequently, a department such as Social Services will not take a position different than the governor's. In this case, the DSS's favor and the governor's neutrality signals that even if the governor eventually opposes the proposal, they will not put forth strong opposition.

budget. This is great news and will be very useful for the December meeting. There is good attendance at the meeting of coalition lobbyists. They begin with introductions and then spend time reviewing the issue and the proposal for multidisciplinary teams to ensure that everyone has the same information. They share information they have on the work of the budget committees and which one is likely to get into social service funding first, and they make a list of all the legislators who will need to be contacted in the near future. They start with the members of the respective budget subcommittees with responsibility for the DSS's budget, placing subcommittee chairpersons as higher priority than other members. Members of the House Committee on Children and Youth are added to the list, then they add the names of the legislative staff persons who work for these two subcommittees and committee.

After making that list, they go around the room and volunteer for those members and staff each will visit. The lobbyists volunteer to visit those they have worked with in the past, are currently working with on another matter, and with whom they maintain positive relations. They discuss the information they wish to convey and what materials will be given to their contacts. They add that their visits will be enhanced if these legislators also hear from a few constituents in their districts expressing support for the funding request. Each agrees to pass the list of names on to their respective association staff to trigger some calls or letters.

The final matter they discuss is how to coordinate communications among themselves and between the lobbyists and their associations. One of the lobbyists for the DSS volunteers to be the coordinator to whom all others relay information. All of the lobbyists need to stay informed of each other's contacts and results so they don't trip over each other. They also need to be able to signal for calls, letters, and visits to the right members at the right time. They agree that once the legislative session starts, they'll have brief status meetings once a week. Finally, they identify the need for a list of advocates and experts who could testify at committee hearings if necessary.

The advocates, lobbyists, coalition, network, and Representative Jones have the advantage of starting early, when many legislators can be contacted and visited while still in their home districts. Once the legislative session starts, the pace and chaos increase exponentially, and it becomes very hard to get a legislator's attention for very long. The feedback from legislators is generally positive—no one has expressed opposition. Some hard questions have been raised, but most are expressing a wait-and-see attitude. Party politics come into play; legislators want to wait until their party caucuses have met over the budget before promising their support. Several have mentioned the relatively small size of the request and that this is advantageous.

Representative Jones contacts the chairperson of the House Committee on Children and Youth to see when her bill could be put on the agenda for that committee. The chair says that legislation related to the committee's interim projects takes precedence but that it might be possible to hear testimony on the bill during the fourth week of the session. Representative Jones is worried that in a 90-day session, and with her bill referred to two committees, this late start might be a problem. She thinks it is important to lobby the members of the committee to support the bill and get it on an early agenda. The lobbyists and coalition are informed of this, and they subsequently trigger phone calls, e-mails, and visits from members of their respective associations and organizations.

House Bill 555 is finally scheduled for a hearing in the committee, and the following week a session is planned during which amendments will be considered and a final vote taken. Lobbying intensifies, and testimony is organized to get the bill out of committee. Lobbyists meet over breakfast a few days before the vote to do a head count. If they don't think they have enough favorable votes, they'll try to postpone the vote. This is better than the bill being defeated. Everything looks positive, however, and the amendments that staff are preparing only clarify some of the language and, therefore, are acceptable. The committee approves HB 555, and it is now to be considered by the House Budget Committee. Everyone involved knows that the funding is the real issue, which is why the bill came out of the Committee on Children and Youth so easily.

The Budget Committees and their respective subcommittees are a long way from completing their work. They are in the process of analyzing the governor's recommended budget, taking related testimony, and developing their budgets. Both Senate and House staff favorably view the funding for the pilot test of multidisciplinary teams in three regions and say that the legislators with whom they're working seem to lean positively as well. No one disputes the existence of the problem, and all acknowledge that the proposed solution is reasonable and no better alternatives have been offered. The biggest suggestion of any opposition is that the approval of this funding for FY 2002 means that in the FY 2003 budget request, the DSS will probably seek to continue in the three regions and expand to three more, if not the whole state. Before we know it, a million dollar request will be $5 million of funding for statewide operation. Many legislators are cautious because they've seen this strategy used before by state agencies. They are skeptical whether an objective evaluation will be conducted and doubt that the program would be terminated if the research results were negative.

Lobbying

The lobbyists in consultation with Representative Jones decide they will focus their efforts on the House subcommittee. There is a specific deadline in legislative rules for legislation to be reported out of committee, and they don't want HB 555 to die for that reason. They seek a meeting with the subcommittee chair to see if he supports the legislation and when his subcommittee will hear testimony. If he is supportive, Representative Jones intends to ask him to sign on as a cosponsor. Other members of the subcommittee are unlikely to oppose legislation cosponsored by him if they want his favor on their own issues. She hopes that the proposal for a team in his district, too, will positively influence him. The lobbyists try to find a couple of influential citizens from the chairperson's district who are involved in this effort and who will either call him or attend the meeting. The local juvenile judge agrees to put in a call.

This meeting goes well and the chair likes the idea, especially since one of the regions to operate a multidisciplinary team includes his home district. He does want to see one change in HB 555, however. He doesn't want the DSS to conduct the evaluation; he wants an independent group to do it. He recently attended a forum sponsored by the School of Social Welfare at the State University and was impressed with the research done by the director of the Office of Child Welfare Research and Development. (He serves on their policy advisory task force.) He says he will support the funding for multidisciplinary teams in three regions if $150,000 is earmarked for the office to conduct the evaluation. The lobbyists thank him for his time and support and indicate that they will get back to him (or his staff) within a few days.

Compromises

A meeting is called, gathering as many of the operatives as possible. For those who can't be there, a conference call and a speakerphone are set up in the conference room. The group has to decide whether to accept the chairperson's proposition. Representative Jones says that she can only be there for 15 minutes and wants to go around the table and quickly hear each group's position. Generally, there is no big objection to the chair's idea. The DSS voices the biggest concern, saying that when outside groups evaluate their programs, the outside groups don't fully understand program operations, are not sensitive to a number of important yet subtle constraints, and make extra work for DSS staff. There are some other small concerns voiced about the proper way to conduct social science research and guarding against "pointy-headed academics who just want publications." The lobbyists, however, are all in favor of moving ahead with the chair's support. Their experience tells them that this is a major victory. Representative Jones agrees and says that she will talk to the chair personally and ask him to cosponsor the bill that will now include his suggestion.

The next step in the process involves presenting brief testimony to the subcommittee and getting a positive vote. Testimony will be brief, because members of the subcommittee were contacted some time ago and given supportive documentation. They have heard positively from their constituents and have expressed their support. The purpose of the testimony will be to comment positively on the amendment suggested by the subcommittee chair, make supportive materials available again, and thank the subcommittee for their work. The only question that arises is that one member notes that the funding recommended in HB 555 is more than the governor included in his proposed budget. The following week the subcommittee formally amends the bill to include funding for the evaluation by the Office of Child Welfare Research and Development and votes positively to send the bill to the full Budget Committee.

The subcommittee chair directs staff to use the funding amounts indicated in HB 555 in the DSS budget on which they are working. Once that is completed, it will be sent to the whole Budget Committee for review and approval. If the committee approves those amounts when it votes on the entire budget, the plan will be for the subcommittee chair to move that HB 555 be tabled. The content of HB 555 will be part of the entire budget bill, and it will not be necessary for it to move forward separately.

The subcommittee in the Senate monitors the action of their counterpart in the House and sees that the subcommittee chair in the House has become very invested in the funding for the multidisciplinary teams. Members of the Senate subcommittee have told the lobbyists that they, too, like the idea of the multidisciplinary teams but aren't sure if funds will be available. As agreed, Senator Smith checks with the Senate subcommittee chair and finds out that, in truth, he, Senator Sneaky, has no problem with the proposal but sees this as an opportunity to gain some bargaining leverage. If they don't include funding for the teams, or propose to fund them at a lower amount, it is likely that during conference committee negotiations the Senate could agree to this funding (if the House agrees to fund something the Senate wants). This sort of posturing for negotiations and trading of budget items goes on quite a bit. Since Senator Sneaky is an odds-on favorite to be selected for the budget conference committee, the lobbyists, network of advocates, and coalition continue to contact him for his support. They do not, however, exert as much pressure in the Senate as they do in the House.

Letters, Calls, and E-mails

The network of advocates and the coalition are being kept informed on the progress of the funding request. At critical times they are asked to write letters, faxes, or e-mails and, if possible, to come to the capital to see their legislator. Everything goes smoothly getting the budget bill out of committee with the multidisciplinary team funding in tact. It is now a very small part of the House appropriations bill, HB 2222.[32] A week later HB 2222 is being

---

32. For the sake of brevity, the remaining steps in the House will be covered only briefly. The tactics used at this stage are the same as those used earlier.

considered by the full House, amendments being offered and debated. The lobbyists remain busy reinforcing the work of the subcommittee and full committee and advocating for and against their other issues. Copies of the supportive editorial are put on every representative's desk. Finally, the House approves HB 2222 with $850,000 of funding for three regional teams and $150,000 for the evaluation.

Once HB 2222 is sent to the Senate, they engage in a number of parliamentary maneuvers and approve their own budget with no funding for the multidisciplinary teams. It is sent to the House for consideration. The House does not concur, and it is time to name a conference committee to work out the compromises. Named to the conference committee are the chairs of the Budget Committees, the six subcommittee chairs, and the ranking minority party member from each of the full committees.

Conference Committee

Unlike other legislative committees, the conference committee does not take testimony, so all efforts are focused on lobbying members. The only exception to this is that there are a few legislators, such as the Speaker of the House and the President of the Senate, who have enough influence to sway the deliberations of the conference committee. Therefore, the lobbyists do everything they can to influence these 12 legislators to include funding for multidisciplinary teams at the House level. All members of the advocacy network and coalition are notified to write, call, fax, or visit these legislators. The reality of the situation is very challenging, however. There are only three days left in the session, and besides finalizing the budget, the legislature is in a crunch to deal with dozens of other important pieces of legislation. Legislators spend long hours on the floor of their respective houses engaged in debates and votes. When not on the floor, the members of the conference committee are meeting and working on the budget.

The lobbyists meet for 15 minutes over breakfast every morning in the capital cafeteria in order to stay coordinated. Not everyone can attend every meeting, of course. One of the lobbyists expresses the fear that the governor's office may be willing to trade the funding for the multidisciplinary teams for another important item. When the House and Senate are working out the budget, the governor is always involved in behind-the-scenes negotiations. If all three parties can reach agreement on the budget legislation, this can avoid vetoes and associated controversies. Several lobbyists volunteer to follow up on the rumor, and all agree that several calls to the governor by influential constituents would really help. The judges' and prosecutors' associations are designated to follow up on this. Other lobbyists are reminded to pass on to legislators the message that this funding request originated at the local level, not from the governor's office, and significant local problems need to be addressed.

Gubernatorial Veto?

In the end, the conference committee accepts the House position on the multidisciplinary team funding, and both the House and Senate approve the conference committee report. Now, the focus is on getting the governor to sign the budget legislation. Most of the lobbyists feel that this shouldn't be a problem since this item was included in his original budget recommendations. They check with the governor's staff to confirm this and to find out if any group is encouraging a line-item veto of the funding. If any opposition were to surface, this would have to be countered in specific ways, besides sending messages of support to the governor. Fortunately, this item appears to be noncontroversial and remains untouched in the signed budget act.

RETURN TO AGENCY ADVOCACY

The specifics of how to implement multidisciplinary teams is now up to the DSS as long as they do not exceed the budget allocation or violate existing laws or administration regulations. Since there will be teams in three regions, the director of child welfare services in the central office will coordinate planning with appropriate persons in the regions—generally the coordinators of child welfare services. Under the director's leadership, the program design will be articulated, job descriptions drafted, and operating protocol established. All of this will be incorporated into a plan.

There are many options available to the advocates at this point so they can monitor implementation, but a major question they must ask themselves is "How much time can any of us devote to monitoring?" They all agree that they don't have time to watch every move and comment on every facet of the plan. Therefore, they want to be sure that valid outcomes are defined, that reliable measures for these outcomes are used, and that outcome data is made available periodically. The advocates convey these ideas in a letter to the state director of child welfare services and send copies to the secretary of the DSS, Representative Jones, the regional administrators, and child welfare coordinators in all three regions. They indicate that they would like to see a copy of the plan (including a description of the outcome measures and data collection procedures) before the plan is finalized. Fortunately, the director of child welfare calls to assure the advocates that they are thinking on the same wavelength—the plan will include these items and the advocates' review and comments are welcome.

They are lucky that several members of the core group of advocates will be involved in implementing the team in Region 5—the juvenile judge, the assistant prosecutor, the regional administrator, and the coordinator of child welfare services. Many other agencies will play important roles, however, and if they are reading from a different philosophical or policy page, the hoped-for outcomes may not be accomplished. A kick-off meeting with the heads of major participating agencies is being planned so they can be informed about the team and involved in the planning. This meeting will include visiting nurses, representatives from the hospitals, psychological services, law enforcement, prosecutor's office, and the DSS, and the judge. The advocates make a request to the coordinator of child welfare services, who is planning the meeting, to be given some time on the agenda to describe the history of their effort and the goals they hope to accomplish. The coordinator is more than happy to do so.

Rather than belabor this chapter, let's leave the advocates to their own devices at this point. They have learned a lot since beginning this effort and are confident that if the team underperforms or gets off track, they have the agency advocacy skills and knowledge to get it back on course. Should the evaluation report positive results, they also have the skills to support continued funding of the team in the next legislative session.

SUMMARY

This chapter described a scenario in which advocates identified a problem, developed a proposal to remedy the situation, and advocated for its adoption. It involved doing advocacy homework and using multiple tactics associated with agency advocacy, community advocacy, and legislative advocacy. Knowledge of the state budget process and how it starts at the local level in a state agency, moves to the central office and the governor, and then to the legislature is critical knowledge that informs the choice and timing of tactics.

The next chapter will draw on this case study by highlighting critical advocacy skills and attitudes that contribute to positive advocacy outcomes. Common pitfalls will also be discussed.

DISCUSSION QUESTIONS

1. Imagine that you are one of the two social workers who were involved in this issue from the beginning. Go back through the chapter and make a list of everything you did as part of this advocacy effort.
2. Identify several instances in the case study at which you would have used different tactics.
3. Are there any alternative approaches (within reason) that could be used to accomplish the same objective?

ADVOCACY SKILLS, CHALLENGES, AND PRACTICE GUIDELINES

CHAPTER OBJECTIVES

By the time you finish studying this chapter, you should
1. Understand the skills and attitudes needed to engage in successful advocacy.
2. Be aware of the common challenges advocates face.
3. Be familiar with a set of principles that guide advocacy practice.

The purpose of this chapter is to highlight numerous advocacy skills and attitudes that contribute to effective change, no matter what strategies or tactics are utilized. These are skills and attitudes that crosscut the four major advocacy strategies discussed in this book. The case study in the previous chapter provides excellent examples of significant advocacy skills. In addition, this chapter discusses common advocacy challenges advocates face and what might be done to avoid or rally from them. Among other things, the challenges of compromising and dealing with conflict are discussed.

The third section of the chapter is used to summarize the book and advocacy practice. This is accomplished by proposing and discussing guidelines for advocacy practice. The last section of the chapter reviews the reasons for which advocacy in the human services is crucial and why all human service professionals should find ways to support or engage in advocacy practice.

CRITICAL ADVOCACY SKILLS AND ATTITUDES

The case study in the previous chapter helps to identify numerous skills needed to engage in successful advocacy. Similarly, effective advocates share several attributes and attitudes. Admittedly, it is difficult to distinguish skills from attitudes from attributes, and for our purposes it is not important to make minute differentiations. The case study painted a rosy picture of advocacy and change. However, it is rarely the case that advocates have the same amount of success at every stage of their effort. A summarized list of critical advocacy skills and attitudes is presented in Figure 10.1. They are not listed or discussed in any prioritized order.

Persistence, Tenacity, and Patience

The advocates in the last chapter devoted more than a year of effort from the time they identified a problem in Region 5 until implementation of a new program began. Even more time will be required to monitor program implementation. Clearly, advocates must be willing to hang in there and roll with the punches. Many veteran advocates and lobbyists claim that it usually takes three legislative sessions to get a bill passed. Patience is needed to endure the budget process, because there are stretches of time during which the decision process must be allowed to play itself out. Ultimately, advocates need to accept the fact that policymakers make decisions and agency staff implement programs.

Upon studying a thesaurus, one finds many useful synonyms for *persistence* and *tenacity* that capture characteristics of effective advocates: deter-

---

1. Persistence, Tenacity, and Patience
2. Persuasiveness
3. Compromising
4. Negotiating
5. Dealing with Conflict
6. Assertiveness
7. Collaboration
8. Prioritizing
9. Flexibility and Agility
10. Resourcefulness

FIGURE **10.1**

Critical advocacy skills and attitudes.

mination, doggedness, indefatigability, vigilance, resolve, and steadfastness. Some people might also suggest stubbornness or obstinacy, but those imply inflexibility; and, as discussed below, the ability to compromise is a critical advocacy skill. Similar synonyms are suggested for *patience:* endurance, forbearance, courage, and fortitude.

Even though advocates have to be ready for the long haul, they also need to realize that their role changes as the process advances. As in the case study, they start by identifying and publicizing client problems. Then they move into the role of proposing and selling solutions. Finally, they become monitors of the solution. Sometimes this last step is tricky. For example, one advocacy group with which the author worked had been a prime mover behind the creation of a particular state program. During the next legislative session, that program came under attack from several interest groups. Many people who were members of the coalition that lobbied for the program expected the advocacy agency to mount an energetic defense of the program. The advocacy group struggled over this but ended up defending the new program only by saying that it was too soon to determine whether it was achieving its desired outcomes. They added that this program needed a minimum of three years of operation before it would be fair to evaluate its effectiveness. If, at that time, the new program was not accomplishing positive client outcomes, the advocacy group was prepared to suggest changes or termination.

What is the source of tenacity? Underneath tenacity is a commitment to clients and to a goal for those clients. Not only do advocates need to feel committed, they need to know how to be persistent. They do this by knowing all the different ways to influence a decision system and which tactics to use at different times. Commitment, knowledge of the system, and the ability to use certain tactics will not be enough, however, if advocates lack credibility. Credible advocates are those who have done their homework thoroughly and who practice advocacy in an ethical manner.

Similarly, Richart and Bing (1989) assert that successful advocates "are value-driven people who possess a sense of mission" and are "guided by a sense of purpose and outrage" (p. 86). The value espoused most strongly here is client-centeredness, and the mission is the accomplishment of all of the advocacy ideals.

Persuasiveness

Many times the success of advocacy is reduced to one's ability to persuade another person to act in a certain way. Lobbying legislators and influencing agency staff involve persuasion. Persuasion sounds simple but is often difficult. One type of presentation may persuade one policymaker, whereas another approach is needed for the next. If we went back through the case study, we would see that persuasiveness was needed dozens of times.

What are the ingredients of persuasiveness? There are several standard arguments used to persuade decision makers. Each approach relies on one or more devices, such as logic, emotion, or values. Using research to demonstrate that a significant need or problem exists is a good start, but unless sympathy is triggered, the policymaker may not act. Advocates have to figure out ways to make policymakers feel and think things like "that isn't fair," "that's dangerous," "society shouldn't be that way," or "we can't let that continue." Logic can also be used to demonstrate both the human and social costs of unaddressed problems and needs. Statistics and research are persuasive in some instances, and case studies work too. Case exemplars are more likely to evoke emotions such as sympathy or outrage, and these are even more powerful if backed up by solid research that shows the prevalence of the need.

Besides convincing policymakers that important needs exist, they have to be shown that the problem is solvable at a reasonable cost and that some types of solutions are better than others. Here is where advocates can run into a very difficult set of values. Policymakers have different beliefs regarding the appropriate role of government. Never assume that once policymakers are convinced that a problem exists and that reasonable solutions are available that they will agree that government should get involved. They need to be persuaded of this, too; it is far from automatic.

The major objective of being persuasive is to show your counterpart that agreeing with your position and acting accordingly is in his or her best interest. In other words, try to achieve a win-win outcome, try to spell out how the policymaker will benifit from agreeing with you. To do this, advocates have to get a sense of the other person's values: what he or she thinks is important, what he or she needs in his or her job, and how he or she wants to be perceived. With this information advocates can creatively frame their arguments to appeal to the policymaker. *Creative framing* is not code for lying or misrepresenting facts. As we know, the same eight-ounce glass with four ounces of water in it is both half full and half empty.

Compromising

Advocates must be able to compromise. One's willingness to compromise may depend on whether one views change as incremental. Believing that change is incremental is much better for advocates' mental health than the alternative.

Another thing that makes compromising a little easier is to remember the clients, both present and future, for whom you advocate. Unwillingness to compromise can result in the defeat of advocates' proposals, and, therefore, no clients are helped. Accepting a partial victory will bring relief to some clients, certainly not as many as advocates had hoped, but there's always a chance for another partial victory in the next legislative session if advocates are tenacious.

In one of the author's classes on advocacy, a student declared, "A noble loss is better than a compromise." The refusal to compromise and accept conditional progress may be acceptable in some circumstances, especially if the loss can be used symbolically as a springboard to mobilize more advocates and continue the advocacy effort. Every advocate has to decide for him or herself what is appropriate in a given situation.

How and what to compromise are very difficult questions, and the answers depend on the unique factors of every case. Richart and Bing (1989), among others, recommend "compromising late, not early" (p. 181; emphasis in original). This sound advice is based on the notion that advocates will give away less by standing firm as long as possible before compromising. The problem with the advice is that knowing when it is too early requires a rare level of judgment and experience. Using information unavailable at the time of the decision, critics will second-guess advocates about when and what they compromised. This inevitability is unavoidable and can be intimidating. Remember that the only real mistake advocates can make is giving up and not advocating for more improvements during the next legislative session.

Negotiating

Negotiating goes hand-in-hand with compromising, and there are specific skills and strategies involved. According to Homan (1999), "Negotiation is the process of bringing parties with different needs and perspectives to an agreement" (p. 323). There needs to be some trust between negotiating parties to achieve a compromise. Again, advocates need to find out what outcomes the other party wants and needs and, by all means, avoid any proposal that could cause the other party to lose face.

There are many approaches to take when negotiating, but one that seems promising is to start with an assumption that both parties share concerns and have similar goals, but each has invested in different means to those goals. Advocates also need something tangible to trade. It is not crucial for advocates to have real power or leverage as long as the other party perceives the advocates as having the ability to help or hurt them. Just having the ability to get them good or bad publicity may be enough to bring the other party to the negotiating table.

Dealing with Conflict

Negotiating and compromising are about disagreements, resistance, and criticism. First, do what you can to avoid taking it personally. Second, remind yourself that if someone's getting mad, it means you're probably onto an important change.

Be aware that those who are opposed to your advocacy effort don't always disagree explicitly or directly counter your arguments. For example, when the author's advocacy organization was advocating for statutory changes that would prohibit commingling juveniles and adults in adult jails, the director of an affected state agency was able to pull strings to have one of the grants audited. It took a lot of staff time to deal with the auditors—taking them away from their advocacy work—and if the auditors had concluded that grant funds were misused, the organization would have had to repay them. This would have greatly compromised, if not crippled, the organization.

Assertiveness

Advocates must be able to ask for what they want, and they must be able to criticize substandard agency performance. Not only should advocates learn to be assertive, they need to be assertive in difficult situations. When the status quo needs to be challenged, advocates are frequently in the minority and often feel like a lone voice. These are the times that the majority, those with the established power of the status quo, says things like, "You're not being reasonable." This should be translated to mean that what's being asked for will require the status quo to operate differently and not be as comfortable as they usually are. It is always reasonable to assert a case that will help clients.

Collaboration

Advocates in the case study had to collaborate with many different parties. Individuals in the core group needed to cooperate with one another in order to work well as a team. Then they decided to enter into a partnership with the Region 5 administrator, who suggested major strategic choices while he worked on the inside of the process. Next, as the coalition of organizations began to form and operate, more collaboration was required. Finally, as the team of lobbyists worked the multidisciplinary team issue in the legislature, a high level of cooperation was necessary.

Collaboration calls for many of the skills already discussed, such as compromising, negotiating, persuading, and being patient. For a new organization to agree to join the coalition, they must be persuaded about the issue and their role negotiated. Inevitably, some compromise will be necessary. Patience is called for when waiting for the organization to go through its deliberations to decide whether to join the coalition. Frequently, the approval of the board of directors must be sought.

Collaboration requires trust and integrity. When two parties make a commitment to one another, they must follow through on it and trust that the other party will do the same. It is important to remember that when agreements are made between multiple parties, they frequently have to be renegotiated as new information becomes available. The scenario of two friends giving each other their word on something is similar. If one friend later discovers a reason for which he can't keep his word, he needs to go to his friend to see if some accommodation can be made.

Try not to underestimate the amount of time necessary to collaborate. It simply takes longer to share and clarify information with multiple parties. If negotiations are required, it will take even longer. In a few instances, collaboration can become a distraction, taking advocates away from the objective. Everyone has seen a work group spend too much time processing and fail to complete its task. Collaboration holds that same danger.

Prioritizing

The need to prioritize and focus limited advocacy resources has been mentioned repeatedly throughout the book, but this chapter affords the author one last chance to beat this drum. The need to prioritize the issues on which advocates work is based on the notion that doing effective advocacy is demanding and time consuming and that advocates' resources are limited.

On what basis should advocates prioritize clients' problems, needs, and issues? None of the factors suggested here are individually determinant, nor do they necessarily carry the same weight. Certainly, if at all possible, talk to clients about their priorities. Another factor to consider, albeit difficult to estimate, is the number of clients currently affected by the problem and the number who will be affected if the problem continues. Next, advocates need to assess the probability of success given the current mood of the public, the agency, and the political environment. For example, if the state is projecting decreased revenue for the next fiscal year, it is not a good time to push for funding new programs. The timing of the advocacy effort vis-à-vis numerous environmental variables should be a major consideration.

Assessing the probability of success also involves knowing advocates' capabilities, strengths, and weaknesses. If an issue is going to require some form of legal advocacy, do the advocates or the advocacy organization have the necessary skills? Will they be able to withstand the predictable controversy?

Flexibility and Agility

Obviously, the ability to negotiate and compromise requires flexibility. Advocates who are true to their goals know there is more than one way to get there. Flexibility allows them to opt for a different strategy when required. Agility is also called for because advocates must be able to change tactics quickly without losing their balance. The different terrains on which advocacy occurs—in agencies, legislatures, courts, one-on-one, etc.—shift quickly. Not only does the terrain vary moment to moment, but the opposition changes strength, direction, and tactics, as does the solution being proposed.

Individual advocates may be nimble, but it is hard for advocacy organizations and coalitions to be. Their decision-making processes, as rational, deliberate, and strong as they are, tend to be cumbersome during negotiations and a fast-paced legislative session. The lobbyists in the case study would have had their hands tied if the coalition had required them to report before making any decisions or agreements. Again, trust will facilitate flexibility.

Resourcefulness

The ability to be resourceful requires creativity, willingness to take risks, and optimism. Successful advocacy frequently requires begging and borrowing (but not stealing). Two social workers' time and skills were borrowed from an agency to support the effort to get new funding for multidisciplinary teams. Most of the professionals and volunteers participating in the effort were giving their time. When people put on their advocacy hats, they are usually in the position of having to borrow resources. They start by begging for them. (Begging is essentially the same as persuasion, it just has a bad name.) They borrow phones, computers, paper, letterhead, offices, staff time, rides, and more.

Advocates also need ingenuity to design tactics that will catch people's attention. There are numerous roadblocks in advocates' paths, and incredible inventiveness has been used to go under, over, around, and through them. Coining a catchy phrase that becomes widely used has helped advocacy efforts more than once. Advocates' resourcefulness is particularly handy when trying to get the media's attention.

ADVOCACY CHALLENGES

Advocacy work is hard work and usually takes a long time. That which is so important is rarely otherwise. The path advocates travel is strewn with many curves, dead ends, blind spots, and potholes. Some are more dangerous than others, but few are terminal. The best strategy is to avoid the problems in the first place, but if advocates do get tripped up, they can get up, make repairs, and move forward. The purpose of this section is to share some warnings about common challenges advocates have faced. Many cautions have been voiced throughout this book, and numerous other authors describe sticky situations for advocates as well (e.g., Richart & Bing, 1989, describe seventeen "pitfalls"). The challenges discussed in this section are listed in Figure 10.2.

1. Dangerous Mind-sets
2. Looking for a Fight
3. Illegal Advocacy
4. Burnout

FIGURE **10.2**

Common advocacy challenges.

Dangerous Mind-sets

Virtually all advocates, no matter what side of the issue they take, feel they are right. This thinking goes too far when advocates stretch this feeling into the idea that they are good and anyone who resists or opposes them is bad. Unfortunately, those who think they have goodness on their side have a tendency to underprepare and to assume that decision makers will automatically see the rightness of their issue and behave accordingly. They tend "to think that good intentions and warmheartedness are substitutes for good strategy and hardheadedness" (Richart & Bing, 1989, p. 70).

Similar to *groupthink* (Janis, 1982), feeling right gives groups a false feeling of invulnerability and leads to weak strategizing and decision making, as well as underestimating the strength or intelligence of the opposition. Fortunately, there are several decision-making ground rules to guard against this mind-set. In these situations, group members often tend to self-censor, so any technique that facilitates broad participation in debate will help. Developing group norms that support constructive criticism decreases the chance that this mind-set will develop. Finally, it's a good idea to structure the discussion of proposals or strategies so that a few minutes are devoted to listing the strengths of the idea, and time is devoted to identifying the weaknesses as well.

Name-calling   A predictable by-product of groups feeling they are good and right is name-calling. One of the author's favorite advocacy colleagues usually called anyone who disagreed or voted against his proposals a "Neanderthal." It's one thing to name-call in order to blow off steam, but to write off these individuals as hopeless is to go too far. Even without name-calling, certain segments of political parties, and sometimes whole parties, may be written off as hopeless. When advocates do this, they are losing potential allies. They need to remember that no one is totally predictable, nor are their positions on different issues absolutely consistent. It is worth the time to have a conversation with policymakers who don't usually vote as desired if for no other reason than to find out what the opposition is saying. Advocates could be surprised, however, and gain an unexpected vote, if not on the immediate issue then a future one.

Cynicism   Cynicism is another dangerous mind-set. One of the main reasons cynicism should be avoided is that pessimism usually comes with it. Advocates need to be careful not to give up hope before giving their cause a full effort. Sometimes it's easy to feel that Agency X will never change, the legislature won't pass good legislation because it threatens those in power, or the system is not designed to serve the needy. If advocates catch themselves feeling cynical and pessimistic, they can remind themselves that the individuals and groups opposing their issues are using the same strategies and tactics that advocates can use to push their own agenda.

Looking for a Fight

It is true that advocacy will involve disagreements and conflict, which creates a potential trap of constantly being disagreeable, outspoken, and controversial. There have been some advocates whose egos get out of control and cause them to derive personal satisfaction from playing these roles. They are against everything and in favor of nothing (Richart & Bing, 1989).

Advocates should monitor agency operations and point out when problems arise and services are substandard. It is wiser in the long run to point this out to the agency, and even make suggestions, rather than immediately approaching the media. Agency advocacy should be attempted before filing a lawsuit. Being constructively critical and suggesting solutions will pay off both in the short and long run. Advocates who thrive on controversy and publicity quickly lose their credibility with policymakers and later will be received with skepticism and great caution if received at all. Frequently, the difference between being an outspoken naysayer and a constructive advocate is a matter of tone and timing.

Illegal Advocacy

Federal law restricts the amount of advocacy carried out by nonprofit organizations. This is explained in the following passage:

> Nonprofit groups classified under Section 501(c)(3) of the Internal Revenue Code are limited strictly in the amount of money they can spend on *legislative lobbying,* both direct and grassroots. Nonprofits can spend up to 20 percent of their first $500,000 in nonfederal funding on lobbying; 15 percent of their second $500,000 of funding; 10 percent of their third $500,000; and 5 percent of any amounts in excess of $1.5 million. Of the total amount allowed for lobbying, only 25 percent may be used for *grassroots* lobbying. (Children's Defense Fund, 1995, p. 6)

Direct lobbying refers to when members of the nonprofit organization communicate their views on legislative proposals to legislators or government officials. **Grassroots lobbying** refers to when the nonprofit organization communicates its view on a specific legislative proposal to the public and also voices a call to action.

There have been recent efforts in Congress to make these rules more restrictive, in an effort to keep nonprofits from engaging in advocacy. Obviously, these rules have significant implications relating to nonprofit staff accounting for the use of their time, as well as other major bookkeeping issues. Since the details of this issue go well beyond the purposes of this book, nonprofits are advised to work closely with their accountants and to seek legal advice.

Hatch Act   The Hatch Act is a federal law originally passed in 1939 and most recently amended in 1993. It restricts the political activities of federal civilian employees. Broadly speaking, it prohibits government employees from engaging in political activity while on duty. It does not prohibit activities such as expressing opinions about issues and candidates or contributing money to political organizations.

States and local governments have similar laws, and advocates who are government employees should familiarize themselves with laws affecting their advocacy activities. The reason behind laws such as the Hatch Act makes sense—government agencies can function more fairly and effectively if employees don't engage in partisan political activities. Fortunately, most advocacy tactics do not involve partisan political activity, but don't assume familiarity with the manner in which laws similar to the Hatch Act are interpreted and applied in specific situations. Sometimes state employees have to take vacation leave in order to attend legislative committee hearings.

Burnout

The discussion above on critical advocacy skills and attitudes underscored the importance of persistence, tenacity, and commitment. At what point, however, does this become unhealthy? Do advocates have to be workaholics to succeed? Professionals engaged in advocacy either full- or part-time can run out of steam. The image of burning out is one of suddenly bursting into flame. Rusting out may be a more accurate colloquialism, because the corrosion takes place slowly until an advocate can no longer function.

Having some of the abilities and attitudes discussed above can prevent burnout. If advocates prioritize and stay focused on a limited number of goals, they can avoid being stretched to their limits. Doing this involves the ever-challenging task of saying "no." Limiting one's advocacy work to high-priority issues and not going beyond the time, energy, and other resources available pays double dividends. Not only will clients benefit from better advocacy, but advocates will maintain themselves for future advocacy efforts. Advocates should try to lead balanced lives with time for family, fun, and personal interests, and they should promise themselves that they won't add any new advocacy issues to their plates without removing something.

One of the author's pet peeves is when someone says, "Don't take it personally." It is more realistic to accept the fact that we do invest ourselves in our work; our egos become involved, and issues that have personal valence are at stake. Many advocates are motivated by a sense of injustice and, therefore, get personally engaged in their efforts to bring about change. If we accept this as part of the advocacy challenge, then we won't be surprised when advocates experience feelings of frustration, loss, and hurt. Those feelings need to be released, and everyone has a unique manner of doing so. Advocates can support one another by setting aside time to express these emotions, rest, and recharge.

Practice Guidelines

As a way to summarize the approach to advocacy practice described throughout this book, this section proposes 12 practice guidelines for advocates to use. Advocates should keep these guidelines in mind as they're engaged in advocacy and as they make decisions regarding strategies and tactics. The guidelines are generally thought to be effective in that they lead to successful advocacy. They are not absolutes, by any means, but should be strongly considered.

Before discussing the specific guidelines, however, it will be useful to review the definition of advocacy used in the book: Advocacy is defined as those purposive efforts to change specific existing or proposed policies or practices on behalf of or with specific clients or groups of clients. As was emphasized in chapter 2, the central idea of advocacy is to bring about change in policies and practices. It is difficult to put enough emphasis on the last phrase, *on behalf of or with specific clients or groups of clients.* Advocacy must be a client-centered type of practice, working with clients or for clients either as case or class advocates.

The plight of clients requires vigorous representation.   Clients served by human service professionals are generally impoverished and have experienced various and multiple forms of oppression for a long time. As individuals they are among society's least powerful, and their chances of effecting change in social policy and agency practices are very small. Even when they coalesce into larger groups, it is difficult to alter the status quo, because so many interest

1. The plight of clients requires vigorous representation.
2. Effective advocates use multiple techniques to hear their clients.
3. Successful advocates target specific policies or practices for change.
4. Effective advocates closely map the decision systems responsible for targeted policies and practices.
5. Effective advocates recast larger problems into solvable pieces.
6. Successful advocates propose concrete solutions to the client problems they address.
7. Effective advocates utilize several strategies, tactics, and skills simultaneously and sequentially.
8. Successful advocates remain aware of and actively counter negative stereotypes about clients and misbeliefs about problems and proposals.
9. Effective advocates use the least conflictual tactics necessary to accomplish their change objective.
10. Effective advocates are culturally aware and respectful as they relate to advocacy colleagues, clients, and decision makers.
11. Effective advocates place a very high priority on impacting budgets.
12. Effective advocates closely monitor the implementation of changed policies and practices.

FIGURE 10.3

Guidelines for advocacy practice.

---

groups are highly invested in it. The emphasis of this practice guideline is on the word *vigorous*. Advocates will not be successful if they take a casual approach, nor will they gain the changes they seek just because they are right. They must be energetic and forceful.

Effective advocates use multiple techniques to hear their clients.
Whether doing case or class advocacy, advocates should make every effort to listen directly to their clients, or their guardians, in order to determine their needs, issues, and problems. If this isn't possible, other approaches should be used to get as close to clients as possible. Those who do work directly with the clients of concern know a great deal about their clients' needs. More indirectly, but the best solution in many situations, different needs assessment techniques ranging from surveys and interviews to agency data on client outcomes can be used. Not only should advocates always listen closely to client needs, but they should also hear their solutions.

Successful advocates target specific policies or practices for change.
This guideline is intended to underscore the critical importance of doing your

advocacy homework. It involves studying and understanding client problems to the point of being able to identify the policies or practices that need to be changed to help clients.

Effective advocates closely map the decision systems responsible for targeted policies and practices.   It is not possible to plan advocacy strategies and tactics without knowing the details of who is involved in making decisions, when the decisions are made, and how they are made. Advocates also must distinguish between the official steps in the process and the informal stages.

Effective advocates recast larger problems into solvable pieces. Clients face many problems that not only *seem* huge, they *are* huge. Take, for example, poverty, racism, or unemployment. How can we expect to change enormous institutionalized forces such as these? Advocates are able to see specific examples of these social problems and how they are articulated in social policy, programs, and practices. For example, as one step toward fighting racism, they advocate for the selection of high school history textbooks that accurately portray the role of African Americans in this country's development. They effectively transform that which is enormous and overwhelming into doable advocacy. Advocates need to be like Stehno (1988) describes Edith Abbott and Sophonisba Breckinridge—"masters at figuring out how to gain incremental victories toward the achievement of a broader goal" (p. 499).

Successful advocates propose concrete solutions to the client problems they address.   To be effective, advocates must be advocating *for* something. The only exception to this guideline is when advocates oppose a proposal that would negatively change existing policies, programs, or practices. In those instances, they are advocating for the status quo. There are two major reasons this guideline should be followed. First, if advocates have really heard their clients and done their homework, they, better than anyone, can suggest solutions that will truly help clients. Second, to have credibility, advocates must be perceived as constructive.

Effective advocates utilize several strategies, tactics, and skills simultaneously and sequentially.   As was seen in the case study in the previous chapter, advocates started with agency advocacy, went on to legislative advocacy, returned to agency advocacy, and used community advocacy throughout their effort. It is usually the case that when advocates are pushing a proposal through the legislative process, they will be engaged in advocacy with the agency responsible for implementation. While networks of advocates are being mobilized and coalitions formed, advocacy homework is being done.

Successful advocates are aware of and actively counter negative stereotypes about clients and misbeliefs about problems and proposals. This guideline was discussed in chapter 7, "Community Advocacy." It relates to the fact that status quo policies and programs are derived from a variety of misinformation about clients, causes of problems and needs, and proposed solutions. Advocates need to use many different tactics to counter these subtle but powerful forces, from the way their advocacy issue is framed to the specific language of position papers.

Effective advocates use the least conflictual tactics necessary to accomplish their change objective. There are two primary reasons for this guideline. First of all collaborative tactics are generally less resource-demanding, and they tend to be faster. Second, conflictual tactics make enemies. If advocacy were a one-shot event, it wouldn't matter if advocates left enemies in their wakes. However, advocacy is a long-term series of incremental changes that will improve clients' situations, and it is very difficult to win back the favor of policymakers and agency leaders who have been placed in no-win situations. Advocates need all the allies and all the help they can get on each and every effort they undertake to help clients.

Effective advocates are culturally aware and respectful as they relate to advocacy colleagues, clients, and decision makers. This idea was discussed in chapter 3 and was based on an examination of several codes of ethics. The guideline is derived from the knowledge that successful advocacy depends heavily on clear communication and respectful relationships. Knowledge of cultural differences as well as the heterogeneity of individuals belonging to a particular culture are prerequisites for advocacy practice.

Effective advocates place a very high priority on impacting budgets. Since virtually all policy is money driven, advocates should be very familiar with targeted agencies' and legislative budget processes. They need to time and execute various tactics to fit into relevant budget processes (Richart & Bing, 1989, pp. 78–79).

Effective advocates closely monitor the implementation of changed policies and practices. As explained in chapter 4, "Agency Advocacy," there is many a slip between the cup and the lip. In this case, the cup is the policy, such as a new state law, and the lip is the actual receipt of services by appropriate clients. Many events and factors can cause implementation to get off track.

SUMMARY

The last section of this book is devoted to reminding readers why it is so important to engage in advocacy. To a very large degree, the clients with whom human service professionals work have led disadvantaged lives and are members of oppressed groups. This creates numerous barriers that prevent them from having a voice in policymaking, the design of programs, funding decisions, and the day-to-day operation of agencies intended to assist them. As groups of citizens they have very little power; as individuals, they have even less. It is an incredible challenge for them to access and impact the governmental mechanisms for change that have been discussed in this book.

Advocates are generally dissatisfied with the status quo. They see injustice in many forms as they read the newspaper and watch television. They know about violations of rights as well as underfunded and ineffective programs. They can make long lists of the negative consequences that result from the skewed distribution of wealth in this prosperous country. They engage in advocacy to make this a better society.

Advocates can teach people how to advocate for themselves; they can advocate with them; and, if circumstances demand, advocates can speak on their behalf. Policy change is now closer to home than it used to be. More and more policy and funding decisions are being devolved to the states. The governmental processes to make and change policy are more accessible to clients and advocates than ever before. With skill and determination, advocates are sure to produce change.

DISCUSSION QUESTIONS

1. Based on your analysis of the case study in chapter 9, can you identify other advocacy skills and attributes not discussed in this chapter? Which of the attributes do you possess, and which ones are challenges for you?
2. Write two more practice guidelines that you hope to remember as you do advocacy.
3. Prepare a pep talk for yourself and write it on a notecard to which you can refer when advocacy is tiring and frustrating or when the chance of success seems bleak.

References

American Counseling Association. (2000). *Code of ethics* [On-line]. Available: http://www.counseling.org/resources/codeofethics.htm

American Institutes for Research. (1983). *Evaluation of the youth advocacy program: Final report*. Washington, DC: American Institutes for Research.

Amidei, N. (1987). The new activism picks up steam: "We aren't in the streets anymore because we're in office—or working to influence those who are." *Public Welfare, 45* (3), 21–26.

Amidei, N. (1991). *So you want to make a difference: Advocacy is the key*. Washington, DC: OMB Watch.

Austin, M. J., & Lowe, J. I. (1994). Should only African-American community organizers work in African-American neighborhoods? In M. J. Austin & J. I. Lowe (Eds.), *Controversial issues in communities and organizations* (pp. 128–141). Boston: Allyn & Bacon.

Barker, R. L. (1995). *The social work dictionary* (3rd ed.). Washington, DC: National Association of Social Work.

Bartlett, J. (1992). *Bartlett's familiar quotations* (16th ed.). (J. Kaplan, General Ed.). Boston: Little, Brown & Co.

Bateman, N. (1995). *Advocacy skills: A handbook for human service professionals*. Brookfield, VT: Ashgate Publishing.

Black, H. C. (1990). *Black's law dictionary* (6th ed.). St. Paul, MN: West Publishing Co.

Brawley, E. A. (1997). Teaching social work students to use advocacy skills through the mass media. *Journal of Social Work Education, 33* (3), 445–460.

Burger, W. R., & Youkeles, M. (2000). *Human services in contemporary America* (5th ed.). Belmont, CA: Brooks/Cole/Wadsworth.

Children's Defense Fund. (1995, September). Nonprofits: Beware. *CDF Reports,* 5–7.

Coates, R. B. (1989). Social work advocacy in juvenile justice: Conceptual underpinnings and practice. In A. R. Roberts (Ed.) *Juvenile justice policies, programs, and services* (pp. 245–277). Chicago: Dorsey.

Davidoff, P. (1965, November). Advocacy and pluralism in planning. *Journal of the American Institute of Planners, 31,* 331–337.

Dear, R. (1997). Personal communication.

Dear, R. P. & Patti, R. J. (1987). Legislative advocacy. *Encyclopedia of social work* (18th ed.). Silver Springs, MD: National Association of Social Workers.

Designs for Change. (1983) *Child advocacy and the schools: Past impact and potential for the 1980's*. Chicago: Designs for Change.

Dluhy, M. J. (1990). *Building coalitions in the human services*. Newbury Park, CA: Sage Publications.

Du Bois, W. E. B. (1905). *The voice of the negro* [On-line]. Available: http://lccr.org/crlibrary/resources/jbond52798.html

Epstein, I. (1981). Advocates on advocacy: An exploratory study. *Social Work Research & Abstracts, 17* (2), 5–12.

Ezell, M. (1991). Administrators as advocates. *Administration in Social Work, 15* (4), 1–18.

Ezell, M. (1993). The political activity of social workers: A post-Reagan update. *Journal of Sociology and Social Welfare, 20* (4), 81–97.

Ezell, M. (1994). Advocacy practice of social workers. *Families in Society, 75* (1), 36–46.

Ezell, M. & Patti, R. J. (1990). State human service agencies: Structure and organization. *Social Service Review, 64* (1), 22–45.

Fernandez, H. C. (1980). *The child advocacy handbook.* New York: Pilgrim.

Gaylin, W., Glasser, I., Marcus, S., & Rothman, D. J. (1978). *Doing good: The limits of benevolence.* New York: Pantheon Books.

Gibelman, M., & Kraft, S. (1996). Advocacy as a core agency program: Planning considerations for voluntary human service agencies. *Administration in Social Work, 20* (4), 43–59.

Haynes, K. S., & Mickelson, J. S. (2000). *Affecting change: Social workers in the political arena* (4th ed.). New York: Longman.

Hepworth, D. H., & Larsen, J. A. (1986). Employing advocacy and social action. In D. H. Hepworth & J. A. Larsen (Eds.), *Direct social work practice: Theory and skills* (pp. 569–574). Chicago: Dorsey.

Herbert, M. D., & Mould, J. W. (1992). The advocacy role in public child welfare. *Child Welfare, 71* (2), 114–130.

Homan, M. (1999). *Promoting community change: Making it happen in the real world* (2nd ed.). Pacific Grove, CA: Brooks/Cole.

Hudson, R. B. (1982). Issues in advocacy, politics and participation. *Administration in Social Work, 6* (2/3), 109–124.

Janis, I. L. (1982). *Groupthink: Psychological studies of policy decisions and fiascoes.* Boston: Houghton Mifflin.

Jansson, B. S. (1999). *Becoming an effective policy advocate: From policy practice to social justice.* Pacific Grove, CA: Brooks/Cole.

Kahn, A. J., Kamerman, S. B., & McGowan, B. G. (1972). *Child advocacy: Report of a national baseline study.* New York: Columbia Univ. School of Social Work.

Kettner, P. M., Daley, J. M., & Nichols, Ann W. (1985). *Initiating change in organizations and communities: A macro practice model.* Monterey, CA: Brooks/Cole.

Knitzer, J. (1976). Child advocacy: A perspective. *American Journal of Orthopsychiatry, 46,* 200–216.

Kutchins, H., & Kutchins, S. (1978). Advocacy and social work. In G. H. Weber & G. J. McCall (Eds.), *Social scientists as advocates: Views from the applied disciplines* (pp. 13–48). Newbury Park, CA: Sage.

Lamott, A. (1994). *Bird by bird: Some instructions on writing and life.* New York: Anchor Books.

Lipsky, M. (1980). *Street-level bureaucracy.* New York: Russell Sage Foundation.

Loewenberg, F. M., & Dolgoff, R. (1996). *Ethical decisions for social work practice* (5th ed.). Itasca, IL: F. E. Peacock.

Lynch, R. S., & Mitchell, J. (1995). Justice system advocacy: A must for NASW and the social work community. *Social Work, 40* (1), 9–12.

McCormick, M. J. (1970, January). Social advocacy: A new dimension in social work. *Social Casework,* 3–11.

McGowan, B. (1978). The case advocacy function in child welfare practice. *Child Welfare, 57* (5) 275–284.

Melton, G. B. (1983). *Child advocacy: Psychological issues and interventions.* New York: Plenum.

Mnookin, R. H. (1985). *In the interest of children: Advocacy, law reform, and public policy.* New York: W. H. Freeman & Company.

Moss, K., & Zurcher, L. A. (1983). The role of social workers in institutional reform litigation. *The Journal of Applied Social Sciences, 8* (1), 43–63.

NASW joins court battles: Legal briefs back the rights of a gay father and a student with disabilities. (1997, September). *NASW News,* 13.

National Association of Social Workers. (1996). *Code of ethics.* Washington, DC: Author.

National Association of Social Workers Ad Hoc Committee on Advocacy. (1969, April). The social worker as advocate: Champion of social victims. *Social Work, 14,* 16–22.

National Conference of State Legislators. (1999). [On-line]. Available: http://www.ncsl.org

National Organization for Human Service Education. (2000). *Ethical standards of human service professionals* [On-line]. Available: http://www.hohse.com/ethstand.html

Netting, F. E., Kettner, P. M., & McMurtry S. L. (1993). *Social work macro practice.* New York: Longman.

Neukrug, E. (2000). *Theory, practice, and trends in human services: An introduction to an emerging profession* (2nd ed.). Belmont, CA: Brooks/Cole/Wadsworth.

Panitch, A. (1974, May). Advocacy in practice. *Social Work, 19,* 326–332.

Patti, R. J. (1974, November). Limitations and prospects of internal advocacy. *Social Casework, 55,* 537–545.

Patti, R., & Dear, R. (1981, July). Legislative advocacy: Seven effective tactics. *Social Work, 26,* 289–296.

Polansky, N. A. (1986). "There is nothing so practical as a good theory." *Child Welfare, 65* (1), 3–15.

Reisch, M. (1986, Winter/Summer). From cause to case and back again: The reemergence of advocacy in social work. *The Urban and Social Change Review, 19,* 20–24.

Reisch, M. (1990). Organizational structure and client advocacy: Lessons from the 1980s. *Social Work, 35* (1), 73–74.

Rhodes, M. L. (1991). *Ethical dilemmas in social work practice.* Milwaukee, WI: Family Service America.

Richan, W. C. (1991). *Lobbying for social change.* New York: Haworth.

Richart, D. W. (1993). *Children's champions: How child advocates protect and increase budgets for children.* Louisville, KY: Kentucky Youth Advocates.

Richart, D. W., & Bing, S. R. (1989). *Fairness is a kid's game: Children, public policy, and child advocacy in the states.* Louisville, KY: Kentucky Youth Advocates.

Rivera, F., & Erlich, J. (1995). *Community organizing in a diverse society* (2nd ed.). Boston: Allyn & Bacon.

Rothman, J., Erlich, J. L., & Tropman, J. E. (Eds.). (1995). *Strategies of community intervention* (5th ed.). Itasca, IL: F. E. Peacock Publishers.

Salcido, R. M. (1984). Social work practice in political campaigns. *Social Work, 29* (2), 189–191.

Schloss, C. N., & Jayne, D. (1994). Models and methods of advocacy. In S. Alper, P. J. Schloss, & C. N. Schloss (Eds.), *Families of students with disabilities: Consultation and advocacy* (pp. 229–250). Boston: Allyn & Bacon.

Schön, D. A. (1983). *The reflective practitioner: How professionals think in action.* New York: Basic Books.

Schram, B., & Mandell, B. R. (1994). *An introduction to human services: Policy and practice* (2nd ed.). New York: Macmillan College Publishing Co.

Snyder, H. N., & Sickmund, M. (1995). *Juvenile offenders and victims: A focus on violence: Statistics summary.* Pittsburgh, PA: National Center for Juvenile Justice.

Society for Applied Sociology. (2000). *Code of ethics* [On-line]. Available: http://www.appliedsoc.org/ethics.htm

Soler, M., & Warboys, L. (1990). Services for violent and severely disturbed children: The *Willie M.* litigation. In S. Dicker, *Stepping stones: Successful advocacy for children* (pp. 61–112). New York: Foundation for Child Development.

Sosin, M., & Caulum, S. (1983). Advocacy: A conceptualization for social work practice. *Social Work, 28* (1), 12–17.

Soukhanov, A. H. et al. (Eds.). (1984). *Webster's II: New Riverside University Dictionary.* Boston: Houghton Mifflin.

Specht, H., & Courtney, M. (1994). *Unfaithful angels: How social work abandoned its mission.* New York: Free.

State Legislative Leaders Foundation. (1995). *State legislative leaders: Keys to effective legislation for children and families.* Centerville, MA: State Legislative Leaders Foundation.

Stehno, S. M. (1988). Public responsibility for dependent black children: The advocacy of Edith Abbott and Sophonisba Breckinridge. *Social Service Review, 62* (3), 485–503.

Sunley, R. (1983) *Advocating today: A human service practitioner's handbook.* New York: Family Service America.

Sunley, R. (1997). Advocacy in the new world of managed care. *Families in Society, 78* (1), 84–94.

Taylor, E. D. (1987). *From issue to action: An advocacy program model.* Lancaster, PA: Family and Children's Service.

Wahl, O. F. (1995). *Media madness: Public images of mental illness.* New Brunswick, NJ: Rutgers Univ. Press.

Walz, T., & Groze, V. (1991). The mission of social work revisited: An agenda for the 1990s. *Social Work, 36* (6), 500–504.

Weissman, H., Epstein, I., & Savage, A. (1983). *Agency-based social work: Neglected aspects of clinical practice.* Philadelphia: Temple Univ. Press.

Index

Administrative Procedures Act, 58–59,
  63–64, 103
Advocacy
  administrative, 28
  agency, 164–169
  case, 25
  challenges, 188–192
  citizen, 27–28
  class, 25
  clinical, 27–28
  defined, xx
  definition, 22–25
  direct service, 27–28
  external, 26
  history, xx–xxii
  illegal, 190–191
  internal, 26
  legal, 28
  legislative, 28
  network, 164–165
  policy, 28
  political, 28
  self, 27–28
  skills and attitudes, 182–188
  systems, 28
Advocacy homework, 138–151
  mapping the system, 148–149
  problem statement, 145
Advocacy ideals, 5–7
Advocacy practice, xviii–xix
Advocacy strategies
  defined, xx
  selecting, 149–150
Advocacy tactics
  selecting, 149–150
Advocacy targets
  defined, xx
  establishing, 146–147
Agency
  discretion, 58–61
  meeting officials, 64–68
  operational policy, 60
  policy, 59–60
  practices, 60–61

procedures, 60–61
regulations, 58–59
responses, 69–71
Agency advocacy
  defined, 53
  targets, 54–58
Amicus curiae brief, 104
Assertiveness, 186
Assumptions, 31–34

Begging, 188
Burnout, 191–192

Case advocacy, 159
Children's Defense Fund, xi
Class advocacy, 159
Coalitions, 92–94, 165–166
Code of ethics
  American Counseling Association, 38,
    47
  National Association of Social
    Workers, 38–41, 42, 44, 47, 49
  Society of Applied Sociology, 38, 47
Collaboration, 186–187
Community advocacy
  case study, 169–171
  direct education, 134–135
  Internet, 136–137
  presentations, 135–136
Community education, 117–122
Compromise, 150, 184–185
Conference committee, 178
Conflict, 185–186
Consent decree, 101
Credibility, 183
Cultural
  awareness, 47–49
  diversity, 47–49
Culture
  defined, 47
Cynicism, 190

Discrimination, 49

Empowering clients, 45

Ethical dilemma, 37
Ethical standards, 40–41, 42, 47, 49

Flexibility, 187–188
Framework for advocacy practice, 34–35
Framing issues, 169–170
   creative framing, 184

Groupthink, 189

Hatch Act, 191
Human services
   defined, x

Inaccessibility, 56
Informed consent, 41–42
Inside advocacy, 69–71, 168

Least intrusive intervention, 7
Legal advocacy, 98–114
   creating rights, 101
   defined, 98–99
   expert witness, 107–108
   opportunities, 100–105
Legal services, 106
Legislative
   bodies, 74
   process, 75–78
   staff, 86–87
Letter writing, 69, 167–168, 177–178
Litigation, 109–113
   defined, 110
Lobbying, 81–83, 175–176
   direct, 191
   grassroots, 191

Media tactics, 122–134
   advertising, 128
   editorials, 125–126, 170–171
   in-depth investigations, 125
   interviews, 134
   letter to the editor, 127–128
   magazines, 129
   newsletters, 129
   newspapers, 124–129
   news releases, 132–134
   news stories, 124–125
   op-ed pieces, 126–127
   personal interest articles, 125
   press conferences, 132–134
   PSAs, 131
   public TV, 131

radio, 131–132
   talk shows, 130–131
   television, 129–131
   TV news, 130
   weekly newspapers, 128–129
Mindfulness, xi
Monitoring
   agency, 61–63, 179–180
   legislative, 173–175
Multidisciplinary team, 159–160

Name-calling, 189–190
Needs assessments, 140–141
Negotiating, 185
Networks, 85–86
   organizing, 88–91
Non-litigious tactics, 105–109

On behalf of clients, 45
Oppression, 49
Overstating the case, 44–45

Patience, 182–183
Persistence, 182–183
Persuasiveness, 183–184
Political campaigns, 95–97
Position papers, 82
Practice guidelines, 192–195
Prioritizing, 142, 187
Problem statement, 158–159
PRWORA, xvii

Racism, 49
Research, 4–5, 142–145
Resourcefulness, 188

Self-determination, 42–44
Self-empowerment, 13–18
Social injustice, 49
State budget process, 160–163

Task forces, 71–72
Telephone trees, 85
Tenacity, 182–183
Testimony, 83–85, 176–177
Types of advocacy, 25–28

Validation rate, 156
Veto
   gubernatorial, 87–88, 179
   line-item, 163

CPSIA information can be obtained
at www.ICGtesting.com
Printed in the USA
FFOW02n0018031214
9224FF